ATHEISTS: THE ORIGIN OF THE SPECIES

Atheists: The Origin of the Species

Nick Spencer

B L O O M S B U R Y

LONDON • NEW DELHI • NEW YORK • SYDNEY

First published in Great Britain 2014

Copyright © Nick Spencer, 2014

The moral right of the author has been asserted

No part of this book may be used or reproduced in any manner
whatsoever without written permission from the Publisher except in the
case of brief quotations embodied in critical articles or reviews. Every
reasonable effort has been made to trace copyright holders of material
reproduced in this book, but if any have been inadvertently overlooked
the Publishers would be glad to hear from them.

A Continuum book

Bloomsbury Publishing Plc
50 Bedford Square
London WC1B 3DP

www.bloomsbury.com

Bloomsbury is a registered trade mark of Bloomsbury Publishing Plc

Bloomsbury Publishing, London, New Delhi, New York and Sydney

A CIP record for this book is available from the British Library.

ISBN 978 14729 029 62

10 9 8 7 6 5 4 3 2 1

Typeset by Fakenham Prepress Solutions, Fakenham,
Norfolk NR21 8NN

Printed and bound in Great Britain by CPI Group (UK) Ltd,
Croydon CR0 4YY

*Dedicated to the memory of
Robin Joyce (1973–2013),
endlessly fascinated by its subject,
present at its conception, not at
its conclusion. Badly missed.*

Atheism is often merely a variety of Christianity. In fact, several varieties. There is the High Church Atheism of Matthew Arnold, there is the Auld Licht Atheism of our friend Mr J. M. Robertson, there is the Tin Chapel Atheism of Mr D. H. Lawrence. And there is the decidedly Low Church Atheism of Mr Russell.

T. S. Eliot, reviewing Bertrand Russell's *Why I Am Not a Christian*, 1927

Atheism should always be encouraged (i.e. rationalistic not emotional atheism) for the sake of the Faith.

T. S. Eliot to Richard Aldington, 24 February 1927

Atheist as I am sir, atheist as I am, no man shall stand between my soul and my God!

Heckler at a Christian Socialist Lecture, quoted in F. C. Bettany, *Stewart Headlam* (John Murray, 1926)

Contents

Acknowledgements   xi

Introduction   xiii

Chapter 1 – Possibilities   1

Types of atheism   1
New worlds   13
Authority and scepticism   22
'Science and Religion'   31
Questioning the Bible   38
Thomas Hobbes' Christian atheism   45
Spinoza, the great leader of our modern unbelievers   52
Crossing the Rubicon   60

Chapter 2 – Pioneers   70

Immoral atheists   70
The reasonable English   75
German toleration   86
French fury   91
British moderation   116
American silence   129

Chapter 3 – Promises   133

The road from revolution   133
The road to revolution (part 1)   142
The road to revolution (part 2)   153
The reaction to reaction   160
Science and religion, once again   179
The high point of British atheism   187

Chapter 4 – Problems   195

Nietzsche's dead god   195
The first death of British atheism   203
The kingdom of godlessness is at hand   214
Germany, Britain, France, America: Mid-century   221
Building godless societies   230
Decline and fall   238
New dawns   243

Notes   259

Index   285

Acknowledgements

There are number of people without whom this book would be larger, weaker, duller or non-existent.

I owe a great deal to Caroline Chartres at Bloomsbury who saw the potential for a history of atheism just as I was trying to pitch a different book altogether. She came up with a title, persuading me out of something much more worthy and much less memorable. No less importantly, she talked me down from the ledge of a much longer book. I don't know which I should be more grateful for. Thanks are also due to Joel Simons who carefully steered the book through production.

I was delighted when my old friend Phill Hatton agreed to do the artwork for the cover, filling the gap that the Cameleopard left in our lives. His work turned out to be even more impressive than I had imagined it would.

A number of people read and commented on the manuscript in whole or in parts. I am grateful to them all but would like to single out three in particular: John Coffey, whose constant supply of advice and encouragement is truly humbling; John Hedley Brooke whose knowledge of the topic and eye for detail knows no peers; and Toby Hole, whose friendship and wisdom is one of the things that makes life worth living.

I was extremely grateful to Charles Devellennes for allowing me to read his unpublished doctoral thesis on the atheism of Jean Meslier and Baron D'Holbach, on which Chapter 2 draws.

My colleagues at Theos – Elizabeth Oldfield, Paul Bickley, Ben Ryan, and Alanna Harris – have been a constant support, as have Katie, Ellen and Jonny without whom none of this is worthwhile.

The dedication contains one final, enormous debt, which was never fully recognized.

Nick Spencer
London, 2013

Introduction

Once upon a time there was a terrible monster that lived in the sky. No one had ever seen it because it lived a long way away, and because it was invisible, but everyone knew it was there because a long time ago it had shown itself to some very clever men.

These very clever men explained how the monster had one head, three bodies and a thousand eyes, with which it could see into people's souls. They told terrible tales of what the monster would do if it got angry but also of how kind it was if people would only worship it without thought or question. They explained how the monster had given them a powerful magic, which, if used rightly, would protect the world from evil.

Sometimes the monster would get angry and when it did the clever men would offer it sacrifices, dragging people into market squares where they would burn them alive, just to show the monster how much they loved it.

The people listened to the very clever men and believed them. But they still yearned to be free of the monster.

And then, one day, a few brave men, who had only ever pretended to believe in the monster, unearthed a chest of strange metal. The chest had been hidden by an earlier, wiser, freer people, who had lived in the land before the monster came, and had known a better way of life.

Ever so slowly, the men began to work the metal, which they called 'reason', using it to forge a new weapon, which they called 'science', and they used 'science' to attack the monster, and the very clever men. They had to be very careful at first because if anyone was caught using 'science', they would be dragged into market squares where they would be burned alive, and indeed this was how many men lost their lives.

But these were brave men, not to be fooled by fables or cowed by threats. Their band multiplied and their weapons grew in number and power until one day, a brilliant, reclusive rebel invented a super-weapon, which he called 'evolution', which could punch clean through the monster's armoured scales.

After that, the attacks increased in frequency and ferocity until one day the rebels were able to show the people what they had long known themselves. The monster had never actually existed. It was just a tale told by the very clever men to keep themselves in riches and power. Slowly the truth spread and although some very clever men still cling to riches and power, and some very stupid ones still believe them, gradually, wonderfully, the world is being set free.

Or so the story goes. Every culture has its ancient creation myth, and this is atheism's, albeit one that is only about 150 years old. Atheism emerged in Europe through the services of reason, science and evolution and in the teeth of often brutal religious opposition. In as far as the history of modern atheism is told, it is often a variant of this myth.

This book tries to tell a different story. This is not to say that atheism's creation myth is wholly untrue. Creation myths are rarely wholly untrue. In this instance the tale is true enough to be believable, even if it's not true enough to be true. Modern atheism did indeed emerge in Europe in the teeth of religious, i.e. Christian, opposition. But it had only a limited amount to do with reason and even less with science. The creation myth in which a few brave souls forged weapons made of a previously unknown material, to which the religious were relentlessly opposed, is an invention of the later nineteenth century, albeit one with ongoing popular appeal. In reality, this book argues, modern atheism was primarily a political and social cause, its development in Europe having rather more to do with the (ab)use of theologically legitimized political authority than it does with developments in science or philosophy.

One way of understanding this is to go back to the earliest years of the Christian church. In the first and second centuries, in as far as Christians were noticed at all, it was for their political disobedience, their apparently cannibalistic and incestuous rites, and their atheism.[1] That Christians, of all people, should be accused of atheism will sound odd to modern readers. The reason lies partly in the fact that, like the Jews who faced similar accusations, early Christians had no visible idols: they appeared to worship nothing.[2] But it also lies in the fact that, in thus limiting their worship, they refused to recognize the divinity of the emperor.

In about AD 160, the octogenarian bishop of Smyrna, Polycarp, was given a choice: either denounce your fellow (Christian) 'atheists' and burn incense to Caesar (thereby acknowledging his divinity), or face the pyre. He chose the latter, preferring instead to call the baying crowd 'atheists'.[3] Even in the ancient world which had – we like to imagine – a tolerant and flexible attitude to religious belief, who you worshipped was intricately tied up with questions of who you obeyed and how you lived. Rejecting the gods constituted a serious threat to public order, one that demanded severest punishment. Ancient atheism, at least in its Christian incarnation, was not only about denying the powers in heaven but also defying the powers on earth.

As with ancient atheism, so with modern: religion, in the form of Christianity, *was* the foundation of European culture in the early modern period. Belief in God determined the way people lived, the way they were governed and the way they structured society. It regulated their days, weeks and years, their births, marriages and deaths. It told them what to hope for and what to fear. It legitimized communities, kingdoms and empires. It explained the past, present and future, earth, heaven and the heavens, human origins, purpose and destiny. It was the key in which all life, human and natural, was composed, if not necessarily played.[4] In the words of the historian turned Conservative politician, John Redwood, early modern Europe was 'God-ridden': 'Whenever a man took up his pen and attempted to write about the weather, the seasons, the structure of the earth, the constitution of the heavens, the nature of political society, the organization of the Church, social morality or ethics he was by definition taking up his pen to write about God.'[5] The implications for atheism were clear. To undermine religion was, in the words of the English Chief Justice in 1676, 'to dissolve all those obligations whereby the civil societies are preserved.'[6]

Recognizing this helps free us from our own (historically rather unusual) conviction that since belief in God is an intellectual activity focused on questions such as 'Who made the world?' or 'Does a supernatural realm exist?', atheism is an intellectual activity that just comes up with different answers. Less about science disproving God, or even about God himself, the history of atheism is best seen as a series of disagreements about authority, the concept in which various concerns – does God exist, how do we know, how should we live and who should we obey – coalesce.

This is sometimes recognized in the more academic literature on the history of atheism. Thus, Victoria Frede, in her fine history of the emergence of Russian atheism between the 1820s and 1860s, has observed that 'to treat atheism as a doctrine is … to miss its most salient feature. In Russia, it was less a statement about the status of God than it was a commentary on the status of educated people in an authoritarian state that sought ever more forcefully to regulate the opinions and beliefs of its subjects.'[7]

For 'Russia' read 'the West': the social and political contexts were critically different from one country to another (which helps explain why atheism took different forms in different places) but the religious-political nexus against which atheism emerged was omnipresent. Wherever you went, to deny God was not simply to deny God. It was to deny the emperor or the king who ruled you, the social structures that ordered your life, the ethical ties that regulated it, the hopes that inspired it and the judgement that reassured it.

This, then, is the first contention of this book: the history of atheism is best understood in social and political terms. It leads to a second contention. Atheism is too readily treated as a merely destructive phenomenon, a stripping away of structures, rituals and beliefs until it arrived at the naked ape that was always there waiting to be revealed. This is misleading. From the outset, atheism was a constructive and creative phenomenon.[8]

The mistake is wholly understandable. Atheism is, in the first instance, a parasitic creed, defined by what it is not, what it is against. Accordingly, a huge amount of energy has been deployed throughout its history – a wearying amount, if the historian is honest – in showing how wicked, stupid, corrupt, violent, ignorant, misleading and malign religion – for the most part Christianity – is. Retarded and self-deluding Christians, malevolent and manipulative priests, incomprehensible and meaningless doctrines, corrupt and hypocritical practices, delusional and dehumanizing hopes: these provide the staple diet of European atheists, many of whose writings have only rarely been burdened by a commitment to balance or a fear of repetition.

Yet, this is only part of the story. Being parasitic in the first instance does not mean being parasitic in everything. Precisely because Christianity was the foundation, the walls, the streets and the public order of European civilization, atheism was faced with the need to construct a different earthly city if its destruction of the existing one was ever going to be successful. 'God does not exist' might be an acceptable stance in the seminar room, but beyond it must either become 'God does not exist so ...' or risk forfeiting public attention. Failure to complete the sentence rendered its first clause irrelevant or unpersuasive or simply dangerous. Anarchy appealed to no one.

The need to complete the sentence, for atheism to construct as well as destroy, leads to a third contention. We should, if we take points one and two seriously, talk about atheisms rather than atheism. The different ways in which different unbelievers have completed the sentence has generated creeds – the word is appropriate in the context – that are sufficiently different enough to be seen as a cluster of positions, rather than a single one. We do better to speak of a family of atheisms, rather than one single, holy, catholic and apostolic atheism.

This 'family' can be glimpsed in the huge range of words that have been used interchangeably with atheist over the last four centuries. These include Bright, Cartesian, communist, determinist, Epicurean, existentialist, fatalist, freethinker, Hobbist, humanist, infidel, irreligious, libertine, materialist, monist, naturalist, Nietzschean, rationalist, sceptic, secularist, Spinozist and unbeliever, to name only the less abusive terms. Few of these are exact synonyms but that is precisely the point. All these terms have been used of people who rejected God, but did so for different reasons, with different strengths of feeling, and drawing different conclusions. All were atheists (or, at least, alleged to be) but they adhered to subtly different atheisms.

If the socio-political nature of the history of atheism is poorly recognized, the existence of atheisms is even less so. Few historical accounts take seriously, or even notice, the range of atheisms present in European culture, one honourable exception being Susan Budd's unjustly neglected study of *Varieties of Unbelief* in Britain in the later nineteenth and earlier twentieth centuries.

Things are changing. A 2012 article in the *History of Human Sciences* charts the differing 'scientific' and 'humanistic' courses within 'the evolution of atheism'.[9] The British Society for the Philosophy of Religion dedicated its 2013 conference to 'Atheisms'. A sociological study recently published by the University of Tennessee outlined six distinct types of atheist: intellectual atheists, anti-theists, activists, seeker-agnostics, non-theists and ritual atheists.[10] Examples like these, together with new academic ventures, such as the Nonreligion and Secularity Research Network, suggest that the study of atheisms is coming of age.

Atheism is not an exclusively modern or Western phenomenon. The classical world had its non-believers, as does the non-Western one, although the precise nature of eastern 'atheism' often puzzled Westerners, and indeed became a major point of debate for the Catholic mission to China in the eighteenth century. That recognized, the focus of this book is modern (post c. 1500) and predominantly 'Western' (from Russia to the US) largely for reasons of length and authorial competence. But more is needed: it is nearly a century since the Austro-Hungarian theatre critic, novelist and sceptical agnostic Fritz Mauthner published his massive four-volume history of atheism.[11] We are overdue another such offering.[12]

This book is separated into four chapters, although not in honour of Mauthner's four volumes, which begin in the classical world. Chapter 1 takes the story from the Renaissance to the start of the eighteenth century and explains how atheism became a possibility in the Western mind. It argues that all the building blocks of an atheistic worldview – God absent, spirits non-existent, souls invented, creation unnecessary, matter everything (and eternal), providence imaginary, universe blind, life chance, miracles impossible, morality an entirely human affair, and humans no more than sophisticated animals – were in place, or at least available, at a very early stage, but that it took the massive theological, epistemological and political crisis precipitated by the Reformation to gather those blocks and turn them into a foundation. Atheism was possible by the late 1600s, certainly by the 1740s, even if it was not legal, let alone desirable.

Chapter 2 takes the story on to the end of the eighteenth century, in which a handful of pioneers, the most prominent in France, put forward the first openly and unapologetically atheist arguments since the classical period. It is also in this period that different countries start to take different paths, France, Britain and the new United States developing different cultures of atheism not so much on account of different philosophical or scientific cultures, but because of the different nature of their theo-political cultures. A rigidly authoritarian Catholic *ancien régime* in France created deep wells of moral indignation on which atheists could draw. The more tolerant settlement in Britain limited those wells, and the 'wall of separation' between church and state in America effectively drained them. If we seek a reason why atheism was the dog that didn't bark in what became the most self-consciously modern, scientifically developed country on earth, it lies here.

Chapter 3 moves into the nineteenth century, the age of atheist promise. Here great systems of thought rubbed shoulders, explaining the past, inspiring the present and predicting the future, putting religious belief in its right place, and then transcending that place, moving people on to a truer understanding of historical progress, a better grasp of economics, or a more rational form of ritual and practice. For all the very real civic and social burdens placed on them at the time, this was the moment to be alive as an atheist, when progress predicted the death of God as humanity moved into broad, sunlit rational uplands.

It didn't turn out quite like that and the final chapter takes the story into the twentieth century, when atheism faced and created problems previously hidden or unimagined. This was the age when Nietzsche lifted the veil on much hypocritical moral posturing by his atheist peers; when logical positivists gleefully hammered home the final nail in the coffin of God-talk, only to find the whole thing was made of papier-mâché and that God hadn't been in the coffin in the first place; when the experience of two world wars left many in Europe, particularly in France, doubting the humanist credentials of atheism; and, most painfully, when attempts to build atheist societies populated with new men (and the occasional new woman) in Russia, China, Albania, North Korea and elsewhere ended up humiliating, enslaving and killing on a scale that made previous religious wars look like playground scuffles. It was an age in which atheism came out and came of age, and it wasn't pretty.

The British philosopher Anthony Kenny ended his *New History of Western Philosophy* by outlining how the American Christian philosopher Alvin Plantinga resurrected the ontological argument for God at the end of the twentieth century. This, Kenny reminds us by quoting Bertrand Russell's own *History of Western Philosophy*, was once thought a closed case. The argument, wrote Russell, 'was invented by Anselm, rejected by Thomas Aquinas, accepted by Descartes, refuted by Kant, and reinstated by Hegel. I think it may be said quite decisively,' Russell opined, 'that ... modern logic has proved this argument invalid.' Plantinga's reformulation, Kenny remarks, serves as 'a salutary warning of the danger that awaits any historian of logic who declares a philosophical issue definitively closed'.[13]

The ontological argument is mercifully absent from these pages, but the salutary warning retains its power. Those who have pronounced the sentence of death on God, or on atheists, have done so prematurely. Both are here to stay.

Possibilities

Types of atheism

'There is nothing but infidelity, infidelity, infidelity': An early modern plague

Early modern Europe was crawling with atheists. In Italy, wrote Roger Ascham, in 1551, 'a man may freely discourse against what he will, against whom he lust, against any Prince, against any government, yea against God himself, and his whole religion'.[1] The Englishmen who lived there, he later lamented, are 'Epicures in living and atheists in doctrine'.[2] It was a land, according to one seventeenth-century writer, of 'pox, poisoning, and atheism'.[3] Voltaire spoke for many when he wrote in *The Sage and the Atheist* that 'Italy, in the fifteenth century, was full of atheists – and what was the consequence? Cases of poisoning were as common as invitations to supper'.[4]

Italy was particularly bad, long infected by pagan authors, but nowhere was immune. Inquisitorial records from fifteenth-century Spain offer examples of universalism, materialism and unbridled scepticism aplenty. France was no better. The Jesuit Francois Garasse identified five different types of atheism in his country – 'furious and enraged atheism', 'atheism of libertinage and corruption of manners', 'atheism of profanation', 'wavering or unbelieving atheism' and 'brutal, lazy, melancholy atheism' – all of which were, of course, reprehensible.[5] Marin Mersenne, a French theologian, philosopher and mathematician of repute, claimed there were as many as 50,000 atheists in Paris in the early seventeenth century.[6]

Northern Europe was not spared the shame. When Jakob

Friedrich Reimann published his history of books in German lands in 1713, he explained how atheism had been a live issue since the twelfth century when it arose in the wake of Averroism and Emperor Friedrich II.[7] According to Matthias Knutzen, himself a prominent atheist, there was an underground society of 700 sworn atheists in late seventeenth-century German academic circles.

Holland was particularly notorious during the seventeenth century as the European capital of free thought and infidelity. It was in Holland, for example, that the Devil, witchcraft and demonic spirits were first methodically denounced and banned, albeit by Balthasar Bekker, a sincere Dutch minister. And it was in Holland that Europe's most formidable and comprehensive atheistic system originated and took root, during Bekker's life.

And then there was England. A *Discourse on the Present State of England*, a report to Lord Burleigh, in 1572, claimed that 'the realm is divided into three parties, the Papists, the Atheists, and the Protestants'.[8] The Puritan Richard Greenham claimed that 'atheism in England is more to be feared than Popery'.[9] Walter, Earl of Essex, complained in 1576 that in England 'there is nothing but infidelity, infidelity, infidelity, atheism, atheism, atheism'.[10] More desperately still, Thomas Nashe wrote in his *Christ's Tears over Jerusalem*, 'there is no sect now in England so scattered as Atheism. In vain do you preach, in vain do you teach ... how many followers this damnable paradox has; how many high wits it hath bewitched.'[11]

So prevalent was atheism among Elizabethan intellectuals that some even formed schools, coteries dedicated to its discussion and dissemination. An official enquiry held at Cerne Abbas in 1594 into Sir Walter Raleigh and his circle of eminent Elizabethan atheists found that they denied the reality of heaven and hell, and argued that 'we die like beasts, and when we are gone there is no remembrance of us'.[12] By 1600, the Bishop of Exeter could complain that in his diocese it was 'a matter very common to dispute whether there be a God or not'. Seventeen years later, a Spanish ambassador estimated that the number of English atheists was somewhere in the region of 900,000,[13] or around a sixth of the population.

Refutations were everywhere. From the late sixteenth century onwards, booksellers sold a growing number of books refuting godlessness. Texts like Philip of Mornay's comprehensively named *A Woorke concerning the trewnesse of the Christian Religion, written in French: Against Atheists, Epicures, Paynims, Jews, Mahumetists, and other Infidels* [originally written in French], or John Dove's *A Confutation of Atheisme*[14] stood on English shelves, just as André D'Abillon's *La Divinité défendue contre les athées* and David Derodon's *L'athéisme convaincu* did in France.[15]

It was all to no avail. Atheism spread, and not just among the ill-educated from whom the authorities should have expected little better. It was one thing for people like John Deryner of Great Bedwyn in Wiltshire to maintain that 'there was no God and no resurrection, and that men died a death like beasts' (although he perhaps shouldn't have voiced such an opinion in front of the parish children); or for Ralph Byckenell of Over Compton in Dorset to tell his minister that 'there was no God, and that he could prove by certain arguments' (although as Byckenell was churchwarden one might have hoped for better).[16] But it was quite another when respectable men like Thomas Harriot (mathematician and astronomer), George Gascoigne (poet and soldier), John Caius (physician), Nicholas Bacon (Lord Keeper of the Great Seal), and the Earl of Oxford were suspect.[17]

There were official enquiries, such as that into the Cerne Abbas circle, but they were of no avail. Atheism spread through Europe like an unspiritual plague. The former Augustinian canon and satirist Ferrante Pallavicino, for example, brought 'heresy and atheism' back to Italy from Germany after he had met a French soldier on campaign there. At least, that was what his biographer claimed.[18]

Living in a pre-scientific age, early modern Europeans would not have known about memes, but had they done so, they surely would have thought atheism spread like one. It was everywhere, a veritable virus of the mind. Indeed, according to Robert Burton, it was best treated like an illness. 'Atheism, idolatry, heresy, hypocrisy, though they have one common root, that is indulgence to corrupt affection, yet their growth is different, they have divers symptoms, occasions, and must have several cures and remedies.'[19]

'The word atheist is now used as the word barbarous was': The meaning of atheism

Or perhaps not: you don't have to read very far in the sixteenth and seventeenth centuries to realize that early modern Europeans did not use the word atheist in the way that we do. Nor do you have to read far to realize that they were not overly cautious in their usage. The word was thrown about with as much abandonment as Communist during the McCarthy years, and to a similar effect.

Atheist was, in essence, a smear. The word could be used of those who (allegedly) denied divine providence, and of those who (allegedly) denied God's involvement in the world; of those who denied the immortality of the soul and of those who denied the existence of hell and heaven; of those who denied the doctrine of creation and of those who denied the existence of the spirit world. It was used by Catholics of Protestants, who denied the authority of God's representative on earth, and by Protestants of Catholics, who evaded and ignored God's word in scripture by placing their trust in a worldly authority. It could, in other words, be used very loosely to denote any heterodox belief that smelled even a little bit like the denial of God.

More extravagantly still, it could be used – indeed was used, universally – to describe those whose behaviour was anti-social or immoral. The Jacobean author Nicholas Breton put this well in his 1616 book of didactic character sketches, *The Good and the Badde, or Descriptions of the Worthies and Unworthies of this Age*. In this he described the Atheist, 'or Most Bad Man', as a figure of desperation, 'who dares to anything even to his soul's damnation', making 'sin a jest, grace a humour, truth a fable, and peace a cowardice'.

Breton was not done with this. The atheist, he explained, 'is the danger of society, the love of vanity, the hate of charity, and the shame of humanity ... The tavern is his palace and his belly is his god ... He knows not God, nor thinks of heaven but walks through the world as a devil towards hell'.[20] Not much had changed by the end of the century. The deist Charles Blount observed in 1680, 'the word atheist is now used, as heretofore the word barbarous was, all persons differing in Opinions, Customs or Manners being then term'd Barbarous, as now Atheists'.[21]

At the same time as early modern Europeans threw the accusation of atheism as wide as a farmer sowing seed, they also took care to define and analyse it with great precision. Francis Bacon identified four causes of atheism in his short essay on the subject – 'divisions in religion', 'scandal of priests', 'custom of profane scoffing in holy matters', and 'learned times, specially with peace and prosperity; for troubles and adversities do more bow men's minds to religion' – adding that 'a little philosophy inclineth man's mind to atheism; but depth in philosophy bringeth men's minds about to religion'.[22] Later in the century, the Cambridge Platonist philosopher Ralph Cudworth, in his massive *True Intellectual System of the Universe* outdid Bacon and outlined 14 grounds on which atheism was possible, ranging from the impossibility of the human mind to comprehend God to the evident defectiveness of Providence.

However many causes of atheism there were, there were undoubtedly numerous kinds of atheist. Perhaps in honour of the Holy Trinity, there were often three kinds. According to Laurent Pollot there were those 'who do not know the true God', those who 'doubt or even feel or speak ill of God's providence', and those who 'force themselves to erase all sentiments of divinity from their heart, and blaspheming miserably, say there is no God'.[23] According to the French Calvinist and theologian David Derodon, there were 'the refined', who were philosophical sceptics; 'the debauched', who lived immorally without care for God's laws; and 'the ignorant' whose belief was weak or inadequate.[24]

Pierre Bayle, one of Europe's arch-atheists himself, at least in the mind of his critics, also spoke of 'three degrees of Atheism' in his influential *Dictionnaire historique et critique*. 'The first is to maintain that there is no God. The second, to deny that the world is the work of God. The third, is to assert that God has created the world by the necessity of his own nature, and not by the inducement of free will.'[25]

Thomas Nashe's *Christ's Tears over Jerusalem* was more cautious, separating out two types of atheist, the careless, who were simply preoccupied and overwhelmed by life and forgot God, and the deliberate, who were more considered in their doubts, coming to believe, by reason, that there was no resurrection, no providence and no God.[26] This division corresponded loosely to the most widespread distinction of the time, made between 'practical' and 'theoretical' atheism.

Practical atheists were wicked. They were the debauched, the adulterous, the drunks, the unapologetic sinners who lived without fear of providence, judgement or the God who underpinned both. They were, according to the Swiss Calvinist Pierre Viret, those who 'do not want to be subjects either of God or of any creature, but [who want] to do everything that pleases them.'[27] Molière's *Don Juan* – described by his valet as 'the greatest scoundrel the earth ever bore, a madman, a dog, a devil, a Turk; a heretic, who believes neither in Heaven nor Hell nor Hobgoblin, who spends his life like the beasts that perish, a swine of Epicurus, a very Sardanapalus,[28] who stops his ears to all the remonstrances that can be made, and treats all we believe in as old wives tales' – was merely a more than usually colourfully drawn type of the age.[29]

By contrast, theoretical atheists – if they existed at all ('one can be an atheist by heart, but one cannot be one by the mind' confidently declared one late seventeenth-century writer[30]), were those who had come to the intellectual conclusion that there was no God.

The two were not necessarily distinct. Indeed, they often blended into one in contemporaries' minds. Atheists are those 'whom debauchery, bad company, or little knowledge of good letters have so corrupted that they dare to deny publicly the Being who gave them their being', wrote Derodon in 1659.[31] Atheism was 'a disorder of the mind conceived in libertinism', according to one French Jesuit.[32] All the meticulous definitions and distinctions of atheism teased out by god-fearing early moderns tended to collapse back into the mess of anti-social libertinism.

It is this that lies at the heart of the wild accusations of atheism that were thrown with such abandon from the early sixteenth to the eighteenth centuries. For, to reject God was not just to reject God. It was to reject the authority structures established in his name. It was to reject the moral code that was revealed in his word and guaranteed by the promise, or threat, of his judgement. Indeed, it was to reject moral realism altogether, replacing absolute right and wrong with personal preference or, worse, moral indifference borne of materialism and determinism. Without God, wrote John Milton, 'there would be no distinction between right and wrong; the estimate of virtue would entirely depend on the blind opinion of men'.[33]

In doing all this, atheism undermined the authority of prelate and prince, denying them the ability and right to maintain social order. It was because belief in God was 'the root and foundation of every polity' that atheism was understood – *felt* – as denial of entire existing order.[34]

This was evident in the matter of oaths. Order depended on justice; justice on functioning judicial proceedings; functioning judicial proceedings on veracity; veracity on reliable oaths; and reliable oaths on that which they were sworn. No God meant, therefore, no justice. 'All moral evidence ... all confidence in human veracity must be weakened by irreligion, and overthrown by infidelity', wrote William Blackstone in his *Commentaries on the Law of England* in the mid-eighteenth century.[35] To be an atheist was, in effect, to declare war on the society and culture of which you were a part. Questions of atheism were as much about what happened in this world as what happened in the next.

This explains why atheism was so feared, so hated and so punished. It also explains why in many of the instances it was used in early modern Europe 'atheist' would be more accurately rendered into modern English as 'godless' or 'ungodly'. Within the early modern mind, what you believed and how you lived were joined together, and it was not until the two could be put asunder that atheism could emerge publicly into European culture.

'All religions have been formed in the brains of men': Atheistic views
Just because someone was called an atheist, then, it doesn't mean they were. But, conversely, just because someone was called an atheist, it doesn't mean they were not. 'Atheist' may have been used with abandonment to label and libel those deemed unorthodox, suspect or immoral, but it does not follow that none of those thus accused was an atheist in the sense that we would use the word.

Whether there were atheists, in the sense of people who did not believe in God, in early modern Europe has been the subject of a significant historical debate since 1942 when Lucien Febvre published a major study entitled *The Problem of Unbelief in the Sixteenth Century: the Religion of Rabelais*.[36] Françoise Rabelais' anti-clerical humour had once been taken to be more than just anti-clerical, a cipher for anti-Christian rationalism. Febvre argued that there was no evidence that Rabelais was not a believer and, more generally, that it was, in effect, impossible to be an atheist at the time. The Christian worldview and culture was so universal, so deep, so thick that it was, for all intents and purposes, impossible to think outside it.[37]

Febvre's book on Rabelais proved influential and scholars spent many years discussing whether his thesis had merit: were there atheists in early modern Europe? The quest was handicapped by the enthusiasm with which the word was used but close historical readings showed that there were people who disavowed Christian doctrine in such a way as to sound like atheists as the modern mind understands the term. The complicating factor was that these would-be atheists seem to go back a long way.

In the early eleventh century, two clergymen in Orléans insisted that the universe had existed from eternity, heaven and hell were fictions and the Trinity was incoherent.[38] The following century, a French monk called Helinant referred disapprovingly to those who believed that there was no other world and no more life after death for men than for animals. The heresy registers of Bishop Fournier of Pamiers in the early fourteenth century include accusations of religious scepticism, materialism and disbelief in the afterlife. Another inquisition, this time in Turin later in the century heard statements from individuals who admitted to believing that Jesus was the natural son of Mary and Joseph and that there was to be no punishment after death.

This was all very well for peasants but the educated also voiced similar opinions. Thomas Semer, alias Taylor, was accused of Lollardy in mid-fifteenth-century England but appeared to be guilty of much worse. He denied the existence of the soul, of heaven, hell and purgatory. He claimed that Christ was nothing but a man born of Joseph and Mary, and said the Eucharist was nothing more than bread. As far as he was concerned, the Bible was just a set of prescriptions for human behaviour of human devising to keep the peace. Semer was not alone. Other Lollards were accused of, and some admitted to, denying the Trinity and resurrection of the body. Semer's doubts, however, seem to have been particularly well developed.[39]

In England, Lollardy was blamed for such opinions. In Spain, it was the Jews. Forced to choose between death, exile and conversion in the fifteenth century, many Spanish Jews converted. Their troubles did not end there. These *conversos* were treated with widespread suspicion and hostility, often accused and often found guilty of unbelief or of showing insufficient respect during mass. Sometimes, the disrespect went further, with some going on record for doubting Jesus' miracles, or claiming that he was crucified as a

Jewish heretic. This was not atheism but it would find its way into atheistic rhetoric a century or two later. Many of these accounts are unreliable, as Jews and others were threatened or tortured into confession. Nevertheless, inquisitorial records report so much anti-clericalism, blasphemy, obscenity, doubts about the resurrection, materialistic views of this life, scepticism about the next, use of magic, sympathy with other religions and religious universalism, that it is impossible to believe it was all an invention.[40]

Such views only grew in the sixteenth and seventeenth centuries as Reformation ideas spread enthusiasm, heterodoxy and panic. Mid-century John Calvin launched an attack on some of the intellectuals of his day, including Rabelais, for their religious scepticism. Among other things, he accused them of publicly asserting that 'all religions have been formed in the brains of men; that we think there is a God because we like to believe it; that hope of life eternal is something to amuse idiots with; that everything said about hell is done to frighten little children'.[41]

Church records show that such views were genuine, rather than the product of the great reformer's febrile imagination. England offers colourful examples aplenty.[42] In 1556, the parson of Tunstall was accused of saying that whoever believed that Christ sat on the right hand of the Lord was a fool. In 1563, Thomas Lovell of Hevingham, Norfolk, remarked that 'God the Son was not believed upon [in] his own country, but driven out; and they [did] better than we do'.[43] Three years later, Robert Master of Woodchurch, Kent, denied 'that God made the sun, the moon, the earth, the water'.[44] Around the same time, a man in Norfolk suggested there were 'divers Christs'. A little later, John Hilton, a London priest, confessed that he had preached a sermon at St Martin-in-the-Fields in which he had claimed that the Old and New Testaments were 'but Fables' and that the doctrine of the Trinity was not true.[45]

Perhaps most notorious, at least in England, was the case of the playwright Christopher Marlowe. A few days before he was stabbed in a Deptford pub, a 'Note' of his religious opinions was delivered to the Lord Keeper of the Great Seal, which claimed that the playwright had denied Christ's divinity and the authority of the Bible, while asserting that Moses was a 'juggler' and religion nothing more than a means of social control. Subsequent evidence claimed that he also rejected miracles, was hostile to prayers and blasphemed the Trinity. More scandalous still, both the note and the evidence of playwright Thomas Kyd recorded that Marlowe was of the opinion that 'St John the Evangelist was bed-fellow to Christ and leaned always in his bosom, [and] that he used him as the sinners of Sodom'.[46] Moreover, Marlowe was not content to keep such views to himself. 'He persuades men to atheism ... and utterly scorning both God and his ministers', the Note claimed.

The 'Baines Note', as it is known, is lurid, and its author a paid informer who admitted elsewhere to scoffing at religion. Other evidence for Marlowe's atheism is hardly cleaner. But, there does seem to be general consensus that Marlowe's religious views, whatever exactly they were, were 'monstrous', 'damnable', 'horrible' and 'dangerous'. Had Marlowe not been stabbed when he was, he might have endured a worse fate still.[47] Such as that of Geoffroy Vallée and Giulo Cesare Vanini: Vallée was a nobleman from Orléans. He was executed as an atheist in 1574 for advocating reason as an 'antidote' to fear and dogma, despite attacking atheism and libertinism, as well as Christianity, in the short pamphlet that earned him the pyre.[48] His case was soon forgotten, unlike Vanini's who became one of Europe's first atheist martyrs. Born in 1585, and educated by Jesuits, Vanini joined the Carmelites, another Catholic order, and then left Venice for England in 1612, haunted by rumours of extreme unorthodoxy. He spent the following years travelling in Flanders, Paris, Liguria, Lyons and Toulouse, and writing two books that were eventually posthumously published.

Vanini appeared to accept the eternity of matter, mocked the doctrine of creation, argued against the existence of non-material beings, and the human soul, claimed that miracles had natural explanations and said that the only true worship was worship of nature. Religions, he claimed, including Christianity, were fictions invented by priests and princes to secure power. Mankind, like other animals, found his earthly origins in putrefaction. Immorality was the product of diet or illness. He even cast doubts over the very existence of God. This was a remarkably comprehensive list of heterodox opinions, hardly less incendiary than Marlowe's provocative blasphemies. Not surprisingly, the authorities were scandalized by them and dragged Vanini to the pyre in 1619.

Vanini sounds as if he were an atheist, although not necessarily a coherent one. But how should one categorize Menocchio, an Italian miller and autodidact who argued with the parish priest, was tried, sentenced, imprisoned, released, and then, eventually retried and burned by the Inquisition? Menocchio was not simply an argumentative troublemaker. He argued that 'earth, air, water, and fire were mixed together' in a chaotic mass – 'just as cheese is made out of milk' – from which worms appeared. 'The most holy majesty decreed that these should be God and the angels', including the God worshipped by humans.

Whether or not these various opinions did constitute a considered 'theoretical' atheism, rather than a contemptuous indifference or 'practical' atheism (or, in the case of Menocchio, just extreme eccentricity) is impossible to say at this distance. It is telling, though, that however much contemporaries dismissed atheists as merely mad, bad or non-existent, they still expended considerable energy in refuting and disproving them. André D'Abillon claimed, like many of his peers, that atheist views were inane, and then spent 250 pages proving God's existence from arguments from miracles, demonology, prophecy and conscience, among others. This was a lot of energy to spend fighting a shadow.

New worlds

'On the Nature of Things': ancient worlds
Whether atheism, in any coherent and recognizably modern sense, existed in early modern Europe is, therefore, questionable; but whether *atheistic views* did is not. Such views – variously sceptical, blasphemous, anti-clerical, materialist – clearly could be heard if you were prepared to spend time in the wrong company. They might sometimes cohere into something more substantial, as with Vanini, or something more comprehensively pugnacious, as with Marlowe, or something more peculiar, as with Menocchio. But most remained variations on a Christian theme, albeit sometimes highly discordant variations.

This is reflected in the history of words. The Middle Ages had a sophisticated vocabulary for heresy, which had developed over the centuries, but it had no specialized language for unbelief.[49] It was not, as we have seen, that there was no one who denied core Christian tenets. Rather, it was that all such beliefs were understood as variants, albeit sometimes enormous ones, of Christianity. So dominant was the Christian culture and worldview in which virtually everyone grew up, that it was all but impossible to think outside it. That began to change slowly in the fifteenth century, from which time visions of different worlds emerged. The word for atheist was coined, in Latin, French and English, in the first half of the sixteenth century, to capture the unprecedented worldview these new worlds presented.[50]

Three of these new worlds would be especially important for the development of atheism. From the mid-fourteenth century onwards educated Europeans became increasingly aware of their rich, long-forgotten and by now entirely foreign cultural past. Scholars scoured monasteries for much-copied manuscripts of long lost texts. Greek scholars moved west ahead of advancing Islamic armies, bringing precious codices. Bibliophiles and poets took it upon themselves to recover and celebrate their classical heritage.

For the most part, this was accommodated within the existing medieval mindset. The majority of humanists were, like Petrarch, devout Christians, and although the cumulative effect of their work was to lift the Augustinian gloom about human nature, the dormant texts that began to circulate from the 1400s did not radically challenge Christian thought.

Or, rather, most of them did not: some ideas and some texts were more threatening than others. Pyrrhonian scepticism, so called because it could (theoretically) trace its origins to Pyrrho of Elis in the third century before Christ, argued that humans could never be sure whether reliable knowledge was possible, and so should withhold judgement on all questions concerning knowledge.[51] For those who liked their religion clear and certain, this was not an appealing prospect. The sole surviving Pyrrhonian texts, written by Sextus Empiricus in the late second century, were all but unknown in the Middle Ages, but they re-emerged in the mid-fifteenth century and were destined to play a significant, if unpredictable, role in the development of atheistic thought.[52]

More directly menacing was the rediscovery of Lucretius' poem *De rerum natura* or *On the Nature of Things* in a monastery in southern Germany in 1417. Lucretius was a Roman poet philosopher of the first century BC of whom little else is known. *De rerum natura* is his only surviving work and although influential at the time – it was praised by Cicero, Virgil and Ovid – it had disappeared with the ancient world.

Over 7,000 lines long, the poem offered a view of the world that was entirely different from the conventional Christian one. Lucretius' universe was made up of tiny, indivisible particles derived from the 'atomos' of Democritus. These were eternal and uncreated, ever combining and separating to make the familiar objects of our universe in endlessly random and unpredictable ways.

The universe itself had no creator, no designer and no plan. Nature was constantly in flux, providence an illusion and human beings as accidental and incidental as anything else. The human soul, made up of the same atomic material as the human body, was no less mortal. Eternal life was a fantasy. Spiritual bodies, such as angels or demons, were illusions. The gods existed but were entirely uninterested in human affairs. Humans could know nothing of them and should not waste their time trying. Organized religion was not only delusional but harmful. The goal of human life was the increase of pleasure and the reduction of pain, best achieved by ridding oneself of delusions and appreciating the true nature of things. Death was nothing to fear.

Technically not atheistic itself, *De rerum natura* nonetheless outlined a coherent worldview that would form and inform atheistic thought in Europe for centuries. Its impact was slow in coming. Considered for, although not added to, the Catholic Church's Index of Prohibited Books in 1549, it attained a kind of contraband caché. Printed editions carried warnings and disavowals of its teaching. Montaigne's *Essays* contain nearly 100 direct quotations from the poem. Latin versions appeared regularly throughout the seventeenth century. When Thomas Creech translated it into English in 1682, it was heralded as the most complete system of atheism in print. All major radical thinkers in the Enlightenment seemed to have read it. Baron D'Holbach translated it into French. His friend Jacques-André Naigeon owned numerous editions and commentaries. Denis Diderot drew on it deeply for his controversial *D'Alembert's Dream*. Claude Adrien Helvétius quoted from it for the epigraph to *On the Mind*. Julien Offray de La Mettrie used it as inspiration for his *The System of Epicurus*.

Taken separately, many of the poem's ideas might be integrated into a Christian worldview. Atomism, for example, while understood as a materialist threat by many, could be accommodated: the world had to be made from something, after all. Francis Bacon was inclined towards atomism for a while, seeing in it a better physical basis for belief in God than the traditional one of 'four mutable elements, and one immutable fifth essence'. A little later, the French philosopher Pierre Gassendi took the atheistic sting out of the doctrine by giving God a prominent role in creating the atoms and in using them to construct the world. More generally, Lucretius had lived before Christ and that always offered a get-out-of-jail free card. Could he be expected to know any better in the age before God's full revelation?

Such tactics were ultimately inadequate to the task, however. Lucretius' universe was coherent in its materialism, its diminution of the human, its abandonment of providence and of moral realism. It presented another universe, from which a coherent atheistic world could be constructed.

'One's nation, one's country, one's home determines one's religion': Foreign worlds

If the ancient world provided the picture of another world, so did other worlds.[53] Long known by rumour, ancient and foreign cultures became more vivid from the early years of the sixteenth century. Increased presence and trade in Southern and Eastern Asia alerted Western Europeans to cultures and traditions of scholarship that were ancient – perhaps even more ancient than those of the Mediterranean – and that had ideas of God that were hard to square with those familiar in Christendom. Worse still, some cultures, such as that reported by missionaries in China, appeared to have no concept of God at all.

This was a serious challenge to the argument that belief in God was universal. Indeed, it was worse even than this. Not only were the Chinese apparently atheistic but they had a longstanding, high-achieving and apparently fully functioning society. This was strong medicine. Continental Europe was convulsed in the 1720s when Christian Wolff argued that Confucius' moral maxims, and the Chinese society they grounded, showed how natural reason, free from revelation and even belief in God, could attain moral truth.[54] Journeys west were easier to accommodate. The cultures they revealed were primitive, so the fact that they had apparently no knowledge of the Christian God mattered less. Indeed, it made positive sense, serving as an open invitation for mission.

New worlds could provide a different kind of provocation, however, with accounts of foreign lands raising issues about pleasure, ethics and moral relativism. Such issues need not be atheistic. One of the earliest literary depictions of the new world was Thomas More's *Utopia*, whose inhabitants, while largely tolerant of different beliefs, drew the line at those who denied the soul's immortality or divine providence. 'For it stands to reason, if you're not afraid of anything but prosecution, and have no hopes of anything after you're dead, you'll always be trying to evade or break the laws of your country, in order to gain your own private ends',[55] remarks More's Raphael Hythloday, neatly capturing the early modern fear of atheism.

More's *Utopia* goaded and questioned Christendom; other new worlds could be more challenging. Unlike those presented by the Chinese or by Lucretius or other ancient writers, the challenge lay not in the prospect of sophisticated and cultured alternatives to Latin Christendom. Rather, it was simply that there were many different ways of seeing the world, each with its own particular intellectual, moral and spiritual dimensions. The religious truths, so long deemed self-evident to Western Christians, were nothing of the kind.

One of the most contentious examples of this was Pierre Charron's *De la sagesse*. Born in 1541, one of 25 children, Charron was educated at the University of Paris and became a respected preacher and theologian, a reputation that was damaged by his magnum opus published in 1603, shortly before he died. Despite the fact that an earlier work had vigorously attacked atheists as part of its broadside against Calvinists, *De la sagesse* was deeply suspect, described as a 'seminary of irreligion', and earning him accusations of being a 'secret atheist'.[56]

Charron was a disciple of Michel de Montaigne and his master's rejection of all forms of dogmatism runs through *De la sagesse*. 'Just think how much we have learnt from the discovery of the New World, the East and West Indies … who can doubt that in the foreseeable future there will be further discoveries,' Charron enthused.[57] Like his master, he was acutely aware of how an expanding horizon relativized everything.

Charron's universe, like Lucretius', was fluid. 'Everything is subject to birth, alteration and death, to the influences of changing times, places, climates, stars, and territorial divisions.'[58] Everything was contestable, 'subject to contradiction and dispute'.[59] This might be an acceptable Christian view if Charron had gone on to explain how such diversity was as a result of the fall, and other cultures were therefore open to judgement and/or ripe for conversion. But he did no more than gesture very vaguely in that direction. In place of judgement, Charron observed how 'whatever is held to be impious, unjust, disgraceful in one place, is pious, just and honourable in another', and that 'one cannot name a single law, custom, or belief that is universally either approved or condemned'.[60]

Most seriously, Charron relativized religion. 'One's nation, one's country, one's home determines one's religion ... We are circumcised or baptized – Jews, or Muslims, or Christians – before we know we are human beings. It is not we who choose our religions.' 'If religion was of divine establishment,' he wrote, 'shining out with God's glory, it would be solidly established in our hearts, and would have consequences that would seem, and would indeed be, miraculous'.[61] Religions were, in effect, all the same. 'All discover and publicise miracles, prodigies, oracles, sacred mysteries, saints, prophets, festivals, articles of faith, and beliefs necessary for salvation ... each pretends to be better and truer than the others'.[62]

The way in which Charron denied universal values, saw superstition within all religious practice and renounced proselytism and efforts to save sinners was too much. *De la sagesse* was soon placed on the Index. The idea that other cultures relativized Christianity, however, was to be a persistent one in atheist polemic. When David Hume wrote, over a century later, that 'some nations have been discovered who entertained no sentiments of religion ... and no two nations, and scarce any two men, have ever agreed precisely in the same sentiments,'[63] he was developing ideas, in an atheistic direction, that the discovery of new worlds had forced upon his predecessors.

'I count religion but a childish toy': Unsettling worlds

Ancient worlds and new worlds opened up alternatives to early modern Christians, but such alternatives need not be so distant in space and time. A more blatant alternative worldview was opened up by a man whose name became synonymous with a particularly cynical form of practical atheism.

Nicolo Machiavelli was a product of renaissance humanism. His father, Barnardo, was a lawyer whose enthusiasm for the *studia humanitatis* shaped his son's education and helped him secure appointment, in 1498, as Secretary of the Ten of War, Florence's foreign affairs and war committee.

In effect the city's highest-ranking diplomat, Machiavelli led embassies to, and spent months in, the courts of the French King, the Pope, the Holy Roman Emperor and others. Over the next 14 years, he was immersed in the cloak-and-dagger world of renaissance diplomacy and realpolitik, noting the folly of weakness, inflexibility and vacillation of some and the strong, decisive, cold-blooded determination of others.

Machiavelli himself fell from grace in 1513, when the republican regime he served collapsed and he was then suspected of conspiracy against their Medici successors, tortured and imprisoned. The experiences marked him, disabusing him of any lingering idealism and precipitating several works that would see him vilified for centuries.

The best known of them, *The Prince*, was written in 1513, although not published until after the author's death. A failed attempt to curry favour with Lorenzo de' Medici, it is an inadvisedly honest tract on statecraft, which carefully and thoroughly subverts the, by then well-established, humanist genre. Machiavelli ridiculed the conventional examples in which virtuous statecraft triumphed.

He talked up some of the most brutal rules of his age and was withering about traditional humanist virtues. Generosity might be essential for the man seeking power, but it is dangerous and foolhardy for the ruler in power. Of compassion he writes limply, 'I'm sure every leader would wish to be seen as compassionate rather than cruel', before going on to explain that 'excessive compassion leads to public disorder, muggings and murder … It's much safer to be feared than loved'. Similarly with honour: it was fine, up to a point, but 'a sensible leader cannot and must not keep his word if by doing so he puts himself at risk'. The ruled were not better than their rulers. Most people were fundamentally self-interested and unreliable, he argued: 'they are ungrateful and unreliable; they lie, they fake, they're greedy for cash and they melt away in the face of danger.'

Saying this kind of thing out loud may have been impolitic and upsetting for humanist presuppositions but that was no crime. Humanism, after all, was itself a reaction to the rather bleaker vision of human sin, which had long dominated the medieval mind, and from which God, through the intercession of his church, rescued humanity. Where Machiavelli's was inexcusably inflammatory was in showing that theological cure was no better than the sinful poison. *The Prince*'s short chapter on 'church states' is a masterpiece of subtle, savage anti-ecclesiastical irony. Church states, Machiavelli observes, are upheld by ancient religious institutions that 'are so strong and well established' they 'keep their rulers in power no matter what they do or how they live'. 'Only Church leaders possess states without defending them and subjects without governing them'.

The New Testament is completely absent from *The Prince* and Machiavelli's few Old Testament examples are lauded for their martial abilities rather than their godliness, being effectively indistinguishable from the book's non-biblical heroes. 'Moses, Cyrus, Theseus and Romulus couldn't have got people to respect their new laws for long if they hadn't possessed armed force.'

Divine interest and intervention made little difference. 'We can hardly say much about Moses, since he merely carried out God's orders,' Machiavelli disarmingly says, before going on to say of the other rulers, 'when we look into the specific actions each took and the institutions they established, we'll see they don't differ that much from what Moses did under divine guidance.'

As if this were not enough, there was the book's deafening silence when it came to any final divine judgement, and the author's notorious willingness, indeed advice, to fake piety: 'There is nothing more important than appearing to be religious.' Altogether, the book wrapped up self-serving amorality, power-worship, false piety and religious disregard into a neat, frightening package.

The Prince failed in its attempts to curry favour and Machiavelli's last 14 years were spent as a man of letters. His later works do not have *The Prince*'s shocking honesty, but nor do they do much to deny its implications. Why were people 'in those ancient times ... greater lovers of Liberty than in these times,' he asks in Book II of his *Discourses on Livy*? The answer is Christianity. For while 'our Religion' has 'glorified more humble and contemplative men rather than men of action', placing 'the highest good in humility, lowliness, and contempt of human things', the religion of the ancients 'places it in the greatness of soul, the strength of body, and all the other things which make men very brave'. The result is 'to have rendered the world weak and a prey to wicked men, who can manage it securely'. This was Nietzsche long before Nietzsche.

Machiavelli's world was cold and amoral, replacing right with might. Religion was a tool of political control. God was, for all intents and purposes, absent. The law was, at best, a temporary, expedient measure. What is good, what is noble, what is generous, what is right: all are irrelevant. What matters is survival and power.

Some modern critics have argued that Machiavelli was a Christian.[64] If so, he certainly wasn't seen as such by his contemporaries, becoming a shorthand for godlessness, feigned piety, amorality, cynicism and political violence. 'I count religion but a childish toy / And hold there is no sin but ignorance ... / Might first made kings, and laws were then most sure/ When, like the Draco's, they were writ in blood,' proclaims Machevil in the Prologue to Marlowe's *The Jew of Malta*. The world revealed by Machiavelli stood as a warning of what Europe would become if it denied God.

Authority and scepticism

'The Holy Ghost is not a Sceptic': Authority and scepticism
In their own ways, Lucretius, Charron and Machiavelli lifted the veil on alternative ungodly possible worlds. They were recognizable, even coherent, but they were also devoid of the comforts, illusory or otherwise, of Christendom. Put another way, they showed that other visions of the world were possible but not actual, still less desirable. The opening up of these different visions of reality also, however, coincided with the biggest crisis in European intellectual and political life in a millennium, which shook the ground on which human knowledge, security and life were based. This was fundamentally a crisis of authority, intellectual, ecclesiastical and political, and it made all the difference for atheism.

Latin Christendom had experienced tremors of authority before the Reformation. Some, like Lollardy, had been suppressed. Others, like the Great Schism in which two, and then three, popes claimed jurisdiction over Christendom, were negotiated. Questions of authority were not, therefore, unprecedented. Martin Luther initially agreed that Christian doctrine should be judged by the criteria of Church tradition, councils and papal decrees but by 1520 he was denying the pope's authority to adjudicate over such matters, and placing scripture over and above tradition as means for evaluating truth.

This, however, left a problem: who could tell what constituted the legitimate interpretation of scripture? Was everyone's opinion equally valid? At first, this did not seem to be a problem but by the mid-1520s, when Europe witnessed a massive uprising that was exacerbated if not caused by doctrinal differences, there seemed to be validity in the accusation that elevating text over tradition meant localizing authority in sects and individuals, which invariably led to violent anarchy.

The Protestant response to this accusation varied. Luther emphasized the compulsion of conscience, and argued that scripture was self-authenticating. Calvin spoke of 'the interior persuasion of the Holy Spirit' and argued that 'the testimony of the Spirit is more eloquent than all reason'.[65] Neither proved a sufficient answer and many accused the reformers of being sceptics or atheists in disguise. When Michael Servetus, a French physician, argued, sincerely and on the basis of reason and inner persuasion, that the doctrine of the Trinity was unbiblical and therefore untenable, he merely reinforced such views, and the reformers in Geneva burned him at the stake.

There were some who tried to take the temperature out of the debate. Sebastian Castellio, a Reformed French preacher, defended Michael Servetus, arguing that the difficulty and opacity of much scripture, all too evident in the public disagreements of Christians, meant that no one could be absolutely sure of religious truth, and that therefore no one merited the stake. It was to little effect. 'A Christian ought … to be certain of what he affirms,' Luther had written contemptuously to Erasmus: 'The Holy Ghost is not a Sceptic'.[66]

If the Holy Ghost wasn't, others were. It was into this militarized crisis of authority that the revival of ancient scepticism spoke. The Latin word 'scepticus' had first appeared in 1430. The work of pre-eminent sceptic Sextus Empiricus had been discussed by some Greek-speaking humanists from the late fifteenth century, but very few knew anything of his thought before the first Latin translation of his work in the 1560s. By that time, politicized fault lines concerning the foundation of human knowledge had spread across Europe, and were swallowing thousands.

Sextus Empiricus had argued not that nothing could be known – an accusation wrongly levelled at many of his sixteenth-century followers – but that humans had insufficient grounds to be sure of their knowledge and so should suspend judgement. This, as historian of scepticism Richard Popkin has observed, was not an inherently anti- or irreligious position, despite latterly being deployed with great effect by irreligious thinkers. Indeed, for much of the sixteenth and seventeenth centuries, scepticism was used to *protect* religious faith, deployed to undermine human reasoning (which could not be trusted) rather than divine revelation (which could). Sceptics could believe as confidently as any religious adherent. They were simply doubtful about the *rational* grounds for belief, and its capacity for certainty. Scepticism was the antithesis of dogmatism, not faith.

Sextus was used to great effect in the doctrinal wars of the late sixteenth century as a means of undermining opponents. Catholics deployed sceptical arguments against Protestants to particularly devastating effect. On what basis did Protestants elevate their own reading of scripture above centuries of tradition? How could they be sure they interpreted it rightly? If church teaching could err, as they insisted, how could they then rely on the Bible in the first place, as it was the church that had chosen the canon?

Protestant ripostes failed to convince. The inner persuasion of the Holy Spirit merely begged the question. Reason, too, was inadequate: it may, as some claimed, be a natural human capacity but the rules of logic were set out by the pagan Aristotle and Jesus did not claim authority on the basis of pagan logic. In any case, was human reason really up to the task of adjudicating on things eternal, especially if the effects of the Fall were as deep-rooted in human nature as many claimed?

Sceptical trade was not just one way, however, and Protestants deployed Sextus' arguments as readily, if less effectively, as Catholics. The Catholic refuge of church tradition as the trustworthy guide to biblical interpretation was itself vulnerable. How could Catholics be sure that the works of Church Fathers were actually by the Church Fathers, or that they had not been altered, or that they were necessary truths? On what basis was ecclesiastical interpretation infallible? If Reformers could not be sure they interpreted scripture rightly, how could Catholics be sure they interpreted the Fathers rightly? Who, in short, should interpret the interpreters?

Military metaphors were popular in this conflict. Pyrrhonic scepticism was a 'machine of war'. Scholars attacked one another and fought back. 'While they wrest such Weapons out of our hands,' wrote one Protestant of the Catholic use of scepticism, 'they at the same time disarm themselves.'[67]

Such theological battles were not merely metaphorical, however, any more than they were merely theological. The early Reformation had placed enormous authority in the hands of the magistrate, largely as a means of wresting it from Rome, and by mid-century confessional blocs emerged across Europe. *Cuius regio eius religio* – 'whose realm, his religion' – became the continent's governing formula. Princes could dictate the confessional allegiance within their territory. Governments and their churches, courts and universities developed or strengthened mechanisms of intellectual and spiritual control. The question of theological authority, never far from that of political authority, became fatefully coterminous with it.

Lutheran Princes in Germany fought the Catholic Habsburg Emperor, from the 1530s onwards. The Swiss Confederacy was divided between confessional factions from the same time. French Protestants were tolerated, then massacred, then tolerated, then exiled. Dutch Calvinists, aided by other northern European Protestants, took the northern Netherlands from Spanish Catholics and split the country. England oscillated between reformed Protestantism, re-established Catholicism and then reformed, if compromised, Protestantism, which then stumbled into civil war. The Thirty Years War dragged in most European powers, although not always on predictable factional lines, and killed around a third of the German population.

Battles were rarely straightforwardly between Catholic and Protestant confessional blocs, with mainstream Protestants fighting one another and other fringe movements, as well as allying with Catholic forces when it was appropriate. Moreover, the extent to which these confessional wars were about confessional issues, as opposed to dynastic and political ones, is endlessly debated. Nevertheless, in as far as they served to be a bloody womb in which atheistic sentiments could germinate, it is irrelevant. Hundreds of Christians wrote thousands of pages demolishing the theological presuppositions of their opponents, arguments that were latterly seized upon by those with a blanket hostility to Christianity. And when intellectual battles became literal ones, thousands more witnessed innumerable public executions ostensibly at least justified for reasons of theological difference. The fact that those theological differences might be a cipher for political or social threats was a nuance easily lost amid the aroma of cooking flesh. Theological certainty could kill, and it wasn't even certain.

'Nothing comes to us except falsified and altered by our senses':
Using scepticism
In the shadow of uncertainty and armies, there emerged a new class of intellectual who, using Sextus' arguments, contended that nothing could be confidently known, a position popularized by and most associated with Michel de Montaigne.

Montaigne's father was a Catholic and his mother a convert to Protestantism from a Spanish Jewish background. Montaigne served as an advisor to nobility and royalty before retiring in his late thirties to a tower in the Dordogne, where he read Sextus, studied the natural theology of the fifteenth-century Catalan monk Raimond Sebond and invented the essay.

Sebond had argued, in his *Theologia Naturalis* written in the 1430s, that not only were faith and reason fully compatible but that Christianity could be proved by natural reason. Montaigne's *Apology* for him politely eviscerated the claim, showing how human reason was fundamentally unsound and Christianity rested on faith alone.

Human senses could not be trusted. 'Nothing comes to us except falsified and altered by our senses', of which we have a limited number to rely on. 'We have formed a truth by the consultation ... of our five senses; but perhaps we needed the agreement of eight or ten senses ... to perceive it certainly and in its essence.'[68] Even if we could rely on our senses, things divine were quite beyond the powers of human reasoning. This conviction concerning human inadequacy, Montaigne insisted, was quite consistent with the Bible's revelation of human nature, quoting St Paul to confirm his point.[69] But it was also a conviction driven by some rather more heterodox views concerning human nature.

Man, Montaigne argued, has few qualities that animals lack. Animals, after all, build, collaborate, grieve and apparently think, like we do. Human reason is a form of animal behaviour. Even human religion is not unique. Elephants, for example, 'are observed to lift up their trunks like arms, and, fixing their eyes towards the rising sun, continue long in meditation and contemplation, at certain hours of the day of their own motion without instruction or precept'. Anticipating Julien Offray de La Mettrie's arguments 150 years later, Montaigne claimed that our own powers change with our bodily and emotional conditions: how, then, can we know whether we ourselves are trustworthy, let alone others? By drawing on examples from the New World, the ancient world and the animal world, Montaigne constructed a tower of ethical relativism on foundations of human uncertainty.

His Christian response was a retreat to (what would one day be called) fideism. Unable to trust our intuition, sense, or reason, we only have revelation, mediated and interpreted by the church, to go on. 'Our religion did not come to us through reasoned arguments or from our own intelligence; it came through outside authority by commandments.'[70]

Sebond ended on the Church's Index of Prohibited Books in 1595 but it took another century before Montaigne's *Essays* were there. His scepticism was fêted by the orthodox at the time and his whimsical heterodoxies tolerated. Some, however, were uncomfortable with his willingness to jettison reason altogether and this became an increasing concern among his followers. Pierre Charron was, as we have seen, labelled a secret atheist. Others, like Gabriel Naudé and François de La Mothe Le Vayer – the so-called *libertines érudits* who dominated intellectual circles in early seventeenth-century France – were also suspect, despite occupying respected positions around the court.

The *libertines érudits* deployed scepticism vigorously to cut through superstition, Protestantism and, many feared, the very Catholic faith they purported to be defending. Naudé was Cardinal Richlieu's librarian, who was openly critical of many religious views and practices, for which he was labelled 'a learned unbeliever'.[71] Isaac La Peyrère, as we shall see, applied his scepticism to the Bible, with, for the time, devastating effect. La Mothe Le Vayer took scepticism to its extremes, denying the point of any scientific research, and arguing that attempts to discover the principles of nature were blasphemous.

Often interpreted as attempts to make Christianity seem ridiculous, which is one of the reasons why some scholars today see them as atheists in fideists' clothing, the *libertines érudits* protested their faithfulness. As ever with figures from this period, the truth demands a view on their integrity and sincerity, the adjudication of which is beyond the available evidence. Yet, even if they were sincere in their Catholic fideism, they still posed a threat to the foundations of religious belief. If Christian revelation was itself mediated by humans, depending on gospel writers who told stories about what Jesus said and (miraculously) did, and if humans couldn't trust their senses, why should they trust accounts of things that were perceived via the senses? Whatever their religious intentions the *libertines érudits* left problems hanging in their air on which others, whose religious intentions were less doubtful, would capitalize.

'An Atheist ... cannot be sure that he is not deceived': Countering scepticism

Some attempts to counter this scepticism proved fruitful. A number of thinkers recognized the full force of the sceptical attacks and acknowledged that definitive and irrefutable knowledge about reality was unattainable, but argued that a lesser, probabilistic knowledge of the way things appeared to be was both possible and adequate. In the hands of men like Marin Mersenne, a brilliant and widely connected French friar, philosopher and mathematician, and Pierre Gassendi, another priest and polymath, this attempt to chart an acceptable course between dogmatism and scepticism resulted in an early form of scientific method, a tentative means of grasping and navigating the perceived world, rather than a metaphysical system requiring secure ultimate foundation and indisputable proof.

Other attempts were more ambitious but also more problematic. René Descartes became aware of the depth of the sceptical challenge in his early thirties, having already made his name as a mathematician and scientist. His response was to establish a foundation so certain as to be incontestable, even in the face of an imagined evil genius, as deceitful as he was powerful, whose entire effort was directed to misleading us about the nature of reality.[72]

His famous response – *'Cogito ergo sum'* – was based on the supposedly indubitable fact of his own doubting, from which he concluded he was thinking and therefore existing. From this foundation he went on to construct a system of reliable knowledge which was dependent on God's own reliability, for it was only God's own perfection that could guarantee the link between what the rational 'I' experienced and thought, and what was real in the world.

In contrast to the fideistic sceptics, for whom the mere fact of revelation was sufficient evidence, Descartes sought to demonstrate God's existence, doing so on the foundations of his own idea of God, from which he constructed an argument for God's existence and perfection. This was not a tentative argument. As he said in response to an early objection to his *Meditations*, 'I regarded God's existence as much more evident than the existence of anything perceptible through the senses'.[73] Unlike the fideists, however, the basis for Descartes' certainty was his own reasoning rather than the simple fact of divine revelation. 'I prefer to use as the foundation of my proof my own existence (rather than sensible things), which is not dependent upon any series of causes, and is so plain to my intelligence that nothing can be plainer'.[74] Entities like God or the sensed world were in orbit around the thinking self.

Descartes, like the *libertines érudits* who so troubled him, insisted on his Christian sincerity and in Descartes' case, there seems little reason to doubt him. God was essential to his system. 'An Atheist ... cannot be sure that he is not deceived in the things that seem most evident to him,' he wrote to Mersenne. 'He can never be safe from it unless he first recognises the existence of God'.[75] His biographer Stephen Gaukroger describes him as having 'a deep religious faith as a Catholic, which he retained to his dying day, along with a resolute, passionate desire to discover the truth'.[76]

This did not, of course, prevent him from being accused of atheism, particularly and persistently by Gisbert Voëtius, the influential rector of the university in Utrecht. This was partly because of his thoroughgoing rejection of scholasticism, which was being assailed across northern Europe at the time, and partly because his demon hypothesis was more dangerously potent than he admitted. It was also because his arguments were apparently circular, as Pierre Bayle put it in his *Dictionary*. 'He is for proving the Being of a God from the Truth of our Faculties, and the Truth of our Faculties from the Being of a God.'[77]

Just as problematically, Descartes had put the thinking human rather than God at the centre of his system. The most promising method of securing certainty, whether of things eternal or earthly, was, apparently, via philosophical or, better, mathematical reasoning. In this fashion, Henry More, one of the so-called Cambridge Platonists and one of the first English thinkers to build on Descartes' work, wrote, in 1653, *An Antidote against Atheism* which was subtitled *An Appeal to the Naturall Faculties of the Minde of Man, whether there be not a God.*

More had rejected his parents' Calvinism and was writing at a time when dogmatic Puritanism and intransigent Royalism had dragged the nation through a ruinous decade of civil war and political chaos. Refuting the atheism that lurked in the shadows of this intellectual, moral and political carnage demanded something much more secure than revelation, which was, it seemed, part of the problem rather than the solution. Scepticism and Cartesian rationalism seemed to be the answer. God would be defended without reference to revelation; atheism defeated on a battleground of its own choosing. It proved a fateful shift. In the words of Michael Buckley, 'Christianity entered into the defence of the existence of the Christian god without appeal to anything Christian'.[78]

So it was that if Lucretius, Charron and Machiavelli had in their own different ways conjured visions of godless worlds (or at least worlds so different from the Christian one as to make no difference) the journey to godlessness was one of unintended consequences. Religious disagreement and polemic, aided by scepticism, undermined the foundations for knowing about God. Religious conflict undermined Christianity's moral authority. Refuge could be found in fideism or rationalism but neither was secure, the former closing its ears to the world, the latter to anything distinctively Christian. Few if any of the thinkers engaged in these battles were atheists but they all, in different ways, were engaged in forging and distributing weapons that would one day be used by people who were.

'Science and Religion'

'Consider the great and wonderful works of God': Co-operation
The crisis of authority – moral, political, epistemological – engendered by the Reformation and reintroduction of scepticism into Western thought generated some of the conditions necessary for

modern atheism, but these were not in themselves sufficient. The re-formation of the European mind in the sixteenth and seventeenth century also generated the idea of a mechanistic universe that was taken by many at the time, and many subsequently, to be the cardinal feature of atheism.

This is where atheism's alleged midwife, 'science', enters the narrative. The received view, with which this book began, is that atheism emerged in early modern Europe because of 'science', a supposedly distinct and obviously anti-religious enterprise. Popularized by some emotive and colourful histories dating from the later nineteenth century, and still heard round atheist campfires today, this tale is better at inspiring infidel passions than explaining historical fact. The reality is that the development of the scientific method was indeed tied up with the emergence of modern atheism but in a decidedly complex and counterintuitive way, precipitated, once again, by the questions of authority thrown up by the Reformation.

The Middle Ages had developed a complex four-fold system of how to read the Bible. Everything, from the insignificant pelican of Psalm 102 (now more often translated desert owl) to the city of Jerusalem itself, could, in theory, be read in a number of symbolic ways.[79] What was important about the pelican, or Jerusalem, was less what it was than what it symbolized.

This mode of reading God's words also shaped the manner in which God's work, the book of nature, was read. 'This whole sensible world,' wrote Hugh of St Victor in the twelfth century, 'is like a kind of book written by the finger of God ... and each particular creature is somewhat like a figure ... instituted by the divine will to manifest the invisible things of God's wisdom.' Nature was to be understood primarily symbolically.

This changed in the sixteenth century, when the Reformers argued that the literal meaning was the only valid sense of scripture. The plain meaning of the text was (at least in theory) the right one, and there was now no need to search for moral, anagogical or allegorical senses. Where scripture led, so nature followed. Henceforth, pelicans were to be understood as pelicans, cities as cities, nature as nature. Nature's intelligibility now came from its taxonomic order, how it related to other bits of nature, rather than from its symbolic power.[80]

This had important ramifications. It desacralized nature, removing most, if not all, religious meaning from it. Nature was still a locus of God's revelation but it was no longer pregnant with spiritual agency. This could be used to undermine the Christian worldview in which God's direct agency was ubiquitous. Giordano Bruno's *The Expulsion of the Triumphant Beast* ridiculed the idea of a detailed, providential universe, in which everything that was done was done by God, in the process implicitly mocking the idea that God was involved with everyday life.[81] Conversely, for many other less provocative thinkers, the idea of a law-governed cosmos, which didn't have to be micro-managed minute by minute by a hyperactive deity, was rather tidier and more appealing.

A desacralized nature allowed, indeed invited study on its own terms. Francis Bacon was as responsible as any other figure for the development of this new approach to knowledge, and expressed his views clearly in his *Advancement of Learning*: 'For as the Psalms and other scriptures do often invite us to consider and magnify the great and wonderful works of God, so if we should rest only in the contemplation of the exterior of them as they first offer themselves to our senses, we should do a like injury unto the majesty of God'.[82] Getting inside God's works was a way of recognizing and honouring his power.

Christian convictions made a 'scientific' approach to nature legitimate and honourable. They also made it possible. Beneath the new approach lay the conviction that nature was characterized by an order that was comprehensible to humans precisely because they were made in the image of its creator. The mind of God gave order to nature and as human minds reflected that mind, albeit imperfectly, they were in a unique position to detect nature's order. Such

convictions may have been unable to persuade the omnivorous
scepticism of a La Mothe Le Vayer but it was enough to get the scientific revolution underway, marking it with the divine imprimatur in
the process.

Contrary to early 'rationalist' histories, in which 'warfare' was
the controlling metaphor for the relationship between science and
Christianity, the truth was that 'far from science breaking free
of religion in the early modern era, its consolidation depended
crucially on religion being in the driving seat'.[83] It was for good
reason that Bacon believed that such studies 'minister a singular
help and preservative against unbelief and error'.[84] Far from being
an atheistic venture with atheistic objectives and predicated an
atheistic commitments, the early development of science was a
pervasively Christian enterprise, although one fraught with pitfalls.

*'Tis a dangerous thing to ingage the authority of Scripture in dispute
about the Natural World': Competition*
Just as Cartesian rationalism sought to establish a secure foundation
for God and ended up nudging him to the periphery, so there were
unintended and potentially deleterious consequences attendant
on the birth of the scientific child for its Christian parent. Having
exhorted the study of nature in his *Advancement*, Bacon went on
to draw on powerful and long-lasting analogy between nature and
scripture. Once again, this had its origins in the Bible. 'Our Saviour
saith, "You err, not knowing the Scriptures, nor the power of God",'
Bacon wrote, commenting that in so doing Christ was 'laying before
us two books or volumes to study, if we will be secured from error:
first the scriptures, revealing the will of God, and then the creatures
expressing His power'.[85]

Scripture and nature were two books, the former revealing God's
will, the latter his power. While this legitimized the study of nature
it also presented a potential problem: what if one disagreed with the
other? How would good Christians negotiate different readings and
conclusions of these two books?

On the surface of it, this should not have been a problem. Each book had the same author. Why would he contradict himself? But having the same author did not translate into having the same message. The Bible might, for instance, tell us how to go to heaven rather than how the heavens go, as Cardinal Cesare Baronio once observed and Galileo subsequently quoted. If one understood this potential for different messages from the different books, all would be well. You could read scripture for what it had to tell you, and nature for what it had to tell you without the two coming into conflict.

If, however, you believed that different books were saying the same thing, and if you believed that the literal and plain meaning of scripture was the only true one (an idea that was, after all, behind the whole enterprise) the potential for conflict was huge. You might, for example, conclude that the early chapters of Genesis were indeed a cosmological treatise and not to be revised according to whatever closet atheists claimed to see through their telescopes.

In reality, the challenge of reconciling the tensions between revelation and reason had been a focus for Christianity from at least the second century. However, they were made more problematic with a rigidly literalistic hermeneutic. Back in the early third century, the theologian Origen had written of the first chapter of Genesis 'What man of intelligence will believe that the first and second and third day and the evening and the morning existed without the sun and moon and stars?'[86] When seventeenth-century Christians, unlike third-century ones, had only a literal reading to fall back on, they could not afford such scorn.

It would take close to 200 years for this potential conflict to become a serious one, when (mostly ordained) geologists in the early nineteenth century began to read from the book of nature a story that certainly did not cohere with the one taken from a literal reading of the book of scripture. But the possibility was there early on and far-sighted thinkers spotted the potential for conflict as early as the late seventeenth century. Thomas Burnet's *Sacred Theory of the Earth*, for example, first published in 1684, was alert to the fact that the two books might not cohere as clearly as many imagined, and counselled against using one simply to correct the other. "Tis a dangerous thing to ingage the authority of scripture in dispute about the Natural World, in opposition to Reason, lest Time, which brings all things to light, should discover that to be evidently false which we had made Scripture to assert".[87] Those who were to ignore his advice would present their atheist opponents with their strongest weapons.

'The prophecies of our religion can[not] be said to be absolutely convincing': Challenges
A further consequence of the scientific revolution only became evident many years after Bacon and Burnet were writing. Science's principles of collaboration, experiment, review and publication helped it develop an image of graceful, swan-like progress, unimpeded by the kind of vicious, petty-minded squabbles that mark the religious world.

A closer reading of the history of science quickly destroys this image. Isaac Newton's unparalleled achievements, for example, were studded with ferocious quarrels with other scientific luminaries, such as Robert Hooke and Leibniz, who was memorably described by Newton's disciple Roger Cotes, in the preface to the second edition *Principia Mathematica*, as a 'miserable reptile'. Scientists knew how to squabble.

Yet, there were important differences. Although national feeling could be drawn on in scientific disputes (as they were in the argument between Newton and Leibniz) scientific theories did not become welded to national identities (at least not before Marxist scientific atheism co-opted Soviet science in the twentieth century). Nations didn't go to war over scientific disagreements. Even if one acknowledges that the European Wars of Religion were not about religion alone, the fact remains that theological, dogmatic and confessional allegiances were stained by the blood.

Moreover, the scientific method, in particular the experiment, seemed to have better prophetic potential than comparable religious methods. This was slow in coming but when Blaise Pascal designed and conducted an experiment to test a hypothesis and demonstrate the existence of a vacuum in 1648, the experiment came of age, and demonstration moved from being the preserve of the mathematical and deductive sciences to the natural ones. Science could tell, rather better than religion, how the world behaved and, consequently, how it should behave.

The fact that Pascal was also one of the most sophisticated Christian thinkers of the seventeenth century was a fine irony. He understood the different grammar of the two books of God, and was later to remark in his *Pensées* that 'the prophecies, even the miracles and proofs of our religion, are not of such a kind that they can be said to be absolutely convincing, but they are at the same time such that it cannot be said to be unreasonable to believe in them'. However, those who did not grasp this point were more easily swayed, and the argument that 'science works' as a defence of atheism was to be deployed often and with great effect.

A final difference is noteworthy. Although science was often marked by personal and poisoned disagreement, consensus and progress did, eventually, emerge. The century-and-a-half tussle over heliocentrism may have been marked by bitterness, envy, false hypotheses and misplaced loyalties but it was finally and satisfactorily settled by the early years of the eighteenth century. Scientific knowledge progressed.

This was not necessarily a problem for religious belief. As we shall note in the next chapter, it was precisely the nature of this Newtonian settlement that helps explain why atheism failed to develop in Britain the way it did in France. However, if one is already wedded to a view that reads scripture and nature, religion and science as *competing* theories, the evident progress in one was easily interpreted as the evident falsity of the other. Scientific progress in the light of religious conflict was to prove a gift to atheist polemicists of a later age.

So it was that a discipline born and borne by Christian convictions would be used, albeit years later, against its parent by those minded to do so. Its apparent success, utility and tendency to consensus marked it out against its Christian parent, and although the extent to which it was used in this way would vary enormously in different countries and at different times, the possibility for conflict was there early on.

Questioning the Bible

'Holy Scripture is full of fables': Early doubts
If the Reformation helped unleash the ambiguous effects of scepticism, rationalism and scientific methods on the Western religious mind, it also, again unintentionally, set free another effect that would prove less ambiguous in the long run.

The theo-political battles of the sixteenth and seventeenth centuries saw confessional blocks do everything in their power to undermine each other's foundations. The Bible was invariably caught in the crossfire of this theological battle, and was damaged in the process.

The discipline of biblical study predated the Reformation, the Renaissance's careful philological scrutiny of classical texts providing a model for biblical study. The year before Luther had pinned his theses to Wittenburg's church door, the greatest European humanist, Desiderius Erasmus, published his *Novum instrumentum* or New Instrument. This printed the New Testament in its original Greek, alongside a new Latin translation, which made about 400 changes to the traditional Vulgate translation, and then followed it up with over 300 pages of notes explaining these changes. Erasmus went as far as to omit the traditional proof texts concerning the Trinity, noting that they did not appear in the early New Testament manuscripts, although he did not of course question the doctrine itself.

Humanist textual criticism was not a problem for Catholics, who understood scripture as having been born within the church's magisterium and so open to being studied accordingly. Nor was it necessarily a problem for reformers, many of whom had been trained as humanist scholars and whose call – *Ad fontes* – To the sources! – entailed the recognition that scripture, being the Word of God, needed to be understood as accurately as possible. It was, after all, a Protestant biblical scholar, Louis Cappel, who compiled a list of thousands of textual variants in the Hebrew and Greek biblical texts. However, when, later in the sixteenth century, different factions began to question each other's basis for biblical interpretation, they also questioned the texts on which their interpretation was founded, and biblical criticism as an anti-Christian discipline was born.

Protestants claimed that the Vulgate, the fourth-century Latin translation that had long been authoritative within the Church, was error-strewn. The Catholic response, articulated at the Council of Trent, was that the original Hebrew text, which St Jerome had drawn on for his translation, and which was now lost, had been superior to the current Hebrew text, which had been corrupted over the centuries. Catholics sought to undermine the Hebrew Masoretic text, which Protestants judged authoritative for the Old Testament, by showing that it was the product of historical process and human interventions, a line further supported by study of the Samaritan Pentateuch, which was first obtained from the Levant in the early seventeenth century. The question of textual reliability, compositional process and authorship thus became another weapon in the confessional battles of the time.

In reality, these had never been entirely absent from Latin Christendom if only on account of the longstanding presence of Jewish scholarship. Some rabbinic scholars had long suggested that not all the Pentateuch was by Moses, not least the last eight verses of Deuteronomy which describe his death and burial. As early as the fifteenth century the Spanish theologian and Hebraic scholar Alfonso Tostado Ribera de Madrigal, better known as Tostatus, alerted readers to the possibility of post-Mosaic additions and alterations, and in the confessional conflicts of the following century interest focused in particular on the role of Ezra the scribe in his formation of Old Testament.

Jewish and Christian theologians had long known of the role of Ezra and his contemporaries in fixing the Old Testament canon as part of their rehabilitation of Israel after the Babylonian exile, something that the Old Testament itself spoke about. Some scholars wrote openly about Ezra adding vowel points to Hebrew (which uses only consonants and therefore requires vowels to clarify meaning) as well as a few other editorial features.

Others, however, argued that Ezra's role was rather more significant than that. The book 2 Esdras, sometimes known as 4 Ezra, has the eponymous hero responding to God's call to go and 'reprove' his people because the law had been burned, and 'no man knoweth the things that are done of thee'. Ezra responds saying 'if I have found grace before thee, send the Holy Ghost into me, and I shall write all that hath been done in the world since the beginning, which were written in thy law'.[88] Ezra's re-writing of the books of the Law after they had been burned in the destruction of the first temple was either miraculous in its fidelity, or questionable (because recorded in a questionable book), but either way it introduced a further element of uncertainty into the textual mix.

Braver scholars made more of this than they should. Flemish Catholic Andreas Masius suggested that rather than touching scripture up, Ezra had 'collected, arranged and united' matter that had been 'dispersed, scattered and mixed together in annals' and went as far as to say 'the Mosaic books, in their present form, were not composed by Moses, but by Ezra, or by some other godly man'.[89]

Once again, such arguments were not necessarily seen as problematic, and were, in fact, adopted by some of the most respected Catholic commentators of the age. The Italian Jesuit Robert Bellarmine argued that Ezra collected and corrected texts after the exile. The Flemish Cornelius à Lapide similarly mused on the extent of Ezra's influence, and argued that Joshua had arranged

Moses' material. The very fact that such discussion raised the idea that scripture was only reliable in as far as it had been dependant on a priest, namely Ezra, played strongly into Catholic polemic.

Such revision was obviously more challenging within Protestant circles but even here it was not necessarily fatal. The reformers had confined some biblical books to the Apocrypha, on the grounds that they were less reliable. The Old Testament referred to other, now lost, sources.[90] The books of Moses used phrases like 'unto this day' which suggested some kind of time gap. And Protestant Hebraic scholars recognized that there was a creative process in fixing the vowel points within the Hebrew. Some Protestant scholars, albeit later in the century, even made the argument that minor errors within the text showed authenticity.

Nevertheless, the questions that loomed over the biblical text hit Protestants harder than they did Catholics. Both parties could, in theory, accommodate the new learning. But both were discomfited by the way in which scholarship appeared to pick at the unit of scripture, casting doubts on its veracity, focusing on its mutability and fragility, and seeing its formation as a human process. Moreover, when textual arguments were deployed by one Christian faction against another, they became weapons of destruction, in much the same way as sceptical arguments had been.

Those who forged such weapons were readily labelled as atheists, in an obvious slander, but some were more genuinely suspect. Noël Journet, a schoolteacher from Ardennes, was burned as a heretic in Metz, in 1582, for casting aspersions on the accuracy and historicity of the Old Testament, claiming, at least according to his indictment, that 'Holy Scripture is full of fables, and of all sorts of fantasies and falsehoods'.[91] It is hard to tell whether his crime was any different from that of countless men, and occasional women, hauled before the ecclesiastical courts for mockery of the sacred. The severity of his punishment seems to suggest the authorities were more than usually alarmed at his combination of contempt (which they were used to) with biblical criticism (which they were not). It was a combination that would prove a potent and endlessly useful weapon within the atheists' armoury.

'A heap of Copie confusedly taken': Three biblical critics
If it is difficult to ascertain Journet's views with any accuracy, it is hardly easier to do so for the courageous scholars who informed the nascent biblical criticism of the seventeenth century. Isaac La Peyrère was (and often is) described as an atheist and was accused but acquitted of the charge at the age of 30. Whether or not an atheist, his views were distinctly unorthodox and seemingly founded on the belief that a messiah was about to appear, recall the Jews to the Holy Land and save all, irrespective of what they believed. Such idiosyncratic beliefs were not unheard of in early modern Europe, and seem anodyne compared to those of Menocchio. What marked La Peyrère out was the way he grounded them in textual criticism, and in his knowledge of ancient and, via explorers' tales, contemporary foreign cultures.

La Peyrère argued for a polygenetic origin of mankind, contending that there were humans before Adam (his most famous and controversial book was called *Prae-Adamitae* or *Men before Adam*).This was not an entirely new idea – Thomas Nashe wrote in 1592 in his pamphlet *Pierce Penilesse* that 'there be Mathematicians abroad, that will prove men before Adam, and they are harboured in high places' – but La Peyrère popularized it. He further argued that the Bible was the history of the Jews only, rather than of all mankind and that, therefore, supposedly universal events, like the Genesis flood or the stationary sun of the book of Joshua, were only localized.[92]

He justified such beliefs by pointing out that there were significant contradictions within the Pentateuch, arguing, pointedly, that:

> I need not trouble the Reader much further to prove a thing in itself sufficiently evident, that the first Five Books of the Bible were not written by Moses, as is thought. Nor need any one wonder after this, when he reads

many things confus'd and out of order, obscure, deficient, many things omitted and misplaced … they are a heap of Copie confusedly taken.[93]

La Peyrère coupled this textual revisionism with ideas about ancient pagan and foreign cultures. The antiquity of Egyptian, Greek and Babylonian cultures had been evident to the early Church, but they were also dismissed as fundamentally untrue, on the grounds that they lacked divine revelation. La Peyrère refused this excuse and treated pagan history seriously, coupling it with reports of ancient Chinese and Mexican cultures, apparently older than the Bible's. It was surely easier to believe that these various people, across time and space, derived from different stocks, rather than from the handful of people who survived the flood.

By drawing together biblical criticism, ancient history and early anthropological evidence La Peyrère outlined a comprehensive if eccentric alternative view of human history. His messianic theology strongly suggests that he was no atheist himself, but his theories offered much grist to the atheist mill. Refutations of his ideas were published for decades after his death and he influenced two of the greatest, and most threatening, biblical scholars of the century.

One of these was Father Richard Simon, a friend of La Peyrère and a better scholar, knowing the history, language and culture of the ancient Near East as well as anyone of the time. Animated by a dislike of the Calvinist insistence on 'scripture alone', Simon's work, most notably his *Critical History of the Old Testament*, which appeared in 1678, argued that behind the biblical text lay disparate source materials. The Old Testament, he argued, was best seen as the product of a long process of textual development, perhaps lasting as long as 800 years, the combination of textual complexity and repeated copying allowing errors and variants to creep in during the process.

Simon's scholarship was of the highest standard, his polemical intent notwithstanding. Even less of an atheist than La Peyrère, his work was to do more than anyone else's in transforming Bible study into a secular subject and, in the process, deflating the claims to inerrancy made by some. Once again, his ideas were to prove a powerful weapon in more hostile hands.

A third scholar, less influential than Simon or La Peyrère, but important and characteristic of a particular turn, was Samuel Fisher. Initially a Baptist minister and then, from 1654, a Quaker, Fisher studied Hebrew, after which he travelled to Holland to convert the Jews. In 1660, he published a 1,000-page book entitled *The Rustick's Alarm to the Rabbies*.

Like Simon, Fisher was attacking the Calvinist view of the value of 'scripture alone'. The Bible has been copied by fallible human beings (especially corrupt Catholic priests). Nothing within it determines the canon (again, decided by untrustworthy clerics). The need to place vowel points made all readings tentative. Altogether, his conclusion was as withering as La Peyrère's. The Bible was 'a Bulk of Heterogeneous Writings, compiled together by men taking what they could find of the several sorts of writings that are therein, trussing them all up into one Touchstone, and … crowding them into a canon or standard for the trial of all spirits, doctrines, truths'.[94]

None of this was a problem for Fisher who found this conclusion as conducive to his Quakerism as Catholics found the role of Ezra in compiling the Old Testament canon to their Catholicism. The Word of God, he insisted, is *in* scripture, not *the same as* scripture. The Bible itself was, Fisher contended, simply a vehicle for the living word of God, which existed beyond the text. It demanded personal interpretation, thereby placing spiritual authority with the individual. What mattered, he reasoned, is 'the Light within, not the bare letter without'.[95]

This was, in effect, a more sophisticated version of what had been going on in England during the 1650s. The collapse of print licensing and church courts in the 1640s had seen a flourishing of wild and wonderful Christian opinions, many of which stressed the ultimate importance of the individual in interpreting scripture. Taken to its extreme, the Bible was unnecessary because Christ or the inner light or personal conscience supplied all that was needed. Thus, six soldiers publicly burned the Bible in Walton-on-Thames in 1649 declaring that 'the Bible containeth beggarly rudiments, milk for babes'. Because Christ 'imparts a fuller measure of his spirit to his saints' than did the Bible, the said saints could legitimately invade the parish church and announce that Sabbath, tithes, ministers and the Bible were to be henceforth abolished.[96] All this was, of course, done on account of the soldiers' unshakeable faith in God. But onlookers could be excused for confusing it with practical atheism of the worst kind.

Thomas Hobbes' Christian atheism

'Life is but a motion of limbs': Matter and determinism
It was precisely the tendency of religious sects to read whatever they wanted into scripture, even to the extent of elevating their personal opinion, or 'conscience', above the text, and then act on their beliefs, that vexed the thinker whose name would become synonymous with atheism in later seventeenth century England.

Thomas Hobbes was the child of a drunken and violent clergyman, and a scholastic education. The former did not stay around long enough to affect his son, but 20 years of schooling, first at Malmesbury, then at Magdalen Hall, Oxford, turned the young man against scholasticism for life. Absurdity, he wrote in *Leviathan*, is caused by 'names that signifie nothing; but are taken up and learned by rote from the Schooles, as *hypostatical, transubstantiate, consubstantiate, eternal-Now*, and the like canting of Schoole-men'.[97]

Hobbes escaped the prison of early modern Aristotelianism and entered the service of William Cavendish, soon to be Duke of Devonshire, with whose family he remained connected for 70 years. As tutor to Cavendish's son he had access to several great libraries, and met a number of leading thinkers, including Marin Mersenne, Pierre Gassendi and Galileo Galilei, on educational tours of Europe. It was on one of these that, according to his biographer John Aubrey, Hobbes chanced upon proposition 47 of Euclid's *Elements*. He duly fell in love with geometry, which appeared to offer a clarity and certainty that was absent from both scholasticism and English Christianity.

During his European travels in the 1630s, Hobbes became a materialist, coming to believe, as he would later say, that 'that which is not Body, is no part of the Universe'.[98] Matter and motion was all. Human experience and imagination were no different. The idea of an 'immaterial substance' was incomprehensible as it combined 'two Names, whose significations are contradictory and inconsistent'.[99]

This posed several problems for traditional Christian theism, problems with which Hobbes struggled not entirely convincingly. If only bodies could exist, that presumably meant that God was a body. But if God was also infinite, as Hobbes acknowledged, that made him into an infinite body. At very least, this was difficult to comprehend, although Hobbes acknowledged that incomprehensibility was not the same as impossibility. Indeed, God was, according to Christian theology, by definition incomprehensible, at least to the finite, fallible human mind. 'Whatsoever we imagine, is *Finite*. Therefore there can be no Idea, or conception of anything we call *Infinite*'.[100]

In itself, this was not totally unorthodox. The sheer otherness of God and the stubborn limitation of human cognition and language were longstanding traditions within Christian theology, to which Hobbes alluded: 'I believe ... that those who worship only the god that they understand are not Christians'.[101] Yet, in Hobbes' hands, the distance placed between God and man felt more sceptical, not so much a humble recognition of human finitude in the presence of divine majesty, as an attempt to tarnish all divine discourse with imprecision and irrelevance. What we think is objective talk of God is really subjective talk of ourselves. 'We understand nothing of *what he is*, but only *that he is*; and therefore the Attributes we give him, are not to tell one another, *what he is*, nor to signifie our opinion of his Nature, but our desire to honor him with such names as we conceive most honorable amongst ourselves.'[102]

Human nature was as affected by Hobbes' materialism as was God's. His masterpiece, *Leviathan*, opens with an uncompromising statement of mankind as a material machine, a view that would become central to some later atheistic thought. 'Seeing life is but a motion of limbs … what is the heart, but a spring; and the nerves, but so many strings; and the joints, but so many wheels, giving motion to the whole body, such as was intended by the Artificer?'[103]

'Whence The Scriptures Derive Their Authority': Drawing political teeth

Such a view challenged the prevailing ideas concerning human nature and the soul but Hobbes' offence went beyond the merely anthropological. Working from the basis of these first principles he argued that humans were equal but, consequently, immured in conflict, from which only an all-powerful sovereign could protect them. People might freely choose to pool their sovereignty in this 'Leviathan', but once they had done so they had no recourse: the sovereign was supreme.

Or at least he should be: writing as he was in the middle years of the century, Hobbes was painfully aware that religious authorities and beliefs were treated as alternative *political* authorities, thereby fatally undermining his own scheme. No kingdom could be 'subject to two Masters' and hope to survive.[104] For this reason, Hobbes spent a great deal of energy re-reading Christian scriptures and doctrine in such a way as to strip them of all that might enable a challenge to the state. His atheistic programme, as it was conceived, was political in intent.

It was in this context that Hobbes dedicated Chapter 33 of *Leviathan* to biblical criticism. Hobbes was the first to go into English print with the revisionist ideas of Mosaic authorship and Old Testament reliability. His criticism strayed beyond the Old

Testament. He renegotiated the meaning of the Kingdom of God
as proclaimed by Jesus, redefining it as an earthly phenomenon,
'properly [God's] civil sovereignty over a peculiar people by pact'.[105]
Heaven and hell were similarly earthed. Regarding the formation of
the New Testament canon, he noted that 'the Councell of Laodicea
is the first we know, that recommended the Bible to the then
Christian Churches ... and this Councell was held in the 364. yeer
after Christ', a demonstrable fact but one that, in Hobbes' hand,
insinuated scriptural unreliability.

There was more uncertainty to be found in the process of
revelation itself and the means by which it was passed on. None
of the traditional means of revelation was entirely trustworthy.
Religious dreams were doubtful – 'to say [God] hath spoken to
[a man] in a Dream, is no more than to say he dreamed that
God spake to him'[106] – and other means, such as 'Visions, Voice,
and Inspiration' were equally vulnerable to human deception.[107]
Miracles, the traditional bulwark of the religious, were uncertain
events, especially in the hands of the ignorant: 'the same thing,
may be a Miracle to one, and not to another'.[108] The ignorant and
superstitious 'make great Wonders of those works', where others
'knowing to proceed from Nature, (which is not the immediate, but
the ordinary work of God,) admire not at all'.[109]

Even if revelation were possible, there were profound problems
over its means of transmission. 'How God speaketh to a man
immediately, may be understood by those well enough, to whom
he hath so spoken,' Hobbes wrote, 'but how the same should be
understood by another, is hard, if not impossible to know.' In reality,
it was impossible rather than merely 'hard'. 'If a man pretend to me,
that God hath spoken to him supernaturally, and immediately, and
I make doubt of it, I cannot easily perceive what argument he can
produce, to oblige me to believe it.'[110]

And if revelation became unreliable when passed from recipient
to his auditor, how much more unreliable would it be when it was
passed down a more extended chain? Hobbes wisely chose the

example of a classical author to make this point. 'If Livy say the Gods made once a Cow speak, and we believe it not; wee distrust not God therein, but Livy. So that it is evident, that whatsoever we believe, upon no other reason, than what is drawn from authority of men onely, and their writings; whether they be sent from God or not, is Faith in men onely.'[111] Faith in God was really no more than faith in man. And man was not particularly trustworthy.

Hobbes' purpose in all this was not to ridicule or disprove religion, much as it may have seemed otherwise, but to disarm it. Writing as he was in the shadow of the Thirty Years War and the English Civil Wars, Hobbes' objective was not anti-biblical or even anti-clerical *per se*, but rather to draw religion's political teeth, by means of theological arguments as much as philosophical ones, so that the Leviathan's authority would remain unchallenged. 'Experience teaches,' he had written in 1641, 'that the dispute for [precedence] between the spiritual and civil power has of late more than any other thing in the world been the cause of civil wars in all places of Christendom.'[112] Hobbes sought to remove that dispute.

Thus, when he argued that to trust revelation was, in effect, to trust other men, he was putting religious commitment on the same level as political loyalty. When, discussing the canon, he noted that personally he could 'acknowledge no other Books of the Old Testament, to be Holy scripture, but those which have been commanded to be acknowledged for such, by the Authority of the Church of England', he was making the point that boundaries of revelation were determined by earthly authority. When redefining heaven, hell and the Kingdom of God he was not abolishing key Christian doctrines so much as 'earthing' them, in such a way as to prevent them from serving as alternatives to worldly power. When, on the vexed question of how the scriptures should be interpreted, he goes as far as to say that the earthly powers should have the final say, he was locating spiritual authority in the temporal. When discussing the 'much disputed' question of 'Whence The Scriptures Derive Their Authority', or 'How Wee Know Them To Be The Word

Of God, or, Why We Beleeve Them To Be So' his answer is always the same: by political authority.

'Do you think I can be an atheist and not know it?': Accusations of Hobbism

This, he insisted, was no atheistic project. Others disagreed. Critics, and there were many, objected to Hobbes' mechanistic determinism, his apparent ethical relativism, his grimly pessimistic view of human nature, and the fact he appeared to worship power on earth rather than in heaven. As early as October 1651, the Anglican clergyman Henry Hammond called *Leviathan* 'a farrago of Christian atheism'.[113] More attacks followed.

Alexander Ross published *Leviathan drawn out with a hook* in 1653. Bishop John Bramhall, who spent much time hunting out the many alleged threats to Anglican orthodoxy, published *The Catching of Leviathan* in 1658 in which he accused Hobbes of being 'an atheist by consequence', and arguing that his principles led to atheism even if they didn't articulate it themselves.

The Earl of Clarendon denounced the philosopher for his 'dangerous and pernicious Errors' in 1676, and objected just as much to Hobbes's allegedly ironic tone. The philosopher's discourse concerning religion was 'naughty and impious', and he handles scripture 'as imperiously as he doth a Text of *Aristotle*, putting such unnatural interpretations on the words'.[114] Invariably, the charges of theoretical atheism brought with them those of practical atheism, as critics accused Hobbes of low standards of personal morality and gross materialism, in spite of the testimony to the contrary by his biographer John Aubrey. Most cuttingly, Hobbes was never invited to join the newly formed Royal Society.

Hobbes responded to his critics, sometimes to particular accusations, sometimes to the wider charge of atheism. In response to the accusation that his materialism implied atheism, he reached for the Church Fathers. 'Whatsoever can be inferr'd from the denying of *Incorporeal Substances*, makes *Tertullian*, one of the ancientest of the Fathers, and most of the Doctors of the Greek Church, as much Atheists as [me]'.[115] He took on Bramhall by pointing out that atheism 'by consequence' was a hopelessly vague accusation, 'a very easy thing to be fallen into, even by the most godly men in the Church'.[116] More generally, he wrote angrily to his critic John Wallis, asking 'Do you think I can be an atheist and not know it? Or knowing it, durst have offered my atheism to the press?'[117]

It was all to little avail. 'Hobbist' became almost synonymous with atheist in the later seventeenth century. In 1669, one Daniel Scargill was expelled from Cambridge University 'for having asserted several impious and atheistical tenets', an intellectual charge not helped by his reputation for drunkenness and loose living. His case received attention and support from the highest levels, however, and the university was told to readmit him, on the basis of a recantation in which he said:

> I, Daniell Scargill … being through the instigation of the Devil possessed with a foolish proud conceit of my own wite, and not having the fear of God before my eyes; Have lately vented and publicly asserted … diverse, wicked, blasphemous, and atheistical positions … professing that I gloried to be a Hobbist and an atheist.[118]

Hobbism neatly united theoretical and practical atheism. Charles Wolseley managed to blame Hobbes for the licentiousness and liber- tinism of the Restoration, saying that 'most of the bad principles of this age are of no earlier a date than one very ill book, and indeed but the spawn of the Leviathan'.[119] Robert Sharrock went further, reading into Hobbes' ethic a kind of Machiavellian immorality rather than simply licence: 'oppress the poor righteous man, spare not the widow and (which is perfect Hobbism) let your strength be the law of justice and what is feeble count it little worth'.[120] Such claims were extreme, to the point of hysterical, but their very hysteria reveals not only the consanguinity of atheism and wickedness in the contemporary mind, but also the terror that lay behind both.

While it is hard to sustain such critics' accusations, it is not clear how far we can believe Hobbes' protestations either. Even in an age in which identifying genuine atheists is difficult, Hobbes is an extreme case, as is testified by the sheer range of scholarly opinion on his beliefs. Some scholars argue that Hobbes' defence was genuine and that he was a believer, even a sincere and orthodox believer.[121] Others hold that he was believer, if a highly eccentric one, with distinctly deistic tendencies.[122] Still others claim that he was as close to an atheist as made no difference.[123]

His contemporaries suffered no such uncertainty. Not only was he widely accused of atheism but he faced, or at least feared, the prospect of capital punishment for his alleged atheism in October 1666, when a Parliamentary committee was 'empowered to receive Information touching such books as tend to Atheism, Blasphemy or Prophanenesse or against the Essence or Attributes of God. And in particular … the booke of Mr Hobbes called the Leviathan'.[124] According to John Aubrey, Hobbes felt sufficiently threatened by these events to destroy a large number of his papers and with them any confidence we might have had concerning what, if any, religious beliefs he held.

Spinoza, the great leader of our modern unbelievers

John Aubrey also told a story of how the poet Edmund Waller once sent Hobbes' patron, Lord Devonshire, a copy of a book entitled *Tractatus Theologico-Politicus* by one 'B.S.' shortly after it was published in 1670, asking what Devonshire's faithful philosopher thought of it. Hobbes apparently replied to his patron with words from Matthew 7.1 ('Judge not that ye be not judged'), but told Aubrey more candidly that author 'had out thrown [me] a bar's length, for [I] durst not write so boldly'.[125]

The B.S. in question was Benedict Spinoza, born Baruch, in November 1632, to a prominent merchant family within Amsterdam's

Portuguese Jewish community, from which he was expelled in the harshest of terms aged 24. Spinoza was thus an outcast from one of Europe's outcast communities, which presumably helps to explain his brilliantly heterodox mind.

The rest of Spinoza's short life – he died aged 46 – was spent grinding lenses and discussing philosophy with a small number of like-minded souls. It was also impeccably upright and respectable, a source of frustration to those who liked their atheists dissolute and immoral. He published one book, on Cartesian philosophy, under his own name in his lifetime, but it was his anonymous *Tractatus Theologico-Politicus* or *Theologico-Political Treatise*, which came out under a false location and false publisher, that would cement his reputation as Europe's foremost atheist.

Ironically, given what the book did to his reputation, Spinoza insisted, in a letter to written to his then friend, Henry Oldenberg, secretary of the Royal Society, that he was writing 'a treatise on my views regarding Scripture [because of] the opinion of me held by the common people, who accuse me of atheism. I am driven to avert this accusation … as far as I can'.[126] That ended up being not very far.

'A whole host of ambiguities': Undermining

The majority of the *Tractatus* is about the Bible, particularly the Old Testament, but the book was no more a mere scriptural demolition job than was *Leviathan*. Rather, the *Tractatus*, as it claimed on the frontispiece, contained 'several discourses which demonstrate that freedom to philosophize may … be allowed without danger to piety and the stability of the republic'. Spinoza's was a constructive project, intended to disaggregate theology from philosophy, religion from politics, and in so doing to establish (a form of) democracy and (a measure of) civil freedom. Spinoza insisted this was not an atheistic project. Everyone else thought otherwise.

Advocating such a political system, which can be called secular without doing too much violence to that much-abused word, required the deconstruction of the existing one and this, in turn, demanded undermining the foundations on which that system was founded. This was why a treatise about the 'freedom to philosophize' spent 15 of its 20 chapters on biblical history and hermeneutics.

Spinoza began by dismantling prophets and prophecy, the pillars on which divine revelation, particularly in the Old Testament, rested. Old Testament prophets had a particular moral wisdom but no special access to the truth. They were 'endowed with unusually vivid imaginations, [rather than] unusually, perfect minds'. That imagination was 'capricious and changeable' and prophecy, accordingly, varied according to the 'disposition of his bodily temperament, his imagination and ... beliefs'. If a prophet were 'cheerful', 'his revelations were of victories and paces'. If he were gloomy his revelations 'concerned, torments and everything bad'.[127] Prophecy was not so much a message from God as from the prophet's imagination, or his stomach.

In the hands of Voltaire or Gibbon this might have simply been a withering put-down but Spinoza meant it earnestly. Prophets could justly be commended for their 'piety and constancy'[128] but prophecy itself revealed nothing more than what was accessible to philosophers and philosophy. To the great mass of mankind, to whom philosophical reasoning was a closed book, revelation was useful and comforting. To those with eyes to see, it was redundant.

Miracles were treated similarly. As God and nature were the same, one could not act in contravention of the other. This meant that what men took as miracles were merely phenomena 'whose natural cause cannot be explained on the pattern of some other familiar thing', or at least not by the person who reports or narrates them.[129] Miracles, like revelation, were a function of ignorance.

All this was scandalous, but more challenging still was Spinoza's textual analysis. Spinoza was an accomplished Hebraist and was clear that 'besides the usual causes of ambiguity common to all tongues, there are certain other features of [the Hebrew] language that produce a whole host of ambiguities',[130] admitting, further, that 'no method will resolve them all'.[131]

Radical uncertainty was introduced into an intellectual discipline that had once been supposed to be the secure basis of certainty. Interpreting the Bible was an impossibly difficult task. The reader needed to know 'the life, character and concerns of each writer',[132] the occasion and audience of whom they wrote, and the context of composition. No surprise then that 'theologians ... for the most part have sought to extract their own thoughts and opinions from the Bible and ... endow them with divine authority'.[133]

Having secularized biblical studies by arguing that the holy book should be treated like any other, and then shown how difficult that was, Spinoza dismissed the traditional claims of authorship of not only the Pentateuch, but also the other books of history and prophecy. 'Everything in these five books', he wrote of the Pentateuch, 'is narrated in a confused manner, without order and without respect for chronology'.[134]

Spinoza held the New Testament in higher regard. This was partly because he clearly bore a particular animus against Judaism and partly because he had no wish to turn the Tractatus into an extended suicide note. But it was also because he had genuine sympathy for some aspects of Christianity, possibly because his circle of confidants comprised a number of Collegiants, a liberal and anti-clerical offshoot of the Remonstrants or anti-Calvinist Dutch Protestants.[135]

Christianity's rejection of Jewish law and ceremony appealed to him, as did the teaching and example of Christ. 'I do not believe that any one save Christ alone ever attained to such superiority over others as to have had the precepts of God which lead to everlasting life, revealed to him immediately, and without the intervention of words or a vision', he wrote in the first chapter. This was hardly the Athanasian Creed but it was a good deal less scandalous than his enemies claimed.

Similarly, New Testament apostles were better than Old Testament prophets, and St Paul's 'long deductions and arguments' were palpably more philosophical than supernatural in nature. Moreover, Paul's argument in the book of Romans, that before God's law was given natural law was sufficient judge, was especially congenial to Spinoza.

There is not much in Spinoza's *Tractatus* without any intellectual prehistory. Spinoza's critique of religion as organized and manipulated superstition echoed Machiavelli's, whose complete works were to be found in his library. His biblical criticism could be found in La Peyrère and Samuel Fisher, although there is debate about whether Spinoza knew their work. It was, however, with Hobbes that the comparisons were most readily drawn.

Spinoza's disparaging attitude to prophets and miracles could be read in *Leviathan*, and his broader objective of drawing religion's political teeth was thoroughly Hobbist. From the later seventeenth century the two philosophers' names were linked as the continent's chief atheists, not simply by the army of heresy hunters who could smell unorthodoxy at 500 miles but by some of the early Enlightenment's most perceptive and reasonable minds. The German mathematician and philosopher Gottfried von Leibniz, for example, wrote of Spinoza in a letter in 1670 'the author follows closely not only the politics, but also the religion of Hobbes ... there is nothing in the astounding critique of Sacred Scripture put into effect by this audacious man, the seeds of which have not been sowed by Hobbes in an entire chapter of *Leviathan*'.[136]

'If every person transfers all the power they possess': Reconstructing
For all that Hobbes and Spinoza were coupled together, however, Spinoza was both more threatening and more influential. Hobbes' ideas were, he contended, conservative, and his life, spent in the service of the Dukes of Devonshire and including employment as tutor to Charles II, had brought him to the heart of the English establishment. Spinoza, by contrast, was an outsider. He wrote from a position of better biblical knowledge and greater theological

sophistication. His vision of the world seemed naturalistic and even deterministic. And his stated intent was to privatize religious belief.

Like every other would-be atheist of the seventeenth century, Spinoza wrote in the shadow of confessional wars. His system underlined with philosophy what recent history had written in blood.

> Disputes and schisms have ceaselessly disturbed the church ever since apostolic times, and will surely never cease to trouble it, until religion is finally separated from philosophical theories and reduced to the extremely few, very simple dogmas that Christ taught to his own.[137]

Religion, properly understood, taught moral living. 'The aim of philosophy is nothing but truth, [whereas] the aim of faith … is simply obedience and piety'.[138] Religion's utility was in instructing the stupid, those incapable of discerning the truth through philosophy. Those who were capable of navigating their way to true knowledge in this way should not be impeded by theology, or churchmen, or rabbis, or any other religious authority. His objective was 'to separate philosophy from theology and to establish the freedom to philosophize which this separation allows',[139] and he did this not simply by undermining the Bible but also by reconstructing a new world.

This began with fish. Fish, Spinoza explained, are 'determined by nature to swim and [for] big fish to eat little ones'. It is therefore 'by sovereign nature right that fish have possession of the water and that big fish eat small fish'.[140] As with fish, so it was with all things in nature, each possessing 'a sovereign right … to exist and to behave as it is naturally determined to behave'.[141]

If this smelled like determinism, that's because it was determin-istic. Spinoza's monistic system did not allow for things to be other than they were. As he wrote in Proposition XXIX of his *Ethics* 'In nature there is nothing contingent, but all things have been determined from the necessity of the divine nature to exist and produce an effect in a certain way.'[142]

It could also, to overly sensitive olfactory organs, smell of libertinism, not least when Spinoza explained how 'the order of nature … prohibits nothing but what no one desires or no one can do'.[143] What if the disreputable found that it was in their desire to thieve, drink and whore their way through life? Was that also their ineradicable and incontestable nature?

Spinoza himself had no desire to erect the libertarian society of which some atheists would subsequently dream. Rather, freedom tempered by reason was his lodestar. People desired to live in security and without fear, so they naturally combined together, the rights to goods being decided collectively, 'by the sole dictate of reason'.[144] Because, however, 'the mind is very often so preoccupied with greed [and] glory … that there is no room for reason'[145] a degree of compulsion is required.

> Human society can thus be formed … only if every person transfers all the power they possess to society, and society alone retains the supreme natural right over all things … unless we wish to be enemies of government and to act against reason … we are obliged to carry out absolutely all the commands of the sovereign power, however absurd they may be.[146]

In case someone will think that this system turns 'subjects into slaves', Spinoza explained that in fact 'anyone who is guided by their own pleasure in this way and cannot see or do what is good for them', is pretty much a slave anyway. Only those who live by reason are truly free. It is not 'acting on command' that 'makes someone a slave', but acting on the wrong, unreasonable, command.[147] If the state acts for the good of the people, it is irrational and immoral to resist it. Just as children are not enslaved by their parents who know what is good for them, so subjects are not enslaved by a right-reasoning 'democratic republic'.

If this sounded suspiciously Hobbist, there were important differences. Spinoza was clear that no one should ever be able 'to transfer his power and … his right to another person in such a way that he ceases to be a human being'.[148] Spinoza's all-powerful state was to be one of toleration, freedom of speech and what we might call inalienable human rights, unlike Hobbes'.

Nevertheless, the two arch-atheists of the seventeenth century were in agreement about the proper place of religion in society. 'Authority in the sacred matters', Spinoza wrote, 'belongs wholly to the sovereign powers', and therefore, 'the external cult of religion must be consistent with the stability of the state'.[149]

He expanded on this briefly in his *Political Treatise*, five years after the *Tractatus*, in which he advocated a form of state religion, a simple, universal, philosophical faith teaching salvation through justice and charity, to which all leading figures must belong. Other (non-state) religions were to be permitted 'to build as many temples as they please', as long as they are small and well separated. By contrast, the national religion's temples 'should be large and costly', its principal rites administered only by patricians or senators, who are to be recognized 'as the priests of the temples and the champions and interpreters of the national religion'. Smaller business and preaching, by contrast, may be conducted by 'the commons', who could serve as 'the senate's deputies', and were therefore 'bound to render it account of everything'.[150] The Cults of Reason, of Humanity, of the Supreme Being, of the supreme leader which would mark the atheist landscape over forthcoming centuries were all here, in germ, in Spinoza's simple, ethical, reasonable state religion. He would have been horrified.

Spinoza's national religion may have 'out thrown' Hobbes' vision of a tame and neutered national church, but it was not this so much as the comprehensive and coherent nature of his system that so shocked and alarmed contemporaries. Spinoza was 'the first that ever reduced atheism into a system' wrote William Carroll in the early eighteenth century;[151] 'the only person among the modern atheists that has pretended to give us a regular scheme of atheism', according to Boyle Lecturer Brampton Gurdon a decade later; 'the great leader of our modern unbelievers' according to Bishop Berkeley's *Alciphron*.[152]

Spinoza revolted against such accusations, seeing his work as a defence of true religion, replying tartly to one correspondent who accused him of renouncing all religion, 'Does that man, pray, renounce all religion who declares that God must be acknowledged as the highest good, and that he must be loved as such in a free spirit?'[153]

Yet if it was a defence, it left the thing defended mauled. In the words of Richard Blackmore's poem *The Creation* Spinoza 'Declares for God, while he that God betrays; / For whom he's pleased such evidence to bring, / As saves the name, while it subverts the thing'.[154] Shorn of supernaturalism and all confessional dogma, the theological animal Spinoza was shepherding was hardly recognizable. Writing to Oldenberg about Christian doctrine, Spinoza had said, 'As to the additional teaching of certain churches, that God took upon himself human nature, I have expressly indicated that I do not understand what they say. Indeed, to tell the truth, they seem to me to speak no less absurdly than one who might tell me that a circle has taken on the nature of a square'.[155]

Crossing the Rubicon

'Ridiculous fables for sacred truths': Clandestine manuscripts
For all it attempted anonymity, the *Tractatus* was soon traced back to Spinoza. Suppression was, at first, slow and piecemeal but the book was officially banned by 1673 and put on the Index in 1679, thereby placing it within the underground network of clandestine publications and manuscripts that was spreading across Europe.

These were anonymous or pseudonymous texts, most hand-copied rather than printed, which were intensely, often abusively, critical of the religious and political authorities, and the ideas that defined and defended them.

Theophrastus redivivus, which put forward the influential and long-lived idea that all philosophers had really been atheists forced to conceal their true beliefs for fear of persecution, was one of the earliest, probably dated from 1659, and many comparable texts originated in the following half-century, when censorship and royal oppression was fiercest in France. The golden age for the clandestine industry, however, was the first half of the eighteenth century, when manuscripts spread rapidly, primarily through the Netherlands and northern France, but also Germany, especially after Frederick the Great ascended to the Prussian throne in 1740.

Some are known to have circulated quite widely. Fifty copies of César Chesneau Du Marsais' *Examen de la Religion* and 35 of Jean Meslier's *Mémoire*, to which we shall return in the next chapter, are known. Undoubtedly the most widespread and famous, however, was the *Traité des Trois Imposteurs*, or *Treaty of the Three Imposters* (sometimes also called *La Via et L'Esprit de Mr Benoit de Spinosa*), of which there were over 200 manuscripts in circulation, the majority in French. The *Traité* was first printed in the early eighteenth century but it had a long manuscript history and an even longer mythological prehistory. Rumours of a Latin work entitled *De Tribus Impostoribus* had been in circulation since the Middle Ages, although no such text has been found. It seems as if, sometime in the last quarter of the seventeenth century, some entrepreneurial individual or group decided to turn myth into reality and wrote the most definitive, aggressive statement of atheism Europe saw before the age of D'Holbach.

Drawing on Hobbes, Naudé, La Mothe le Vayer and Vanini, and of course Spinoza, the author attacked religion, authority, tradition and tyranny with inexhaustible energy. The criticism was total and the tone marked by vitriolic, pugnacious, bellicose rhetoric throughout. The Bible, the author tells us, is full of contradictions. Miracles are impossible. Revelation should be rejected in favour of reason. Religion is a superstition, and the church an organized deception for political control. 'These men who exhibit and spread about ridiculous *Fables* for sacred truths divinely revealed are all of them except some few ignorant dunces ... people of villainous principles, who maliciously abuse and impose on a credulous populace'.[156]

The world of the *Traité* is unapologetically materialistic, mechanist, determinist and non-providential. Matter is all that exists. Good and evil are relative and not absolute concepts. Civil law was the only legitimate basis of authority. The purpose of life is to make earthly existence liveable. The *Traité* traced many of the themes that were to mark the pioneering atheistic work of the eighteenth century.

It was not, however, a treatise for political liberation so much as an attempt to be as shocking as possible. It worked. Those who came into contact with it were scandalized, feeling, in the words of the German scholar Johann Lorenz Mosheim, that it 'surpasses infinitely in atheistical profanity even those works of Spinoza', with whom it was wrongly connected.[157]

The *Traité* did not limit its critique to Christianity or its parent religion but also attacked Islam. There were, after all, *three* imposters: Christ, Moses and Mohammed. This may have been because the Turks were, at the time, pressing hard at south-east Europe but it also reflected the Enlightenment's attitude to Islam, or rather part of it.

On the one hand, Islam was just another religion, an even worse example of theologically justified political and social exploitation than either Judaism or Christianity. In the *Tractatus*, Spinoza chose the example of the Turks, who 'clog men's minds with dogmatic formulas', to illustrate religion's intellectual oppression of mind,[158] and wrote in a letter how Islam exceeded even the Catholic Church in its capacity to 'mislead the common people and keep men's minds in its grip'.[159]

On the other hand, Islam was a useful stick with which to beat Christianity, in the manner in which the ancient world and foreign cultures had been used by sceptics. Indeed, it could even be seen as genuinely superior to Christianity, unencumbered by and antipathetic towards Trinitarian dogmas as it was. Henri de Boulainvilliers' *Vie de Mahomed*, published in 1730, spoke warmly of Islam and its founder as purifying Christianity. Islam would not re-enter the European atheist's conscience again in any significant way until the final decades of the twentieth century. But when it did, there would be no such ambiguity.

'It is not more strange for an Atheist to live virtuously, than for a Christian to abandon himself to crime': Pierre Bayle

One of those who saw the positive side of Islam was Pierre Bayle. He wrote in his entry on Mahomet in his 1697 *Dictionnaire* that Muslims ignored the fundamentally violent tenet of their faith by tolerating other religions whereas Christians ignored the fundamentally peaceable tenet of theirs by persecuting others. It was the kind of paradox in which Bayle delighted, frustrating his contemporaries and helping him become one of the most important (alleged) atheists of the seventeenth century.

Bayle's studied ambiguity derived, in part, from the fact he had seen denominations from both sides. Born in 1647 to a French Protestant minister, he attended a Calvinist School, then a Jesuit college, before converting to Catholicism, and then four months later converting back again.

Such a relapse was highly risky in Louis XIV's France and Bayle moved to Geneva, before returning to Sedan in France, until this last Protestant university was closed, after which he became a professor in Rotterdam. Given that his brothers and father were killed in subsequent Huguenot persecution, it was a lucky escape, though not the end of his problems.

Bayle was temperamentally sceptical. Leibniz once remarked that if you asserted something in conversation with him, Bayle would analyse and question it until you were ready to give up or assert its opposite, at which point Bayle would then analyse this.[160] His experiences gave him good reason to doubt. His life's work was marked by incredulity, not only towards popular superstitions but, more provocatively, to any rational defence of theological truth. Philosophy, he observed in an article on Uriel Acosta, was a universal acid, similar to those powders 'that are so corrosive that, after they have eaten away the infected flesh of a wound, they then devour the living flesh, rot the bones, and penetrate to the very marrow'. At first it refutes error. Then it attacks truths.

Reason was thus useless for defending faith, which could be sustained on unquestioning acceptance of revealed doctrine alone. This was a tenable position in the seventeenth century – just – and, as we have seen, not a novel one at the time he was writing. But Bayle undermined the rational proofs for Christianity with such vigour and seeming glee that most contemporaries suspected more sinister intent.

It was not so much his omni-scepticism (or proto-fideism) that so offended the authorities in Rotterdam, where he lost his chair in 1693. Rather it was his generous, even admiring, attitude towards atheism. This first emerged in his *Various Thoughts on the Occasion of A Comet*, published anonymously in 1680. Primarily a debunking of the popular superstitions prompted by the appearance of Halley's Comet that year, the book also spoke of Spinoza as a virtuous atheist, described Vanini as an atheist martyr, and raised the idea that a society of atheists might, in theory, be a well-regulated one.

These ideas were developed further in his four-volume *Dictionnaire historique et critique*, published between 1695 and 1702, for which he became best known, the work being reprinted numerous times in the eighteenth century and treated almost like a handbook for atheists. Superficially the *Dictionnaire* was a biographical digest of important historical and philosophical figures, albeit one that carried nearly 90 per cent of the text in its footnotes and overlooked many major figures in favour of lesser-known ones. More subtly, it was a stage on which Bayle could parade all range of subversive opinions, while remaining comfortably in the critical background.

On one side, the Bible could be tenderly mocked and undermined. Bayle describes King David as 'one of the greatest men in the world' before painting the miseries of his reign in the most lurid colours, all the time sticking faithfully to the biblical narrative. In a similar way, his entry on Abimelech criticizes the Jewish historian Josephus, and ancient historians more broadly, for 'tack[ing] on superstitions, and, not finding facts developed and embellished according to their fancy, … enlarge[ing] and dress[ing] them up as they pleased'.[161] Those with eyes to see, could read what he was suggesting.

On the other side of the religious coin, he gave an extended hearing to various materialist, fatalistic, naturalist and atheist philosophers, both ancient, like Epicurus and Lucretius, or more modern, like Vanini, Pietro Pomponazzi, Hobbes and Spinoza, who earned the longest entry in the *Dictionnaire*. Although always careful to refute their views, Bayle was also willing to defend them, reminding readers, for example, of Vanini's exemplary morality or defending Pomponazzi (among others) from the charge of impiety.

Readers search the *Dictionnaire* in vain for a coherent position. Bayle was too elliptical and too sceptical for polemic. But venomous anti-theism, such as was to be found in *Traité*, was not the only way to insinuate atheism. Arguably more powerful was to make the case that atheism was not necessarily immoral, and atheists not necessarily anti-social.

Bayle's contemporary Jean de La Bruyère once wrote how 'I would like to see a sober, moderate, chaste, equitable man utter the phrase that there is no God', and concluded that 'this man cannot be found'.[162] This was, of course, the standard view in early modern Europe. Atheism, as we have seen, could mean many subtly different things to many different people, but at its core was a rejection of the foundation for the moral, social and political life of every community, city and country on the continent. Atheism was feared and loathed not because it was a rejection of God, but because it was a rejection of everything that belief in God was supposed to guarantee: human uniqueness, free will, a conclusive reason to choose the right over the pleasurable, ultimate justice, social order and political authority – as well, of course, as eternal life and peace. Atheism was as much a moral, social and political threat as a theological one.

That was why the exemplary life of a Spinoza or a Vanini was important. If such alleged atheists were good, perhaps an atheistic society was not such a threat after all. It was also why the lion's share of atheist and proto-atheist criticism in the seventeenth century and beyond dwelt on the multiple moral failings of church and Christians. Where there were live traditions of criticism and anti-clericalism within Christian denominations, such attacks were not necessarily atheistic. But where such criticism was muted and forbidden, especially by violent means, atheistic critiques were given an enormous fillip.

It was a moral critique that Bayle appeared to adopt, although in a typically surreptitious way. His entry on Atheism in the *Dictionnaire* began by arguing that atheism was 'less injurious than idolatry'. The most horrendous Roman emperors, like Nero and Caligula, were, after all, heathens not atheists. He then proceeded to point out that atheism was not as bad as 'false religion'. Creatures from another world might assume that Christians lived by the gospel but were they to visit and see 'the real and proximate sources of action, they would quickly discover, that in this world the doings of men are regulated by other springs'.

Not that such hypocrisy was confined to Christians. 'The Jew, the Mahometan, the Turk, the Moor, the Christian, the Infidel, the Indian, the Tartar, the Islander, and the inhabitant of Terra Firma, the nobleman and the plebian' – all these 'are so alike in regard to the operation of the passions, that they are in that respect copies of each other'. Or, more bluntly, religion makes precious little difference to ethics.

Having danced around the issue, Bayle came straight out. 'It has been asserted,' he wrote, 'that a mere Atheist would be a monster beyond the power of nature to create: I reply, that it is not more strange for an Atheist to live virtuously, than for a Christian to abandon himself to crime'.

The Sadducees may not have been atheists, but they 'openly denied the immortality of the soul' (which was more or less the same thing to many of Bayle's contemporaries). And yet, Bayle reasoned, even 'with this offensive opinion, I cannot perceive that they led a more corrupt life than the other Jews'. Moral atheists existed in the ancient world. Indeed, some 'appeared so admirable in the eyes of Clement of Alexandria, that he denied their right to the appellation'. The case thus made, Bayle emphasized that he did not think that atheists are necessarily 'moral and austere'. Indeed, 'there may be, among them, every species of criminal'. Rather, he was simply making the point that atheism is not a necessary cause of immorality, but simply an incidental one.

This was a useful distancing device, and Bayle needed it. To mount such a defence was to attack one of Europe's most cherished beliefs: belief in God was necessary for the secure running of society. Not surprisingly, given his views, Bayle's doctrine of toleration was among the most generous of his time, granting liberty of conscience to atheists in the way that John Locke's more influential *Letter Concerning Toleration* did not. The difference is instructive. Locke denied atheists toleration for the very specific reason that 'promises, covenants, and oaths, which are the bonds of human society, can have no hold upon an atheist'.[163] For Bayle, by contrast, because what you believed had no necessary link to how trustworthy or moral you were, atheists merited as much toleration as the faithful.

Bayle knew such sentiments would land him in trouble and strenuously denied the charge of atheism, writing in his *Dictionnaire* that 'in order to remove all suspicions of a vicious affectation, I have taken care to mention, as often as possible, the bad morals of Atheists'. But even this denial had a sting in its tail. 'If I have not done it oftener, it was because I wanted more materials.'

How sincere were Bayle's affirmations of faith is unanswerable. His self-defence was certainly vigorous and not just for public show. He wrote to a friend a few days before he died, 'I am dying as a Christian philosopher, convinced of and pierced by the bounties and mercy of God'.[164] Yet he was still stripped of his professorship and spent much of the last decade of his life defending himself against critics. It was not without reason that figures of the early Enlightenment seized on him as an early, closet atheist whose memory they honoured.

With Bayle, the history of atheism crossed a watershed. Atheism was still at best scandalous, even in the Netherlands, and at worst punishable by death. There was no discernible, let alone obvious difference, before and after Bayle's *Dictionnaire*. Yet, Bayle had put forward the most significant atheistic argument of the early modern period. Machiavelli may have exposed ecclesiastical hypocrisy, Lucretius conjured a new vision of reality, Empiricus sown seeds of scepticism, Charron the seeds of relativism, Hobbes cast doubt on divinity, Simon on the Bible, and Spinoza offered the most coherent and consistently atheistic system before the eighteenth century (in spite of its profoundly theistic language and his insistence otherwise). However, it fell to Bayle to make the *moral* case for atheism or, rather, undermine the moral argument against it.

Given that early modern atheism had emerged within a society, or collection of societies, in which belief in God infused every aspect of life, from personal morality and the stability of the family, to property rights and political authority, atheism could not help but have a profoundly moral, social and political significance. To deny God was to make a statement about how one should or should not live; about how society should or should not be organized; about who should rule and how. Atheism meant both not believing in God and not behaving as if you believed in God: both 'atheistic' and 'ungodly'.

It was Bayle who first, cautiously, and sceptically, publically mooted the idea that belief had little impact on how people lived and constructed society. Public atheism did not become respectable after that, but it did become possible.

2

Pioneers

Immoral atheists

'You admired the stupidity of the world in being so long deluded':
The terrible fate of Thomas Aikenhead
On 8 January 1697, a young man was taken from his cell in the
Old Tolbooth in Edinburgh to the gallows situated on the road to
Leith. He carried a Bible, with which he allegedly died. His name
was Thomas Aikenhead. He was 20 years old and his crime was
blasphemy.

Writing 150 years later, the historian Thomas Babington
Macaulay recreated the story in suitably pathetic colours. The boy's
habits were 'studious', his morals 'irreproachable'. His crime was
transparently not a capital one. Given no counsel, he was unable to
defend himself. 'It was in vain that he with tears abjured his errors
and begged piteously for mercy.' Divines denied him a short delay
in sentence in which he might make his peace with God. At the
gallows he 'professed deep penitence, and suffered with the Bible in
his hand'. To no avail: the preachers 'who were the boy's murderers
crowded round him at the gallows, and while he was struggling in
the last agony, insulted Heaven with [their] prayers'.[1] Aikenhead
was certainly deemed an atheist, although, as with many people
during this period of transition, it is not clear whether he was or, if
he was, what his atheism consisted of.

Matriculating at Edinburgh University in 1693, he was summoned
before the Scottish Privy Council for offences that he had allegedly
been committing for over a year. Witnesses claimed that he had
called theology 'a rhapsody of feigned and ill-invented nonsense',
made up 'partly of the moral doctrine of philosophers, and partly

of poetical fictions and extravagant chimeras'. Indeed, it was 'worse than the fictions of the poets'. At least they had 'some connection' to reality. The scriptures had none. Aikenhead had, the Council was told, ridiculed the Bible, claiming that it was 'so stuffed with madness, nonsense, and contradictions, that you admired the stupidity of the world in being so long deluded by them'. He called the Old Testament 'Ezra's fables', neatly eliding the accusation of late authorship with the mockery of being no better than Aesop. The New Testament was a history of 'the Impostor Christ', who, having learned magic in Egypt, 'picked up a few ignorant blockish fisher fellows', and 'by the help of exalted imagination ... play'd his pranks' on them. The Trinity was 'not worth any man's refutation'; the incarnation 'as great a contradiction as the hircocervus' (the half-goat, half-stag of mythology); Mohammed to be preferred to Christ; and Christianity destined to be 'utterly extirpat[ed]' by the year 1800.[2]

Whether this pugnacity was underpinned by anything more substantial than contempt is unclear. His indictment claimed that Aikenhead had maintained 'that God, the world, and nature are but one thing, and that the world was from eternity', ideas that blended Aristotle and Spinoza. But his philosophical views were not the issue.

The 1661 Blasphemy Act, confirmed a few years before Aikenhead's trial, allowed severest punishment for those who would 'deny, impugn or quarrel, argue or reason, against the being of God, or any of the persons of the blessed Trinity, or the Authority of the Holy Scriptures of the old and new Testaments, or the providence of God in the Government of the World'. Such draconian legislation reflected a particularly nervy period in English and Scottish Christian life, in which the spectre of atheism loomed large.

In 1690, the General Assembly had expressed concern about 'dreadful atheistical boldness' of those who 'disputed the being of God and his Providence, the divine authority of the Scriptures, the life to come and the immortality of the soul'. Around the same time, Privy Council had begun an inquisition of booksellers in

Edinburgh, in which 'atheistical, erroneous or profane and vicious' publications were seized and burned. Aikenhead's crimes were not unique. A year before, the Council had heard the case of one John Frazer, who made similar claims. An immediate and fulsome recantation saved him from the gallows. Aitkenhead had either been less penitent or just one atheist too many.[3]

His fate was briefly the subject of animated and indignant conversation in London's coffee houses but he never became a martyr and his case was soon forgotten. The reasons for this, and why atheism began to take a different path in England (and Scotland) to that of, say, France during the eighteenth century, are intimately connected.

'Tis all one to debauch, or to be civil': Dissolute atheism
The Restoration of the monarchy in 1660 saw the English turn their backs on religious 'enthusiasm'. The Anglican Church reasserted itself, dissenters were subject to varying levels of civil restriction, and those Protestant ministers unable to sign up to the Book of Common Prayer and the 39 articles were ejected from their parishes. Nevertheless, the King did not have the spirit, nor the nation the stomach, for a new age of spiritual tyranny. Government was not there to establish a community of saints reigning on earth, but to maintain order, liberty and property, at least among the right people. Earthly pleasure nudged aside heavenly bliss.

This did not, of course, eliminate the need for punitive or moralizing legislation. The established church reasserted its authority, and the population was again legally required to attend services, pay tithes, and solemnize baptisms, marriages and funerals according to its rite. The Licensing Act of 1662 reasserted control of the press. Later in the century, the Societies for Reformation of Manners and the Promotion of Christian Knowledge were established. These, however, were the products of a hierarchy worrying about social unrest rather than trying to legislate the nation into piety.

In place of a godly spirit, there emerged a commercial one. Desire, self-interest and consumption drifted from the realm of sin to that of nature, becoming reasonable and then necessary human impulses. It was through the pursuit of material comfort that the commonwealth was to be secured. Greed was acceptable, if not actually good.

Not everyone shared this view. The Court, critics complained, should have led by example. In a sense, it did. Holiness was not an immediate priority for the Caroline monarchy, and Charles' court became renowned for its libertine culture. Drink, gaming, whoring, swearing and blasphemy: the court either ignored or indulged vice, and where court led, society followed.

Inns, taverns and, now, coffee houses were dens of unregulated wit and ridicule. Playhouses were worse still. Restoration drama abounded in sexual discord, dalliance, duplicity and deceit. The longstanding Puritan critique of the theatre – that its atmosphere of show, of levity, of mockery undermined all that which was serious and godly – was never truer. Theatre became the epitome of practical atheism. '[Men] are now taught how they might be without a Creator ... They make very bold with the Grace of God, and crave inspiration to serve the ends of lust and revenge', complained the author of the pamphlet, *Some considerations about the danger of going to plays* in 1704.[4]

Church was no antidote. The parish system was characterized by pluralism and non-residence. Convocation was prorogued in 1717 leaving the church without any form of self-government. Ecclesiastical authorities were criticized for poor catechizing and badly educated clergy. Milton may have been a particularly puritanical observer, so to speak, but he voiced the concerns of many when he wrote in 1673, 'it is a general complaint that this nation of late years is grown more numerously and excessively vicious than heretofore: Pride, Luxury, Drunkeness, Whoredom, Cursing, Swearing, bold and open atheism everywhere abounding'.[5]

Milton's 'open atheism' was, of course, the practical atheism of longstanding Christian concern. But scratch the skin of a practical atheist and you might just see a theoretical atheist bleed. John Wilmot, 2nd Earl of Rochester – satirical, lascivious and by his own account drunk continuously for five years – appears to have been one such atheist, at least until his death-bed conversion at the age of 33.

Rochester was as contemptuous of philosophical reason as he was of puritanical orthodoxy and hypocritical 'priestcraft'. His *A Satyr Against Reason and Mankind* was a relentless attack on the rational pretensions of the age. Reason, he wrote, is an '*ignis fatuus*', or will-o'-the-wisp. It is conceited and deceiving, a 'supernatural gift, that makes a mite,/ Think he's the image of the Infinite'. It was utterly unable to prevent the inevitable: 'Huddled in dirt the reasoning engine lies, / Who was so proud, so witty, and so wise'. If reason did have a role it was strictly limited to 'bound[ing] desires' so as to 'keep them more in vigour'. Beyond that, it was as much an illusion as was revelation.

Although promiscuous priests, bullying bishops and churchmen 'who hunt good livings, but abhor good lives' were all eloquently skewered in Rochester's satire, his ambition went beyond the anti-clerical. Rochester deflated all human pretensions, his *Satyr* repeatedly comparing human nature to that of animals, rarely to the former's advantage. Having begun by saying he would rather 'be a dog, a monkey, or a bear, / Or anything but that vain animal / Who is so proud of being rational,' he went on to ask 'which is the basest creature, man or beast?' The answer was never in doubt. 'Birds feed on birds, beasts on each other prey, / But savage man alone does man betray'. The poem concludes with a motif that would become an atheist mantra, although for more substantial reasons than Rochester's: 'Man differs more from man, than man from beast.'

Rochester's atheism was egoistic, hedonistic and earthy. 'Our sphere of Action is life's happiness,' he wrote at one point, 'And he who thinks beyond, thinks like an ass.' Rochester did not seek to replace religious authority with philosophical reason, but rather to mock, ignore and undermine all authority, and dreams of human dignity, to make space for an ethic and polity that enabled people to live as they wanted.

It is this kind of dissolute atheism that was to inform the notorious Hell-fire clubs of the eighteenth century, with their deliberate rejection of Christian morality in favour of a libertinism founded on a motto drawn originally from Rabelais – *Fais ce que tu voudras* or 'Do what thou wilt' – and rather engagingly characterized by Lord Vaughan's ditty: 'There's no such thing as good or evil, / But that which do's please, or displease, / There's no God, Heaven, or a Devil, / 'Tis all one to debauch, or to be civil.'[6]

The reasonable English

'The works of God plainly argue the vileness and perverseness of the atheist': Hubris

Not all Restoration culture was so frivolous, and some of Rochester's peers had bigger ambitions than lust and luxury. The Royal Society was founded in 1660 and granted a Royal Charter two years later. Its method of 'Physico-Mathematical Experimental Learning' was based on the new science of Francis Bacon and others. From a very early stage it was considered a momentous new intellectual departure.

Such a venture, with its presuppositions that nature can be understood without recourse to revelation or creeds, might have become the cornerstone of a new atheism, with elite 'scientists' (the word was yet to be invented) dismantling Christendom brick by brick. That was certainly how it was seen by later historians with an atheistic and Whiggish bent. Unfortunately for this narrative, most of those behind the so-called scientific revolution were serious Christians, whose endeavours, as we noted in Chapter 1, were justified, directed and encouraged by their Christian convictions. This was to prove of utmost importance for the development of British atheism.

The Society consciously eschewed debates over revelation and confessional allegiance. A somewhat premature history of the

Society – written seven years after its foundation – by Bishop Thomas Sprat explained that it was 'cautious not to intermeddle in Spiritual things'. An early memorandum noted that Fellows scrupulously avoided 'medding with Divinity, Metaphysics, [and] Moralls'.[7]

Aversion was not revulsion, however. The 1663 Charter declared that the Society's activities shall be devoted 'to the glory of God the Creator' and its officers were required to swear an oath on the gospels. This was more than mere window dressing. Defences of and justifications for scientific activity repeatedly drew on Christian convictions. Investigating and understanding the mechanics of the natural world in this way was to think God's thought after him. It was to recover Adam's knowledge lost at the Fall, and re-establish his dominion over nature. It was, to borrow the title of Henry More's important book from 1653, an *Antidote against Atheism*.

Most influential in this endeavour was Robert Boyle, a key figure in the group that met in Oxford in the later 1650s and formed the founding quorum of the Royal Society. Boyle was convinced that the new philosophy would 'furnish us with some new Weapons for the defence of our ancientest Creed'.[8] Boyle died in 1691 but in his will left funds for a lecture series intended 'for the defence of the Christian religion against atheists and other unbelievers'.[9] The Boyle lectures began the following year, with Richard Bentley speaking on the *Confutation of Atheism*, and continued, on and off, for the next two centuries, being resurrected in 2004.

It was during its first 40 years that the series was most influential. Early lectures included *The Atheistical Objections against the Being of God and His Attributes Fairly Considered and Fully Refuted* (John Harris, 1698) and *Physico-Theology, or a Demonstration of the Being and Attributes of God from his Works of Creation* (William Derham, 1711). By no means all lectures sought to do battle with atheism on the field of natural philosophy – a number sought to defend the credibility, sufficiency and perfection of revelation – but the Boyle lectures became renowned and remembered primarily for using science to fortify Christianity. 'The works of God are so visible to all the world ... that they plainly argue the vileness and perverseness of the atheist,' Derham wrote confidently.[10] In the long run, this would prove short-sighted, but at the time it was a hugely effective means of disarming atheist arguments and sentiments.

'Contrary to the Holy Scriptures themselves': Questions

For lecturers, auditors and many an erudite gentleman, this blossoming field of natural theology was not only compatible with theistic belief, but its best defence. The intricate structure of the cosmos, of nature and latterly of individual organisms revealed the wonder of creation, confirming and strengthening human appreciation of its creator and his goodness. The uncertainty and violence that had attended confessional theology earlier in the seventeenth century had demanded a revision of the way people thought about God. The natural sciences provided one.

Not everyone was so sure. The observation, and the fossils, and the antiquarianism that was slowly morphing into archaeology posed uncomfortable questions about the natural and human past and some luminaries were thinking suspiciously unorthodox thoughts. Robert Hooke, for example, speculated on the possibility of species dying out and of processes of creation that took into account the violence of earthquakes, thereby jeopardizing the beneficent, once-and-for-all-creation of Christian doctrine. John Woodward, who became Gresham Professor of Physic in 1692 and was another fellow of the Royal Society, theorized about marine fossils found far inland, seeking a natural cause to explain the phenomenon.

This was unnerving but at least Woodward tried to reconcile his causes with a literal reading of Genesis. Some didn't even do that. The Mosaic account of creation, already under pressure from biblical criticism, found itself fighting a war on two fronts. William Whiston, Lucasian Professor of Mathematics and 1707 Boyle lecturer, wrote that 'the notions [people] have entertain'd of the Nature, Stile, and Extent of the Creation of the World in six days, are false, precarious, and no less contrary to the Holy Scriptures themselves, than to sound reason and true philosophy'.[11] Thomas Burnet said the same, only in a still more irreverent spirit.

Such ideas were threatening in themselves but so, more pervasively, was the wholesale shift from primary to secondary causes. Natural theology revealed God but it was a discomfortingly grey God, perched on the edge of nature's frame, comfortable in his role as creator, but somewhat redundant as Father, Son, or Holy Spirit.

Just as this was happening, studies of pre-Nicene Church Fathers raised questions about whether the early Christians had had any concept of the Trinity at all. Intellectual giants, like Milton and Newton, worked methodically through scripture, compiling systematic theologies that remained stubbornly anti-Trinitarian, and unpublished. William Whiston studied the fourth-century *Apostolic Constitutions*, and came to the conclusion that Arianism had been the early church's creed, for which he was then removed from his professorship, expelled from the university and never invited to be a member of the Royal Society.[12]

Early Christian history joined natural theology in nudging Christianity back to the long-suppressed Arian heresy of the early church, and Arianism, it was widely imagined, was merely – as Erasmus Darwin would describe Unitarianism a century later – a featherbed to catch a falling Christian. Still, at least it was a featherbed. Without it, many more might have fallen further and harder on to the cold stone floor of atheism beyond which there was nowhere to go.

'The Human Soul an invention of the Heathens': Renegotiations

Even if these questions could be answered, and physico-theology judged the saviour of beliefs that had been battered by decades of confessional conflict, the question remained, at what cost?

Doctrinal orthodoxy mattered but it mattered as much for providing the sinews and joints that bound society together as for intrinsic reasons of truth or salvation. Again, here, physico-theology, for all its demonstration of God's might and glory, was worrying. Where, for example, did it leave divine providence? God might, at a push, retain the capacity for general providence, rewarding and punishing the good and wicked by means of the laws and processes he had set up, but this was a blunt instrument at best, denying divinity the weapon of special providence, and effectively de-moralizing creation. Some, like Thomas Burnet, tried to ride both horses, seeing in Noah's flood, for example, both a natural event and divine punishment. But this lacked the pleasing, unqualified moral clarity of earlier explanations. Atheistic claims had long denied the efficacy or reality of God as the *moral governor* of the universe. Natural philosophy was apparently proving them right.

If providence was threatened, so was the soul. Spinoza had pointed out that that the Hebrew word often translated as soul or spirit, 'ruach', literally means 'wind' but could be used figuratively to mean breath, life, breathing, courage, strength, ability, capacity, a 'sentiment' of the mind, the mind or soul itself.[13] Natural philosophy, unable to locate anything that looked like a soul within the human frame, seemed to point in a similar direction.

William Coward's *Second Thoughts Concerning the Human Soul*, published in 1702, explained, in its interminable subtitle, that it would demonstrate 'the notion of Human Soul, as believ'd to be a Spiritual, Immortal Substance, united to a Human Body, to be an invention of the Heathens, and not consonant to the principles of Philosophy, Reason, or Religion, but the ground of many absurd, and superstitious opinions, abominable to the reformed churches and derogatory in general to true Christianity'.

As it happens, Coward was more accurate than he or his contemporaries really knew. The biblical notion of the human as an animated body had given way to the Platonic idea of a soul-body dualism in the early Christian centuries and would not resurface as the authentic position until well into the twentieth century, and even then only controversially. In the meantime, criticism of Coward's ideas was severe. Where did they leave resurrection, judgement and eternal life? It was bad enough to relinquish divine providence in this life. Doing so in the next was completely unacceptable.

The author anticipated many of these criticisms, replying that 'this life will to the Righteous be chang'd into life everlasting at the day of the general Resurrection'.[14] Again, he was closer to the New Testament view than his critics, not that they were satisfied. *Second Thoughts* was condemned. Coward was ridiculed, and then called to the House of Commons after his next book, *Grand Essay; or a Vindication of Reason and Religion against Impostures of Philosophy*. His books were then burned by the hangman. He escaped.

'Vice is beneficial found': Attacks

The hubristic attitude to reason that characterized the later seventeenth century placed revelation in a bind. If reason and revelation disagreed, revelation must be at fault. If they were at one, why bother with revelation in the first place?

The acceptable answer was that revelation showed what reason could not. In the words of one early eighteenth-century pamphleteer, 'All the doctrines I can name in revelation, whether *discoverable by reason or not*, are agreeable to the nature and reason of things'.[15] The parenthesis – 'whether discoverable by reason or not' – was crucial, but hardly rang with confidence. What seemed, at first, to be harmonious union could readily dissolve into acrimonious divorce, revelation evicted for being an ineffective or abusive partner. This was precisely what a loose group of deist thinkers did in the early decades of the eighteenth century, provoking an 'atheist scare', and publishing phenomenon, unmatched until the early years of the next millennium.

The deists deployed a range of arguments that were familiar but now embedded in a more confident and coherent intellectual framework. There was the knowing comparison with the ancient world. Charles Blount translated the first two books of Philostratus's *Life of Apollonius Tyraneus*, a first-century Greek philosopher, who became, under the pen of his biographer and subsequent anti-Christian writers in antiquity, a holy, wonder-working rival to Christ. Blount's innocent dissemination of his life was not so innocent. His subsequent *Great is Diana of the Ephesians* used a similar tactic, ridiculing Christian practice, especially the Eucharist, under the guise of attacking heathen sacrifice. Conyers Middleton, a Fellow of Trinity College, wrote in his *Letters from Rome* how paganism was, in effect, an earlier form of Catholicism, its demi-gods saints, its pagan worship Catholic ceremony. This was not necessarily atheistic. Reformed Protestants had delighted in comparing the ways of modern Rome to those of its ancient predecessor. But 'priestcraft', as it became disparaged, need not be a Romish sin alone.

Comparing religions invited an anthropological reading of them. John Toland's *Letters to Serena* argued that all superstition originated in funerary rites. Religious enthusiasm was happily psychologized. 'Thus is Religion also Pannick,' explained the 3rd Earl Shaftesbury in *A Letter Concerning Enthusiasm*.[16] So was superstition: John Trenchard's *Natural History* of the subject contended that there was something innate in human nature that led to superstition, and interpreted religious visions as if they were psychic states.[17]

If religious phenomena were naturalized, so were religious texts, though rarely with Spinoza's erudition or subtlety. Daring criticism of the New Testament majored on miracles. No longer the unanswerable arguments of Christian apologetics, they were seen by rationalists as slightly embarrassing and unconvincing examples of the primitive mind, unnecessary for and beneath the dignity of a God of reason. Blount's *Miracles, No Violations of the Laws of Nature* comprised a free translation of Chapter VI of Spinoza's *Tractatus* (the earliest in English), interpolated with passages from Hobbes' *Leviathan*. Thomas Woolston's *The Moderator between an Infidel and an Apostate* implied that the miracles of Jesus should not be taken literally, and argued (rightly) that many Church Fathers had read them with an allegorical bent.

Just as seriously, some claimed that religion was not necessary to social order. None of the deists had Bayle's lightness of touch but that didn't affect the weight of their argument. 'Men's relation to, their interest in, their dependence upon, and their obligations to society,' wrote Thomas Chubb, are 'exactly the same, whether they believe these points [God, a providence, and a judgement to come], or not.'[18]

In reality, deist writers went some way beyond the suggestion that religion was not necessary for social harmony, proposing reason as the alternative, and better, foundation. Reason required freedom of thought. 'It is every Man's natural right and duty to think, and judge for himself in matters of opinion,' wrote Antony Collins in 1724. Freedom of thought was inadequate if not coupled with freedom of discussion and expression. 'So,' Collins continued, 'he should be allow'd freely to profess his opinions, and to endeavour, when he judges proper, to convince others also of their truth; provided those opinions do not tend to the disturbance of society.'[19] Freedom of discussion in the growing urban, mercantile society of early eighteenth-century England meant, or should mean, freedom of the press. 'There is no freedom either in civil or ecclesiastical, but where the liberty of the press is maintain'd,' wrote Matthew Tindal in 1704.[20]

Reason demanded freedom, then, but it also demanded a moral system that was based on self-interest rather than eternal rules, a self-ish basis for morality. 'The perfection and happiness of all rational beings, supreme, as well as subordinate,' wrote Tindal, 'consists in living up to the dictates of their nature.'[21] Personal happiness was dependent on personal pursuit of personally chosen ends. Pleasure, not virtue, was the lodestar, although not quite in the way the Earl of Rochester had favoured. Most influential here was Bernard Mandeville, a philosopher and economist who grew up in Rotterdam and was taught by Bayle, and who subsequently wrote a poem and extended commentary entitled *Fable of the Bees, or, Private Vices, Public Benefits*.

In contradiction to every tenet of Christian morality, Mandeville argued that the dissolute individual could be a great public asset in their generation of wealth. 'Do we not owe the Growth of Wine/ To the dry shabby crooked Vine?' Vice was more profitable than virtue. True, this vice was not the unrestrained libertinism of Christian nightmares. It required discipline. 'Vice is beneficial found/ When it's by Justice lopt and bound'. Nonetheless the view of humans as appetite-driven animals was scandalous enough and the book was attacked, denounced and convicted as a nuisance by the grand jury of Middlesex in 1723. Mandeville protested but didn't help himself by going on to publish his *Free Thoughts on Religion, the Church, and National Happiness*, which argued that faith in the Trinity and the creeds should be treated as 'matters indifferent' to the Christian religion; a *Modest Defense of Public Stews*, not a title calculated to calm fears; and *An Enquiry into the Origin of Honour, and the Usefulness of Christianity in War* (his answer was that it was not particularly useful).

These deists were not atheists and did not become atheists. They saw their ideas not as a rejection of Christianity but a return to it, albeit to a Christianity, that was, in the title of Matthew Tindal's book, 'as old as creation'. They saw reason as Christianity's best ally. 'Ignorance is the foundation of Atheism and Free-Thinking the Cure of it,' wrote Collins in his *Discourse of Free-Thinking*.[22] Many believed themselves not so very far from contemporary orthodoxy, with good reason. No less a person than John Tillotson, Archbishop of Canterbury, had written that 'all the duties of Christian religion ... are no other but what natural light prompts men to, excepting the two sacraments, and praying to God in the name and by the mediation of Christ'.[23]

Nevertheless, it was clear that the intellectual climate of England in the late seventeenth and early eighteenth centuries had all the ingredients for sustained and systematic atheism (such as would emerge within a couple of generations in France): hostility to enthusiasm and superstition; denigration of priestcraft and confessional religion; sceptical biblical critique; a rejection of the spiritual apparatus of the Christian universe; a quasi-deification of reason and its defiant elevation over revelation; an understanding of personal and public morality that was indifferent or actively hostile to traditional Christian concepts of the good. The fact that these sentiments did not morph into full-blown atheism has much to do with the intellectual, political and social settlement of the time, which was epitomized by two figures in particular.

'I esteem ... toleration to be the chief characteristic mark of the true Church': Defence

Isaac Newton was secretive, unstable and insecure.[24] He had some form of religious crisis aged 19 in which he wrote out all the sins he could remember having committed, but remained intensely religious throughout his life, beginning serious biblical studies from about 30, and writing more about biblical chronology, prophecy, apocalypse and church history than he did on mathematics and optics.

It was, of course, the latter work that earned him his reputation and although his *Principia*, first published in 1687, was slow to take off, when it did it established him as one of Europe's pre-eminent minds. Newton was cagey about his religious views, not least because his biblical studies had taken him in an anti-Trinitarian direction, but was nevertheless open and clear that he thought his scientific work not simply compatible with, but confirmation of, his Christianity.

Richard Bentley was a distinguished classics scholar and one of Newton's scientific protégés and he sought his master's help in preparing his inaugural Boyle lectures. Newton obliged with four detailed letters that were subsequently published. The first of these began 'When I wrote my treatise about our Systeme I had an eye upon such Principles as might work with considering men for the beleife of a Deity & nothing can rejoyce me more then to find it usefull for that purpose.'[25] It was a persistent theme in his scientific writing. 'This most beautiful system of the sun, planets, and comets, could only proceed from the counsel and dominion of an intelligent Being,' he wrote in Book III of his *Principia*, going on to describe a 'living, intelligent and powerful Being' in terms that would not have been out of place in the pulpit, or even a mystic's vision. He 'governs all things ... is not eternity or infinity, but eternal and infinite ... is not duration or space, but he endures and is present ... In him are all things contained and moved'.[26] If the greatest scientist in Europe thought this, who was anyone to say otherwise?

That recognized, Newton probably had less of an impact on the late development of atheism in Britain than his friend, the philosopher John Locke. Just as Newton exemplified the compatibility of belief in God with the intellectual revolution, Locke did the same for the political one.

A few years before Newton and Locke began corresponding, Louis XIV had revoked the Edict of Nantes, forcing France's vulnerable Protestants to choose between conversion, persecution and exile, and thereby cementing in the English mind the longstanding connection between France, Catholicism and tyranny. Three years later, at the moment that Locke burst upon the public imagination with his *Letter Concerning Toleration*, his *Two Treatises of Government* and his *Essay Concerning Human Understanding*, the Catholic James II was ousted peaceably and the Protestant William and Mary placed on the throne. A Bill of Rights and Act of Toleration were rapidly passed, although both rights and toleration were severely limited in practice. A few years later the Licensing Act was allowed to lapse creating a relatively free market in printing. Within a few decades publications such as the *Freethinker*, which lasted from 1718 to 1721, were freely available. Britain settled into a self-conscious national identity rooted in and proud of its commitment to law and liberty.

Locke proved the lead theorist of this, his political ideas explicitly rooted in biblical Christianity. His first *Treatise of Government* was a careful justification of equality which drew repeatedly on 'scripture-proofs'. It was on this foundation that he constructed his arguments concerning property, political society and the legislative power of the commonwealth in the *Second Treatise*. His *Letter Concerning Toleration* was, if anything, more biblical still, grounding its arguments in detailed exegesis, on account of which Locke wrote how he 'esteem[ed] … toleration to be the chief characteristic mark of the true Church'.[27] The equality, liberty and toleration that supposedly marked British political culture was not won in spite of Christianity, but because of it.

Eighteenth-century Britain was not, of course, a liberal society. The Blasphemy Act was passed in 1697. Ecclesiastical courts retained the power to imprison for atheism, blasphemy and heresy. Books were still burned. Yet, compared to the rest of Europe, excepting the Netherlands, England (and then Britain) was a beacon of liberty, with an established and limited constitutional monarchy, which tolerated Christian dissenters whose own traditions of anti-clericalism could be as vigorous as those of any proto-atheist. No wonder Voltaire was so impressed and influenced by the English model.

When Jonathan Swift bemoaned, in 1722, that 'no age, since the founding and forming of the Christian church was ever like, in avowed atheism, blasphemies, and heresies to the age we now live in', he wasn't just being cantankerous.[28] In different circumstances, any number of those loosely accused of atheism – Rochester, Blount, Chubb, Toland, Tindal, Collins, Mandeville – might have become atheists, such as those who sat round Baron D'Holbach's table two generations later.

Yet, they did not and the reason they did not is that the Christian establishment was too flexible and accommodating, intellectually and politically, to give them reason to. Ultimately, it was because Thomas Aikenhead's punishment was so exceptional, that his beliefs remained exceptional, at least for a century.

German toleration

Continental Europe fell in love with British thought, particularly that of Locke and Newton, in the early eighteenth century, and the German territories in particular followed the British example closely.

Both lands had been scarred by bloody, confessional wars. Both saw a new dawn in natural philosophy, the Prussian Academy of Sciences being founded in 1700. Both feared infidelity. The scholar Veit Ludwig von Seckendorff observed in 1685 that there was a growing tendency among ordinary people to mock scripture, reject the devil, deny spirits and doubt the immortality of the soul. And both linked this to wickedness. Immanuel Weber, chamberlain of the principality of Schwartzburg-Sonderhausen, wrote a treatise on atheism in 1696 in which he condemned the philosophy, as well as a range of other modern fashions, such as opera, ballet, theatre and masquerades, all of which were essentially ungodly at heart. A few years later Johann Georg Leuckfeld, a Lutheran pastor and theologian, wrote about the advent of atheism in German society, connecting the intellectual sickness of universities and moral illness of court life in his critique.

Like everywhere else at the time, atheism in Germany was deemed, in the words of theologian Valentin Loescher, 'pernicious both to virtue and the republic'.[29] But, like everywhere else at the time, it is difficult to discern when the tradition of atheistic thought began, and how wide, and genuine, it was.

According to Jakob Reimann, the early German historian of atheism, things began in 1670 with Matthias Knutzen. Knutzen is sometimes called the first publicly acknowledged atheist in early modern Europe, but not enough is known of his life and thought to be sure of this. What is known is that his sermons (he had studied theology and took up a temporary post as a preacher) criticized the ecclesiastical authorities and, having been dismissed from his post, he wrote a number of short tracts, in the guise of letters and conversations, denying God and the immortality of the soul, together with the legitimacy of princes and magistrates, and the authority of the church. Life after death was a fantasy, he declared, and marriage meaningless, as married intimacy was no different from extramarital. Reason, he declared, was better than the Bible: conscience the only legitimate authority. In a particularly creative moment, he left his tracts on the professors' church pews in Jena in 1674, after which foolhardy venture little is heard of him.

Knutzen had successors, if not followers. Johann Lorenz Schmidt was a preacher's son, theology student and learned Hebraist who detected in natural religion the elegant mathematical perfection of reason which had been perfected by Greek philosophers but subsequently corrupted by Jews and Christians. He compiled what become known at the Werthem Bible, a translation and commentary on the Pentateuch, which contemporaries saw as a systematic attempt to dilute and explain away everything miraculous in the Torah, and which was banned in 1737.

Gabriel Wagner was a thoroughgoing materialist who denied spirit, souls and apparently the existence of God. Friedrich Willhelm Stosch was similarly inclined, contending that 'nothing is absolutely good or bad itself, but only respectively in so far as it is useful or damaging to another thing'.[30] Johann Wachter suggested that Christianity originated with the Essene sect and that Jesus was himself an Essene, which helped explain why the gospels record him arguing with the Pharisees and Sadducees but never the Essenes (a theory later favoured by Voltaire and Frederick the Great). Johann Christian Edelman's *The Revealed Face of Moses* argued that Christ was only a man and the Bible was merely a human book of human rules. He too dismissed the need for marriage and advocated sexual licence. The anonymous clandestine manuscript *Symbolum sapiente*, dating from around 1700 in Germany, though not translated into German until 1749, rehearsed the various accusations of deception, manipulation, subjugation and imposture beloved of that genre.

There was, then, a live tradition of deistic, and possibly atheistic, thought in Germany in the later seventeenth and early eighteenth centuries. It was less confident and less visible than in Britain and also less original. *Symbolum sapiente* was reminiscent of *Traité des Trois Imposteurs* and indebted to Spinozist thought, if not necessarily Spinoza. Theodor Ludwig Lau, another alleged atheist, denied he was a Spinozist (not entirely convincingly) but clearly drew on the work of Lucretius, Lord Herbert, Hobbes and Toland. In his *Praenotiones*, Valentin Loescher cited Hobbes as a factor in the advent of philosophical incredulity in Germany. The English deists became influential from the 1720s, and Mathew Tindal in particular from the 1740s.

Germany thus paralleled Britain in developing a sub-atheist tradition of thought in the decades around the turn of the century. More tellingly, however, it also followed Britain in *not* developing a sustained or unambiguous atheistic movement until much later. The reasons are, again, similar.

The German lands had suffered as much, if not more, in the Thirty Year War as England had in its civil wars. The former's conclusion was inconclusive, in as far as no one emerged as undisputed victor (which further eroded divine authority: whose side was God on exactly?) and the ensuing Treaty of Westphalia, cementing confessional blocks across Germany.

This led to a mosaic of political regimes in which censorship, and to an extent philosophical culture, rested in the hands of individual princes or city governments. These regimes could be severe, but many weren't and in any case the patchwork nature of authority meant that it made it relatively easy for those accused of atheism to escape. Thus, Johann Lorenz Schmidt fled to Holland after the Werthem Bible controversy but returned a few years later to Germany, settling in Altona, which was at the time under Danish jurisdiction. Theodor Lau led an almost peripatetic life moving from court to court across Germany as he escaped the accusations of atheism that followed him. Johann Edelman settled in Sayn-Wittgenstein-Berleberg, which was ruled by the unusually liberal and tolerant Count Casmir, until he was obliged to leave for another liberal principality, Neuwied, and then obliged to leave once again, finally throwing himself on the mercy of the greatest free-thinking prince of the age, Frederick the Great. Edelman thought Frederick was a tyrant, but he was at least a freethinking tyrant, and the monarch took him in on the condition of silence.

Frederick acceded to the throne in 1740 and immediately fostered a culture of religious toleration, which was born of the king's deep loathing of confessionalism and equal contempt for all religions. In contrast to his Pietist and authoritarian father, with whom he had been on epically bad terms, Frederick adopted some of Europe's most wanted thinkers, including Edelman, Voltaire, Jean-Baptiste le Rond D'Alembert, and Julien Offray de La Mettrie. Political censorship remained tight but theological and philosophical restrictions were minimal. Such freedom to think, unimpeded by religious authorities, was the reason why a vigorous atheistic tradition did not take hold in Germany, as it did in France.

Or, rather, it was part of the reason: the second was the existence of a 'moderate' Christian enlightenment in Germany, which embraced and legitimized new philosophical, mathematical and scientific ideas. Where Britain has its Locke and its Newton, Germany has its Christian Wolff, Christian Thomasius and its Gottfried Wilhelm von Leibniz.

This Christian enlightenment was far from straightforward. Christian Wolff, a professor at the University of Halle, was dismissed from his chair in 1723 and forced to leave the Prussian kingdom within 48 hours or face the scaffold, accused of atheism and determinism, having argued, among other things, that (atheistic) Confucianism served as an efficient basis for a moral society. Wolff was no Bayle, however, and although he was adamant that philosophy and morality were independent of theology and revelation, he put forward arguments from natural theology for the existence of God seriously and sincerely. Fleeing to Hesse-Cassel after his exile he was given a chair at the University of Marburg, and although academic Europe was angrily divided over him for the next 20 years, Frederick the Great recalled him to the kingdom and his reputation was fully rehabilitated.

Christian Thomasius was professor of natural law at Leipzig. He advocated a measure of toleration for atheists, and strongly critiqued the pedantry and bigotry of much confessional thinking.

He sought free thought and, in particular, jurisprudence from the Lutheran theological straitjacket in which it was held. Like Wolff, he was forced into exile. And yet, again like Wolff, Thomasius was no radical, being shaped by the Pietist movement that was altering the face of German Christianity at the time.

Most influentially, Leibniz, was, in the words of historian Jonathan Israel, the 'pre-eminent architect of the mainstream, moderate Enlightenment'.[31] A brilliant mathematician, whose discovery of calculus at the same time as Newton fed their animosity, he was polymathic, prolific and convinced that faith and reason were compatible. Leibniz's reputation faded quickly in the eighteenth century as his rationalism was eclipsed by Locke's empiricism, by Newton's apparent victory in the battle over calculus, and by Voltaire, who mercilessly mocked his cosmic optimism in *Candide*. Yet, his writings at the time showed those who fretted at the new philosophy that they need not embrace materialist, Spinozist or atheist creeds but could legitimately hold together reason and revelation.

Like Britain, then, the German tradition of atheism was impeded by pious mathematicians, natural theology and political moderation. It was because people like Wolff, Thomasius and Leibniz carved out a legitimate moderate Christian enlightenment, working within a political patchwork that enabled a degree of toleration, albeit more by accident than design, that the atheism with which German intellectual culture was pregnant in the early eighteenth century would not be born for another hundred years or so.

French fury

'Hung and strangled with the entrails of priests': Jean Meslier's posthumous revelation
The Wars of Religion had dislocated many people and created numerous diasporas across the continent. A disproportionate number of these found their way to the Low Countries. Formerly

a Spanish province, it already hosted many wealthy Sephardic Jews who had refused to convert during the Reconquista. They were joined by poorer Ashkenazi Jews and Polish-German Socinians fleeing from an increasingly intolerant Catholic Counter-Reformation in north-eastern Europe.[32] To them were added English Puritans disaffected with early Stuart Anglicanism and then French Protestants who came in their numbers after Louis XIV revoked the Edict of Nantes in 1685.

Such diverse theological commitments were further fermented by a period of unprecedented trade and economic growth, urbanization and a political system of provincial and municipal autonomy. The Dutch Republic became a beacon of toleration, liberty – and of atheism – by 1700. And yet, it was not the Netherlands that developed the most vigorous and pugnacious atheistic culture of the eighteenth century but France where the garrotte tying together royal absolutism and ecclesiastical authority was drawn tighter than anywhere else in Western Europe.

Louis XIV became ever more pious in the later years of his reign, banning many of the entertainments he had previously enjoyed. He had forbidden the teaching of Cartesianism in French colleges and universities in 1671, enforcing an (already outmoded) Aristotelianism which was, in any case, kept thoroughly subordinate to theology. The French Church was gloriously wealthy, owning close to ten per cent of land, exercising the right to tithe over most of the rest, enjoying significant tax exemptions, and nourishing popular hostility to Protestants.

Not that this calmed fears of atheism: books leaked in from the Netherlands, finding their way to booksellers, who were regularly searched; to readers, who hid them well; and to the hangman, who burned them in public. Preachers denounced atheism, theologians disproved it and the authorities worried. Censorship was relaxed a little in 1713, after the end of the War of Spanish Succession, and more so two years later when Louis was eventually succeeded by his nephew, Philippe, Duke of Orléans, but throne and altar still dominated the spiritual, intellectual and political landscape.

There was an irony – or, more accurately, a reeking hypocrisy – in all this, however. Philippe was a sceptic who had the works of Rabelais bound into his Bible so he could read them during Mass. He was not alone in his infidelity. Several contemporary sources remark how French nobles, officials and diplomats hardly bothered to conceal their freethinking, libertine views. There is nothing more important than appearing to be religious, Machiavelli had written. The French nobility knew it.

Even under the moderate liberalization of the press from 1715, which was undertaken for economic rather than political or religious reasons, France still enjoyed less freedom than other countries. Whereas most of its neighbours symbolically tore or burned books, or imprisoned their authors, France still allowed torture and execution for confessional crimes. As late as 1766, Chevalier de la Barre was publicly tortured for reputedly singing blasphemous songs, disrespecting a religious procession and owning a copy of Voltaire's *Philosophical Dictionary*.

This helps explain why the tradition of atheism that developed in France was so much angrier and more uncompromising than that of Britain, Germany or the Dutch Republic. Christian belief was the foundation for an authoritarianism which was that much more prejudiced and despotic than across the Channel, a deep well of tyranny from which sceptics could draw limitless indignation.

This in itself was not enough, however. Crucially and again unlike Britain or Germany, France developed no indigenous Locke and Newton or, more precisely, no tradition of a moderate, demonstrably Christian enlightenment, in which reason and revelation, science and scripture, philosophy and theology were reconciled. The royal ban on Cartesianism in favour of a crumbling scholastic consensus, combined with a bitter rivalry between Jesuits and Jansenists, drained the culture of an ameliorative intellectual

presence, one that might have offered a third way between intellectually incredible and morally repugnant orthodoxy, and blunt
materialist atheism.[33]

Voltaire, whose profound Anglophilia and determined deism
seemed to be taking French intellectual life in that direction in the
1730s, was no diplomat and ill-suited to broker any settlement. His
true position – far too close to non-providential deism for official
comfort – combined with his habit of ridiculing those foolish
enough to disagree with him meant that long after its neighbours
had introduced a measure of intellectual and political toleration,
France had virtually none.

In such conditions it was sensible to keep silent, which is precisely
what Jean Meslier did. Meslier was born in 1664. He took Holy
Orders in January 1689 and spent his entire life as a priest in a poor
community at Etrépigny, in Champagne. Apart from a couple of
archepiscopal reports condemning his use of under-aged females
as servants, his life was unremarkable. He died in 1729 leaving his
Mémoire in which he offered 'clear and Evident Demonstrations of
the Vanity and Falsity of All the Gods and of All the Religions of
the World'.[34] Meslier is the first modern European about whom it is
possible to say, without doubt or qualification, he was an atheist.

The *Mémoire* is long, thorough and uncompromising. Early on
Meslier wrote of how a man 'with neither science nor education
but who ... did not lack common sense' once told him that he
wished 'all of the greats of the earth, and all of the nobles were hung
and strangled with the entrails of priests'. This was shocking and
vulgar, Meslier admitted, but it did at least show what such people
deserved.[35] Denis Diderot agreed, deriving from it his better known
hope that the people would strangle the neck of the last king with
the guts of the last priest.

At the heart of his *Mémoire*, Meslier offered a savage critique
of religious exploitation. 'Know, my dear friends,' he wrote, 'that
everything that is happening in the world concerning the cult
and the adoration of gods, is nothing but error, abuse, illusion,

mendacity, and betrayal'.[36] On one side, the priests terrify their flock into political obedience on pain of eternal damnation. On the other, princes enforce religious order, give priests 'good appointments and good revenues, and maintain them in the vain function of their false ministry'.[37] Trapped between them, bullied, terrified, docile, the people suffered.

Such arguments were familiar, even if they were only to be found expressed with such vigour in the clandestine tradition which the *Mémoire* joined, but they did not exhaust Meslier's passion. Adopting many sceptical arguments from the previous century, and adapting some of those used in the long-running dispute between the Jansenists and Jesuits, Meslier unburdened himself.

There were problems with revelation. Why was it necessary to reveal morality when it could have been engraved into every human heart directly? Why was God's revelation through an intermediary people rather than directly to all humans? If that revealed moral code was so essential to salvation, why keep the majority of the world in ignorance of it for so long?

Meslier found the idea of exceptionalism morally repugnant, little more than naked prejudice against all peoples other than the chosen ones. Faith, he said, was simply another word for 'blind belief'.[38] Miracles meant nothing as they were easily replicated by other religions, as the Bible itself recognized. There was no soul. There was no free will. There was no redemption or benefit in suffering. And there was, of course, no God, who, if he had existed, would have been capricious, inept and impotent.

Colourful as these objections were, they were also a bit generic. Meslier's personal pet hates were more engaging. He thought sacrifice was a revolting idea. How could God enjoy the bloody slaughter of animal sacrifices?[39] Some Old Testament prophets, he acknowledged, expressed a similar distaste and this redeemed them, slightly.

Meslier's hatred of Israel was strong even by his standards. The Hebrews were a 'vile and miserable little people', circumcision 'despicable and ridiculous'.[40] His attack on the New Testament was hardly more moderate. Jesus, ('son of Mary, nicknamed the Christ, and leader of the Christian sect') came more to mislead than to save men.[41] His call for self-renunciation was no more than a grotesque form of self-mortification. The crucifixion was 'guilt sacrifice … in its most revolting, barbaric form', little better than 'gruesome paganism'.

The benefit promised from Christ's sacrifice was entirely illusory. At least the people of Israel received substantive promises from God, albeit false ones. Christians had, and continued to content themselves with, 'imaginary goods, imaginary victories, an imaginary redeemer, and by consequence a redemption that is itself only imaginary'.[42]

Christ's disciples were 'common and ignorant men'.[43] Throughout the book Meslier uses the neologism 'christicole' – untranslatable but perhaps best rendered as 'pathetic little Christlings' – to describe Christians. St Paul was, of course, the 'arch-christicole', but other, lesser christicoles were not beyond disdain, right up to his own his flock, whose existence of toil, viciousness and ignorance bred squalid lives of superstition, stupidity and cowardice.

A new reformation, purifying Christianity with the scourge of reason, such as was advocated by many contemporary deists, would make no difference. Returning to a purer Christianity would merely lead to different evils as the religion's teachings were simply incompatible with those of natural morality. Christianity was not a good idea that failed or had been corrupted by wicked men, though there was no shortage of failures and wicked men. It was just a bad idea.

For all his contempt and ferocity, Meslier sought to construct as well as destroy, in so doing anticipating many ideas that would became familiar in the later history of atheism. Meslier was a secularist, though one who was capable of imagining a limited role for religion in the public realm. He was a hedonist of sorts, repeatedly condemning the church's glorification of suffering, and its condemnation of the flesh. Earthly pleasures were to be enjoyed, not damned, and Meslier defended a liberal view of sex. He drew the line at complete *libertinage*, saying that it is wise to contain oneself in these matters, but admitted that it was daft not at least to taste such pleasures.

His attitude to pleasure was linked to a primitive utilitarianism, a moral theory that was frequently the flip side of the atheistic coin in the eighteenth century. Only that which increased pleasure on earth was worthy of respect. Meslier's objection to clerics was at least in part on account of what he deemed their social redundancy. The only priestly role he could envisage was that of educator, providing that such reformed clerics forewent any Christian teaching and grounded their lessons in reason rather than revelation.

Alongside his libertinism and utilitarianism, Meslier advocated a form of communism, which elicited a rare word of praise for the early Christians who, according to the Acts of the Apostles, had kept their goods in common. Since then, of course, Christianity had degenerated, and accepted, indeed legitimized, the misappropriation, and gross inequality, of wealth. Meslier denounced this robbery, by priest and prince alike, arguing that everyone should equally possess and enjoy the material goods of the earth in common.

Full of aggressive language and imagery, the *Mémoire* also has a streak of violent anarchism within it, a streak that went beyond the lurid vision of kings strangled with priestly intestines. Meslier described how he would personally like to have Hercules' strength and club with which he would beat tyrants and priests. This sounded like more than rhetoric. Where, he mused, were these generous murderers of tyrants, defenders of public liberty when they were most needed?

This combination of materialism, communism and anarchism is familiar to us in the form of Marxism, and Meslier did at times sounds like a proto-Marxist calling his contemporaries to action. 'Try to unite yourselves, as many as you are, you and your likes, to entirely shake off the yoke of the tyrannical domination of your

kings and princes'.[44] Although without any comparably sophisticated theory, still less a belief in the inevitability of revolution,
Meslier still exhibited a form of political messianism as he sought
an earthly saviour in lieu of the imaginary redemption preached by
the 'christicoles'.

Perhaps the only aspect of his constructive atheism not familiar
from later tracts was his attack on animal cruelty. Meslier had no
time for the Christian idea that humans were in any way special
or unique. His proto-utilitarianism based on pain and pleasure led
him to defend the idea that animals are our equals when it comes
to suffering. He felt that domesticated animals were our loyal
companions and also capable of knowledge, possessing a form of
natural language. Consequently, he judged it a gross injustice to
slaughter them, in particular for religious sacrifice, and he came
close to advocating a form of animal rights.

'Animation is a physical property of matter': Denis Diderot and the materialist turn

Meslier was influential in the eighteenth century if not quite in the
way he would have wanted. Although his book was read in full by
a small number, many more read the version published by Voltaire
in 1761. Voltaire feared atheism almost as much as the clerics he
lampooned, once famously remarking that 'I want my lawyer, my
tailor, my servants, even my wife to believe in God, because it
means that I shall be cheated and robbed and cuckolded less often.'
He thought Meslier's style was that of 'a carthorse, but of one that
kicks rightly', the best kicks being against the church rather than
God.[45] Accordingly, he cut and refashioned the text 'purg[ing] it of
the poison of atheism' so that it would support his cause.[46]

That cause influenced virtually everybody in the 1730s and
'40s, including Denis Diderot whose devout family background,
formative years in the church (he was later affectionately addressed
by peers as *abbé* Diderot) but growing dislike of authoritarianism
initially disposed him towards Voltaire's deism. It was not to

last. Voltaire contributed to Diderot's *Encyclopédie* but denounced his materialism. Diderot admired Voltaire's wit and courage but thought him untrustworthy. Each resented the other as a threat to his enlightenment throne.

Not much is known of Diderot's intellectual life before the age of 30 so it is unclear how early his anti-Christianity emerged. He left his ecclesiastical education at 19 and after an abortive attempt to study law decided on becoming a writer and lived a poor, bohemian existence in 1730s Paris. This coincided with the height of a Jansenist religious revival, in which many Parisians, mostly women and workmen, convulsed hysterically around reported miracles during zealous public gatherings held, at first, around the tomb of a pious Jansenist hermit and then, when the authorities closed the cemetery, in various clandestine gatherings. If anything was calculated to harden Diderot's contempt for religion, particularly in its more emotional manifestations, it was this.

An accomplished linguist, he translated Temple Stanyan's *Grecian History* in the late 1730s, which stimulated his interest in the classical world and problems of biblical chronology. This was followed by a multi-volume medical dictionary and then the Earl of Shaftesbury's *An Inquiry Concerning Virtue and Merit* in 1745. This was a work of empirical and utilitarian bent, which Diderot took upon himself to annotate, the resulting notes forming *Pensées philosophiques*, his first major work, immediately followed by a short essay on the sufficiency of natural religion. These texts are not atheistic but they mark their author as a religious sceptic and an admirer of Bayle, some way down the long road from Christian belief to outright materialism.

Such materialism became easier by the later 1740s on account of the scientific developments of the decade. In 1740, Abraham Trembley, a young Genevan employed as a tutor in Holland, noticed that a freshwater polyp, now known as a Hydra, which had been classified 40 years earlier as a plant, behaved rather like an animal. Not only did it move, but it was sensitive to movement.

To complicate matters, however, it clearly had the capacity for regeneration. Cut it up and it simply regrew. 'From each portion of an animal cut in 2, 3, 4, 10, 20, 30, 40 parts, and, so to speak, chopped up, just as many complete animals are reborn,' wrote one contemporary journal.[47] Trembley sent 50 in jars to scientists across Europe and caused a sensation, the normally reserved *Memoires de l'Academie des Sciences* ejaculating, 'the story of the Phoenix who is reborn from his ashes, as fabulous as it might be, offers nothing more marvellous'.[48]

The little polyp captured the scientific imagination, and the philosophical one. The manner in which it blurred and disrupted categories of nature cast doubts on the separate creation outlined in Genesis Chapter 1. The manner in which it exhibited complexity, and the enviable ability to regenerate, cast questions against the hierarchical ladder of creation that humans inferred from Genesis, by means of which they understood the natural – not to mention the social and political – order.

There was more. Trembley's polyp insinuated possibility of change across species, or 'transformism' as the idea was known at the time. This was a particular sensitive issue at the time because of Benoît de Maillet's 1748 publication *Telliamed, or Conversations between an Indian Philosopher and a French Missionary on the Diminution of the Sea*. This drew on the author's time as a diplomat in Egypt and sought to explain the existence of fossils at high altitudes by proposing an ancient age for earth, at least two billion years in fact. De Maillet went further to suggest that the earth had been shaped by chance rather than ordered design, and that all animals, including humans, had developed from primitive sea creatures. *Telliamed* was the first published account of what would become the theory of evolution, a scientific idea whose importance to the development of atheism is so great that it became, in the eyes of some, almost a substitute religion.

Perhaps worse than any of this, however, the little polyp's seemingly miraculous ability to regenerate pointed, albeit vaguely, in the direction of self-creation. Living things begat living things: that much was obvious. But were the tentacles that curious scientists lopped off the little creature actually living? In the normal run of things, if you lopped off a limb it died. But if these tentacles were dead, how could they come to life? It was all rather disconcerting.

As if de Maillet's transformism and Trembley's polyp weren't enough, the influential naturalist Georges-Louis Leclerc, Comte de Buffon, published in 1749 the first volumes of his *Histoire naturelle*, which would stretch to an impressive 36 volumes over the next 40 years. These drew on recent microscopic observations of seminal fluids which demonstrated, he argued, that 'living and animation, instead of being a metaphysical degree of being, is a physical property of matter'.[49] Nature was innately active and did not, it seemed, require God's intervention at any point.

Buffon and de Maillet and Trembley would influence some of Diderot's peers more than they did him, but they still clearly informed his thought. For all its anti-Christianity, his *Pensées philosophiques* had been a deistic work, resting its burden of proof on the 'wing of a butterfly' and the 'divinity imprinted in the eye of a mite'.[50] That didn't save it from the hangman's pyre or protect its author's reputation, but it did place mark him as a believer, just.

The materialist turn in French science of the 1740s helped undermine this, as did his increasingly fraught encounters with the authorities. Diderot was a more practised writer than his radical peers, with a wider range and better grasp of literary form and voice, which he used to good effect. This was on show in his *Letter on the Blind For the Use of Those Who See*. The book offered an imaginary conversation between the blind Cambridge mathematician Nicholas Saunderson and a priest who argued for God by beauty in nature. The author used the mathematician's blindness not only to challenge the argument by design but to insinuate that all human moral systems are ultimately dependent on our social and physical context, and therefore relative. Such relativism undermined Christianity, and with it Christian and royal authority. This was a threat which neither Diderot's wit nor his clever literary devices could disguise, and the book earned him three months in prison.

His literary wit was also evident in the *Encyclopédie*, the monumental project that originated in Diderot's commission to translate Ephraim Chambers' two-volume *Cyclopaedia* and which ended up a 17-volume, 18,000-page, 20-million word monster.[51] Diderot commissioned and wrote many of the 70,000 or so articles for the *Encyclopédie*, working closely with D'Alembert to manage the project, and although such a vast enterprise defies summary, the project is marked by the kind of subversive scepticism typical of its chief editor. For example, Christianity, the relevant entry informs the reader, 'may be considered in its relation either to sublime and revealed truths, or to political interests', which it immediately goes on to explain as meaning either 'the felicities of the other life, or to the happiness that it may procure in this one'. Calvinists, we are told, borrowed a portion of their errors from the heretics who preceded them, to which they added new ones. A factual and respectful entry on the Bible is followed by short entries on the Arabic, Armenian, Chaldean, Coptic, Ethiopian, Gothic, Greek, Latin, Muscovite, Oriental, Persian and Syriac Bibles. The entry on Priests is self-consciously vague, explaining that it refers 'to all those who fulfil the functions of religious cults established by the different peoples of the world'. This then enables a discussion of corrupt priests, who 'knew how to turn the good opinion they had fostered in the mind of their fellow men to their advantage', the examples given being of pagan priests, the impression given a broader one. None of this was actionable, so to speak, but those with eyes to read – and the *Encyclopédie* was popular for a publication of its size – knew what Diderot and his allies were saying.

The materialist ideas of the 1740s and Diderot's time in prison further eroded whatever was left of Diderot's deism, and yet lingering doubts remained. On a visit to his hometown, Langres, after his father's death in 1759, Diderot attended church with his siblings, remarking 'my head wants one thing, my heart another'.[52]

Such longings notwithstanding, it was clear where Diderot's loyalties lay. Even in the period during which he still clung on to some vague belief in the divine, he was happier among the sceptics. 'I believe in God,' he wrote to Voltaire in 1749, but 'I live very well with atheists.'[53]

'That barbarous divinity': D'Holbach and his salon

Foremost among those atheists was his friend and collaborator Paul-Henri Thiry, Baron D'Holbach. Born Paul Heinrich Dietrich in 1723, D'Holbach was raised in Paris by his uncle, after which he attended Leiden University in the Netherlands from 1744 to 1748, at the time a leading centre of European education. His early religious doubts were informed by geology, though he was also influenced by Lucretius and John Toland's *Letters to Serena*. He returned from Leiden a deist but he soon, it is unclear when, converted to atheism.

Receiving an annual income of 60,000 livres from the family coffers, D'Holbach established a salon in early 1750s Paris to which the most unorthodox thinkers of the age gravitated for evenings of wit, scepticism and gastronomic excess. The list of attendees reads like a Who's Who of eighteenth-century European radical intellectual life. In addition to Diderot, there was the mathematician and philosopher Jean-Baptiste le Rond D'Alembert, who collaborated with Diderot on the *Encyclopédie*; the brilliant but mercurial Jean-Jacques Rousseau; Friedrich Melchior, Baron von Grimm, who established and ran the influential *Correspondance littéraire*, an intellectual newsletter that was hand-copied to avoid the censor; Georges-Louis Leclerc, director of the Royal Botanical Gardens; André Morellet, an economist and like Diderot an *abbé*; Jean-François Marmontel, who subsequently became permanent secretary of the *Académie française*; Guillaume Thomas Raynal, a writer and defrocked priest; the philosopher and mathematician Marie Jean Antoine Nicolas de Caritat, Marquis de Condorcet; the philosopher Étienne Bonnot de Condillac; and the economist Anne-Robert-Jacques Turgot. Visitors from overseas included the Italian economist Ferdinando Galiani; the Italian legal reformer Cesare Beccaria; the Scottish economist Adam Smith; Scottish historian David Hume; English historian, Edward Gibbon; and the English radical writer and politician John Wilkes.

Not all of these stayed at D'Holbach's table for very long. Some left quietly. The Catholic Beccaria, fêted for his proposal to reform penal law along rational and proportional lines, was scared away by the group's atheism. Others fell out more spectacularly, Rousseau spending decades denouncing his former friends. Not all diners were materialists and not all were atheists but such differences notwithstanding, the group shared an antipathy towards Christianity, particularly the authoritarian and royalist form it took in France.

It was a view that, according to the historian Philipp Blom, who has charted the life of this 'wicked company', may have had some shared biographical roots. Many around D'Holbach's table 'had left their homes, defied their fathers, [and] constructed their own lives far away ... There was ... a certain animus against the idea of the powerful father at the baron's table'.[54] Between them these men met, discussed new ideas, de-divinized human nature and ethics, ridiculed Christianity, lambasted ecclesiastical hypocrisy and enjoyed the pleasures of board and bed.

If anti-Christianity was their creed, D'Holbach was their pope. He never published under his own name but was nonetheless prolific, contributing over 400 articles in Diderot's *Encyclopédie* and writing more than 6,500 pages in total. Many of these were as angrily anti-Christian as Meslier's *Memoire*, and D'Holbach's friends soon dubbed him the 'personal enemy of God'.

Throughout the 1760s, beginning with his first atheistic work *Christianisme dévoilé* (*Christianity Unveiled*) and culminating in his substantial, two-volume *Système de la nature* (*The System of Nature*) in 1770, D'Holbach wrote some of the most uncompromising tracts of the radical Enlightenment. They were written, copied, printed and distributed under strictest secrecy. People discovered with them could be, and sometimes were, pilloried, flogged and branded. One apprentice was condemned to nine years on the galleys for possessing *Christianity Unveiled*. The context helps explain their tone of relentless, angry mockery and sarcasm.

This could be witty. In the relevant entry in *Portable Theology* from 1768, D'Holbach explained that 'vampires' are 'dead people that play at sucking the blood of the living', adding that 'free spirits will perhaps doubt such a marvel, but if they open their eyes they will see a dead body sucking the living body of society. See *Monks*, *Priests*, *Clergy*, etc.'.[55] It could also, though, be wearisome. D'Holbach was not as practised a writer as Diderot and his furious indignation could wear thin after the 500th page.

According to D'Holbach, religion was simply the result of superstition and ignorance, accepted through custom alone, and defenceless against serious thought. Faith is the opposite to reason, repeatedly described as a form of blindness (blind submission, blind belief, blind trust, blind commitment, etc.), demanding the abandonment of common sense and submission to corrupt ecclesiastical authorities. Faith demeaned and degraded. Man-made gods, which were merely personifications of nature, and religions altered them according their needs.[56] This not only stupefied people but justified horrendous and/or irrational practices such as circumcision, ritual cleansing, eating prohibitions and baptism.

D'Holbach damned actual religions as well as just theoretical ones. Islam was criticized for its incoherence and violence. Ancient polytheisms might have been more tolerant but practised human sacrifices and idolatry. Greek Platonism, with its belief in an immortal soul, was not only ridiculous but harmful in so far as it denied people earthly pleasures.

None of these, however, could compare to Christianity. D'Holbach had read Meslier, although it is not certain in which version, and the *curé*'s sentiments are visible throughout. D'Holbach's take on the Old Testament drew heavily on Meslier. The biblical Jews were a nation of thieves, brigands and bandits, stupid and superstitious, ignorant and intolerant, unreasoning and unhappy, the mockery of other nations and for good reason. Their institutions enslaved them, their God was cannibalistic, and their religious stories appear to have been invented only to amuse an obtuse and credulous people. Not much had changed since then. Contemporary Jews, D'Holbach claimed, ignored their ethical duties towards non-Jews, such as was demanded by natural morality, another grotesque example of how revelation perverted the truths of reason.[57]

The Old Testament helped D'Holbach clear the dust from his throat before pronouncing on the New. He described Jesus (the 'hero of the novel') as a vile craftsman, a skilful phoney, an Egyptian magician, not merely a God for the poor but a poor God. The saviour's arguments with priests and religious leaders – something that might, one would have thought, have endeared him to D'Holbach – revealed him as nothing more than vindictive and rowdy.[58] Not that the accounts of his life could be believed, of course. The four evangelists were fabulists, their gospels riven with differences, the manuscripts corrupt, the canon late, dogma invented and St Paul, naturally, the real founder of the religion. Christianity was little more than a schismatic Jewish sect, sharing all the faults of its parent, but adding viscous factionalism, life-denying Platonism and strange pagan customs into the mix.

Like Meslier, D'Holbach had no interest in reforming Christianity. As far as he was concerned, the uncorrupted original was just as toxic as the version that now held France in its grip. True Christianity bred intellectual slavery, moral corruption and fanatical enthusiasm, just as much as false. There was no reforming to be done here.

D'Holbach did sometimes engage in philosophical rather than theological arguments. He returned to perennial favourites such as who created the creator, or what attributes could logically be attributed to God (certainly not the inconceivable ones suggested by the church) and he could write intriguingly on the nature of language. D'Holbach inherited Locke's empiricism, if not his faith, which contended that all ideas entered the mind through the senses. Words only meant anything when they correlated with identifiable sense experiences. The rest of the time they were abstract to the point of being literally meaningless. 'Every time that a word or its idea does not furnish any sensible object to which one can refer it,' D'Holbach wrote, 'this word or this idea is derived from nothing, is void of sense; one should banish the idea from one's mind and the word from the language, since it signifies nothing.'[59]

Such theological broadside and philosophical skirmishes noted, D'Holbach's attack was, at heart, an ethical one. Christianity's defective morality, he contended, was based on its defective, cruel, capricious, ferocious, bloodthirsty God. At best he was inherently unstable. 'This God, who is in turn styled the God of *Vengeance*, the God of *Mercies*, the God of *Arms*, and the God of *Peace*, is ever at variance with himself.' More usually he was simply wicked. Small wonder his followers were so morally retarded. '[God's] conduct being so strange, cruel, and opposite to all reason, is it surprising to see the worshippers of this God ignorant of their duties, destitute of humanity and justice, and striving to assimilate themselves to the model of that barbarous divinity which they adore?'

'To love one another ... [and] live in peace': Atheist paths to virtue and happiness
For all that D'Holbach and his coterie liked to ridicule and wished to raze the religious edifice that cast its shadow over mid-century France, they sought also to replace it with something better. The questions were with what, and how?

The answers to this lay in nature. According to the unapologetically materialist systems that clustered round D'Holbach's table, man was a purely physical creature, his life constructed via his senses. His good was to be found in self-love and the pursuit of happiness, and only those things *useful* in the goal of achieving happiness were of value. With no belief in an afterlife, no time for metaphysics, no belief in revelation, and of course no time for religiously dictated or enforced morality, 'public utility ... [became] the principle on which all human virtues are founded, and the basis of all legislations'.[60]

Humans were naturally sociable and naturally good. They needed no supernatural intervention to encourage virtue. On the contrary, it was precisely supernatural intervention that distorted natural virtue. Goodness would be the default position were it not for the ignorance and superstition bred by religion. Thus, according to Jacques-André Naigeon, a fellow contributor to the *Encyclopédie* and one of D'Holbach's coterie, with whom the baron often collaborated, humans were predisposed 'to love one another ... [and] live in peace', tendencies destroyed by belief in the tyrannous God of Christianity. Atheism alone could liberate mankind for the happiness that was naturally his.

There was much consensus over what this demanded. First, and most obviously, it required the death of religion. The *philosophes* differed in the extent to which they believed religious belief could, or should, be allowed to survive in a tolerant, godless society, and even the most antagonistic were by no means sure it could ever truly be vanquished. 'He who combats religion,' D'Holbach once wrote, 'resembles a man who uses a sword to kill fruit-flies: as soon as the blow is struck, the fruit-flies ... return'.[61] Nevertheless, the goal was to be sought even if never to be realized on this earth.

Second, there was a need for good government. Government was a fundamentally moral business for D'Holbach, and good government was good, not simply by virtue of having struggled free of theological talons, but by understanding true human nature and legislating accordingly. Good government 'will be good when it will bring happiness to the greatest number,' D'Holbach wrote.[62] It could and should reward talents and virtue, discourage inutility and punish vice, teach morality, and enlighten the masses with reason.

'Governing is to force the members of a society to loyally fulfil the conditions of the social pact.'[63]

The *philosophes* disagreed over whether this demanded any form of democratic accountability. D'Holbach wrote angrily against tyranny and despotism, and was willing to advocate a form of mixed government, despite favouring the enlightened despot, but he was adamant that government had no need of commoners. Even by the standards of his enlightened peers, D'Holbach was contemptuous of '*le vulgaire*'. They were ignorant and imprudent, gullible and stupid: given to drunkenness and fanaticism, lacking in foresight, in need of guidance. A happy, godless society needed good government of the people, and for the people, but emphatically not by the people.

His friend Claude Adrien Helvétius disagreed. Not as animated by theological dogma as D'Holbach, nor as acerbic, Helvétius was nonetheless thoroughly materialist and atheist in his thinking. This thinking steered him towards democratic ideas, if not full democracy. To bring the 'moral aptitude of the governors' to its maximum, he reasoned, sovereign power must be given to those whose interest it is that the general happiness be maximized – the people.

There were similar disagreements about whether nature demanded equality and, if so, of what nature. D'Holbach may have shared Meslier's loathing of Christianity but unlike the priest of Etrépigny, the wealthy Baron had no particular passion for material equality, let alone proto-communism. Where Meslier had momentarily praised the early Christian communities for holding possessions in common, D'Holbach criticized them. Such behaviour was not natural. D'Holbach knew property was essential to patriotism and citizenship and that equality, at least of this kind, was against nature.

Again, Helvétius differed. Like his friend, Helvétius was well provided for, and having served as Farmer-General, a tax collecting post that earned 100,000 crowns a year, he stepped down to live philosophically. This did not prevent him from at least gesturing towards a more thoroughgoing egalitarianism than the baron, however. How can the lot of the unfortunate be improved, he asked rhetorically in *A Treatise on Man: His Intellectual Faculties and His Education*. The answer, apparently, was to 'diminish the riches of some; augment that of others [and] put the poor in such a state of ease, that they may by seven or eight hours' labour abundantly provide for the wants of themselves and their families'.[64]

There was less disagreement about education. All the *philosophes* recognized the need to (re)educate the people, but Helvétius was particularly focused on this. Given that education was presently in the hands of corrupt, ignorant, lazy and fanatical priests, it was no wonder vice was rife. Were the people to be educated with reason and science, they would naturally seek the good of society. 'Instead of causing children to be taught a senseless religion, [we] should give them equitable laws, teach them a pure morality uncontaminated with fanaticism, deter them from vice by suitable punishments, and invite them to the practice of virtue by proper rewards'.[65] The need to remove children from religious educators (even, when necessary, their parents) would become a recurring theme in atheist rhetoric over the next 250 years.

The need for education was not limited simply to children. Helvétius took from Locke the idea that humans were a blank slate on which sensation imprinted meaning. This meant that humans were near-infinitely malleable. People acted wickedly because of poor education and a lack of philosophical knowledge. Society's laws were formed before science so 'we have, in a manner, the morals of the world in its infancy'. Universal education and rational laws are what would make a better society. 'Education makes us what we are,' he wrote in his notorious book, *De l'esprit*, or *On the Mind*.[66]

There was a downside to this, however. Helvétius' belief in human malleability and the omni-competence of education and legislation was paralleled by a questionable attachment to freedom. Indeed, Isaiah Berlin would label him as one of his six enemies of human liberty in his 1952 lectures on the subject.[67] The philosopher was the architect and builder of human society, using education and law to condition subjects in true virtue, knowledge and happiness. Man was an object, and mankind material to be moulded in the philosophically defined image of true happiness. The logic was, in Berlin's words, that 'scientists know the truth, therefore scientists are virtuous, therefore scientists make us happy ... What we need is a universe governed by scientists, because to be a good man, to be a wise man, to be a scientist, to be a virtuous man are, in the end, the same thing'.[68] Thus, a godless world was not simply a world without god, but one without priestcraft (obviously), without ignorance (hopefully), without inequality (possibly) and perhaps even without freedom.

'We are natural machines': Atheist paths to vice and happiness

De l'esprit was notorious less for its attitude to freedom than for its attitude to free will. The book took a rigorously empirical view, arguing that the mind comprised nothing but a flow of sensations that combined with a store of 'continuing images' which constituted memory. These phenomena were ordered and grouped into classes, with vocabulary and grammar providing labels for them, treating each as if it were real.

This meant that many problems in philosophy were caused by simple misunderstanding of grammar. Abstractions like beauty, for example, were simply grammatical constructs, with no actual existence outside language. Once this was realized, a whole universe of metaphysical – and, of course, theological – claims and counter-claims could be swept away.

It also meant that the human capacity to determine its own ends was an illusion. Helvétius believed he had discovered the laws of human nature, just as Newton had discovered those of the physical world. In both cases, they were rigid and determinist. Humans were the way they were on account of the vast panoply of sticks and carrots that was their environment. Their own beliefs and motives were irrelevant.

Helvétius was not alone in this. D'Holbach's materialism left little room for free will which he saw as a theological con-trick, necessary for the heaven, hell and the gross system of bribery and threat they supported but indefensible otherwise. Human thought and action were in principle explicable through the study of the brain, nervous system and senses within, and the forces of education, custom and government from without. 'We are natural machines, we do not have free will, and therefore our actions depend on the society we live in and its values.'[69] An ignorant and superstitious society bred ignorant and superstitious people; an enlightened and virtuous society enlightened and virtuous people; hence the need for morally enlightened and virtuous government, even if it was not entirely clear how enlightened and virtuous rulers were enlightened and virtuous without also being free.

D'Holbach was at pains to emphasize that our happiness should be based on well-being rather than pleasure or libertinism but this was not entirely convincing, not least as, on occasion, he allowed the mask to slip. 'It would perhaps be unjust, to demand that a man should be virtuous,' D'Holbach wrote in *System of Nature*, 'if he could not be so without rendering himself miserable. Whenever he thinks vice renders him happy, he must necessarily love vice.'[70]

The fear of 'necessarily lov[ing] vice' had been the beating heart of anti-atheist polemic for two centuries but D'Holbach was not the first to confirm those fears. Indeed, it was over 20 years since Europeans had been openly scandalized by such outrageous views by a man whose very similarity to them provoked the *philosophes'* hostility.

Julien Offray de La Mettrie was born in 1709. He began by studying theology before turning to philosophy and natural sciences, taking up medicine in Paris and Leiden, 20 years before D'Holbach arrived there. Like Diderot he had witnessed the Jansenist religious fervour of the 1730s with distaste and like him he apparently dawdled in the foothills of public atheism rather than striking out for its visible summit. In reality, his writings are as godless as those of his peers, albeit with more of a medical than philosophical flavour.

La Mettrie married in 1739 but left his wife and two children in 1742 when he gained employment as an army surgeon, an experience that shaped both his attitude to violence and to what human beings were made of. A few years later, he caught a fever and, paying close attention to the effect it had on his thought processes, came to the conclusion that the soul and all mental activity were merely an aspect of physical activity.

His anonymous *Natural History of the Soul* pursued this idea but the book was not anonymous enough, and it was condemned and burned by court order. The author left for Leiden. The experience radicalized him further, as did his encounter with Meslier's *Mémoire* and Trembley's polyp. Over the following years he penned a number of brutally honest materialist books, the best known of which (indeed, the only one of his works still read today) he called *L'Homme Machine* or *Man a Machine*, in which he sought to show that humans were nothing more than biological machines, seeking pleasure and fleeing pain.

This was not a new idea. Du Marsais, a philosopher and clandestine author, had written, 20 years earlier, how the philosopher was 'a human machine like any other man but a machine which, by its mechanical construction, reflects on its movements'.[71] La Mettrie took this idea and built on it. Rather than the summit of creation, humans were merely another part of the natural world, differing only by degree. He drew on examples of comparative anatomy, of animal intelligence and of how the soul, such as one could speak of it, 'depends essentially on the organs of the body', concluding that humans had no immortal soul, no afterlife and no spiritual nature.

La Mettrie's arguments about God had a Bayle-like quality to them. He could range from supercilious piety ('I do not mean to call in question the existence of a supreme being'), to innocent agnosticism ('who can be sure that the reason for man's existence is not simply the fact that he exists?'), feigned intellectual humility ('Let us not lose ourselves in the infinite, for we are not made to have the least idea thereof'), and detached indifference ('I am taking no sides').

Similarly, when setting out arguments on both sides, in a fair and balanced way of course, La Mettrie spoke warmly of the naturalists who argued (with Lucretius) that the eye was not expressly made for its apparent purpose, whereas of the religious apologists he spoke of the 'boring repetitions by zealous writers who add to each other only verbiage which is more likely to strengthen than undermine the foundations of atheism'.[72]

Although without the encyclopedia that Bayle and Diderot found so useful, La Mettrie could still ventriloquize. Thus, he recounted the disreputable opinions of 'a French friend of mine' who said 'the universe will never be happy, unless it is atheistic', going on to explain 'this wretch's' reasons at length:

> If atheism, said he, were generally accepted, all the branches of religion would be destroyed and their roots cut off. Result: no more theological wars, no more soldiers of religion ... Nature, now infected by sacred poison, would regain its rights and its purity. Peaceful mortals, deaf to all other voices, would only follow the spontaneous promptings of their own individual being, which are the only ones that we ignore at our peril and which alone can lead us to happiness along the pleasant paths of virtue.[73]

Such sentiments were not, of course, unfamiliar (or unwelcome) to La Mettrie's radical contemporaries, any more than they are to ours. What marked him out from them was his willingness to follow the materialist thread to its ethical destination. The 'spontaneous dictates' of our being might not necessarily, he recognized, be virtuous. If humans were indeed animals, and if our nature was shaped by pleasure and pain rather than by revelation or divine dictate, they might just as readily (and justifiably) seek the sensual pleasure as moral good. If there were no afterlife to aspire to or no immortal soul to protect, humans should only live for the present. But living for the present was not necessarily the same as living for the good, let alone living for the wider good. The logical consequences of a godless material universe could just as easily be hedonism as virtue or utility.

Once again, others had been here before him. In *Le Philosophe*, written around 1720, for example, Du Marsais had explained how men being machines, 'in all [their] actions ... they search only their own present satisfaction ... [it is] the present attraction following the mechanical disposition in which they find themselves, that makes them act'.[74] La Mettrie merely drove home the message, with admirable rigour and candour. People were not morally free. Remorse was useless as it only made people suffer needlessly. Nothing could gainsay pleasure, 'the sovereign master of men and gods, in front of whom everything vanishes, even reason itself'.[75] And if someone's pleasure included sensual indulgence, debauchery and even crime, so be it. Society could protect itself from such behaviour, but it could not condemn it. This was the kind of thing that the atheist hunters of the previous century had put into their quarries' mouths. Now they actually heard it.

It was strong meat, even for the radicals. La Mettrie had written to Diderot thanking and praising him for his *Letter on the Blind*. The appreciation was not mutual. Diderot was not alone in despising La Mettrie for having brought naturalism into disrepute – or, more precisely, confirming the disrepute in which it was already held. Despite this, however, Diderot himself could come perilously close to La Mettrie's amoralism.

D'Alembert's Dream, written in 1769 but not published until 1830, explored the question that had so motivated La Mettrie in the 1740s: what happens to a fevered mind? Diderot's book involved three related dialogues primarily between D'Alembert's mistress, Julie de Lespinasse, nursing him through fever and his physician, Bordeu. The book was a thoroughgoing materialist work, seeing humans as complex material beings made up of smaller ones, 'an infinity of human animalcules' in much the same way as a swarm is made up of bees. It had a transformationist view of life, seeing humankind as a machine 'which develops toward perfection through an infinity of successive developments' in such a way as became tenable after Trembley. It even speculated on the existence of 'human polyps', asking whether such things exist on Jupiter and Saturn.

All this might have been written by La Mettrie, as could the book's attitude to pleasure. 'Everything changes, everything passes,' Julie de Lespinasse said at one point. 'The world begins and ends without cease … In this immense ocean of matter, no molecule resembles another … There is nothing dependable but drinking, eating, living, loving and sleeping'.[76] If Diderot maintained his practised ventriloquism concerning such sentiments, and did not follow La Mettrie further along this path, nor was he so far behind. As he wrote privately in a Letter to Mr Landois in 1756 'there is no vice or virtue, nothing that must be rewarded or punished'.[77]

La Mettrie would have approved. Sadly, by the time Diderot wrote that, he had passed away. Too honest even for Leiden, the medic was forced into exile again in 1748, this time at the court of Prussian king Frederick the Great, where he was welcomed, by his patron if not his peers, and worked as a physician. Even at the court of this most tolerant, sceptical and enlightened of despots, however, La Mettrie led a precarious existence, conscious of his vulnerability and unpopularity. After three years, he developed a gastric illness after a feast held in his honour and died, leaving his many enemies to gloat about the inevitable consequences of godlessness.

British moderation

'Make the infidel abashed of his vain cavails': Human nature
Of the many famous guests to enjoy D'Holbach's hospitality, one of the most fêted was a Scottish embassy secretary to Paris, who had arrived in 1763. Flattered by the attention paid him by this notorious gathering, he once remarked that he didn't believe in the existence of atheists. D'Holbach asked him to count the number of

guests at the table. There were 18. 'It is a good start to be able to show you 15 straightaway,' D'Holbach told him. 'The other three haven't yet made up their minds.'[78]

The odd thing about this conversation was that the inquirer had, a decade or so earlier, mocked religious philosophers who energetically 'refute the fallacies of Atheists', while at the same time 'disput[ing] whether any man can be so blinded as to be a speculative atheist'. 'How shall we reconcile these contradictions?' he asked rhetorically, before comparing the theologians to 'knights-errant' who 'wandered about to clear the world of dragons and giants'.[79] No naïve ingénue, then, the Scottish guest was Britain's most renowned sceptical philosopher, David Hume, although at that time better known for his history than his philosophy.

The first great hero of British atheism, he had an antipathy to Christianity almost as deep as his host's. 'The Church is my Aversion,' he had confided to a close friend in 1747.[80] While in Paris he complained to his friend the Rev. Hugh Blair that the English were 'relapsing into the deepest Stupidity, Christianity & Ignorance'.[81]

It was a longstanding antipathy. Brought up in a devout Christian household, Hume appears to have lost whatever faith he had by the age of 20. Living in France in the 1730s he was familiar with the Jansenist religious ecstasies and miracles, writing later in his *Enquiry Concerning Human Understanding* that it was extraordinary that 'many of the miracles were immediately proved upon the spot, before judges of unquestioned integrity, attested by witnesses of credit and distinction, in a learned age'. 'What have we to oppose to such a cloud of witnesses,' he asked, consciously echoing the New Testament Epistle to the Hebrews, 'but the absolute impossibility or miraculous nature of the events, which they relate?'[82]

Hume's hostility to Christianity was never to leave him. James Boswell, Samuel Johnson's biographer, visited the dying philosopher in 1776, curious to confirm rumours of his infidelity and to witness how an unbeliever died. With complete equanimity was the answer. 'David Hume said to me he was no more uneasy to think he should not be after this life, than that he had not been before he began to exist'.[83]

What complicates matters is that Hume was not an atheist. As ever, there is the matter of 'innocent dissimulation', as Hume described it to a friend in 1764, to negotiate.[84] Coming out as an atheist was to risk less in mid-eighteenth-century Britain than France, but it was still to dice your job prospects if not necessarily your life, as Hume discovered when he failed to secure the chair of moral philosophy at Edinburgh in 1744.[85]

Sometimes, in Hume's case, dissemblance and irony gave over to downright untruth, such as when he introduced his *Natural History of Religion* by declaring 'The whole frame of nature bespeaks an intelligent author; and no rational enquirer can, after serious reflection, suspend his belief a moment with regard to the primary principles of genuine Theism and Religion'.[86] Few were taken in by this, but it was a useful thing to say nonetheless.

It is not just the dissemblance that confuses the matter with Hume, however. According to his biographer, Ernest Mossner, 'Hume, in the strict conventional sense of the terms, was neither a believer nor an unbeliever, that is to say, neither a theist nor an atheist'.[87] Whether he would have accepted the label agnostic – the term was not coined for another 100 years – is a matter of speculation. Whatever the nature of his scepticism, and his scepticism about scepticism, it did little to blunt his critique of theism or theology.

Hume's anti-Christianity occupied the same territory as others. He wrote against enthusiasm and its 'raptures, transports, and surprising flights of fancy'. He wrote against superstition, its genesis in 'weakness, fear, melancholy, [and] ignorance', and its manifestation in 'ceremonies, observances, mortifications, [and] sacrifices'.[88] He wrote against clergy, dedicating a lengthy footnote to the hypocrisy of the clergy in his essay 'Of National Characters'. He wrote against supernatural agency as a factor within human history.

In all this he was recognizably a man of his age, singing from the same hymn sheet as many a French radical, not to mention English latitudinarian divine.[89] What distinguished Hume was the sophistication of his argumentation and, in particular, his attack on the argument from design, the keystone of so much contemporary rational religion.

His essay 'Of Miracles' was a fine example of that sophistication. Originally intended for and erased from his early *Treatise Concerning Human Nature* ('I am at present castrating my Work ... endeavouring it shall give as little Offence as possible,' he wrote to Henry Home in 1737), the essay was included in his 1748 *Philosophical Essays concerning Human Understanding* against the advice of friends who knew it would brand its author an infidel.

Hume's central argument was 'that no testimony is sufficient to establish a miracle, unless the testimony be of such a kind, that its falsehood would be more miraculous, than the fact, which it endeavours to establish'.[90] The quality of the testimony was crucial and, in Hume's opinion, no example from history passed muster. No miracle was attested 'by a sufficient number of men, of such unquestioned good-sense, education, and learning ... [and] of such credit and reputation in the eyes of mankind', as to be prove credible.[91]

This was a high hurdle for a religion such as Christianity, that was not only 'first attended with miracles', but 'even at this day cannot be believed by any reasonable person without one'. The olive branch Hume offered – faith can go where reason fears to tread, offering the devout what philosophy and history could not – was illusory. 'Whoever is moved by Faith to assent to it, is conscious of a continued miracle in his own person, which subverts all the principles of his understanding, and gives him a determination to believe what is most contrary to custom and experience'.[92] Faith was fine, so long as you were prepared to take leave of your sense.

His attack on the argument from design was no less methodical, so provocative that Hume postponed the publication of his *Dialogues*

Concerning Natural Religion until after his death. This trialogue between Demea, Cleanthes and Philo helps kick over Hume's own footprints, and scholars have long debated which character or characters best speak for their author. The sceptical Philo seems the likeliest option, but whether or not he is Hume's mouthpiece, or shares that honour with his interlocutors, or whether no combination of speakers satisfactorily articulates the author's true views, the *Dialogues* presents arguments against natural religion that were to weaken this, by then, rather overused apologia.

Ultimately, however, the book seemed unwilling to abandon the argument altogether. In a paragraph that appears to have been later added to the initial manuscript of 1757, Philo remarks, apparently without irony:

> If the whole of natural theology ... resolves itself into one simple ... proposition, that the cause or causes of order in the universe probably bear some remote analogy to human intelligence: If this proposition be not capable of extension, variation, or more particular explication: If it afford no inference that affects human life, or can be the source of any action or forbearance: And if the analogy, imperfect as it is, can be carried no farther than to the human intelligence; and cannot be transferred, with any appearance of probability, to the other qualities of the mind: If this really be the case, what can the most inquisitive, contemplative, and religious man do more than give a plain, philosophical assent to the proposition ... and believe that the arguments, on which it is established, exceed the objections which lie against it?

Whether one reads this as an honest admission of heavily attenuated deism, or the murder of natural theology by a thousand qualifications, or simply another piece of sophisticated ventriloquism will depend on perspective. Even if it were the first of these, however, it was hardly much comfort to contemporary Christian apologists.

Hume treated the human soul in the same way as miracles and design. Another posthumously published essay, 'On the immortality of the soul', sought to demolish this most personal and cherished belief. Nothing earthly, Hume pointed out in his essay on the soul, is 'perpetual'. Everything is 'in continual flux and change'. The mind is no different, its demise marked by 'disorder, weakness, insensibility and stupidity', all foreboding 'annihilation'. And, in any case, consciousness was no better explained by the claim that 'it emerges from non-material as opposed to material substance'. All in all, while impossible to say authoritatively that the soul did not exist or was not immortal, the essay left few options as to how it could be either.

The idea of eternal damnation was abhorrent to him. 'Punishment ... should bear some proportion to the offence,' he wrote in his essay on the soul. Eternal punishment for temporary offences was unacceptable for 'so frail a creature as man'. So disproportionate was the sentence that it underlined his argument that religion destroyed rather than edified human morality. 'Virtuous conduct is deemed no more than what we owe to society and to ourselves'. The 'morality of every religion was bad,' the astonished Boswell reported him as saying. 'When he heard a man was religious, he concluded he was a rascal, though he had known some instances of very good men being religious.'[93]

If Hume had a few nagging reservations about the moral sufficiency of godlessness – he once wrote in his *Natural History of Religion*, 'Look out for a people entirely void of religion: if you find them at all, be assured that they are but few degrees removed from brutes' – he had none about the moral insufficiency of godliness.[94] A loathing of religiosity, in particular popular religiosity, permeated his writing. 'Survey most nations and most ages,' he advised in *Natural History*:

Examine the religious principles which have, in fact, prevailed in the world. You will scarcely be persuaded that they are other than sick men's dreams; or perhaps will regard them more as the playsome whimsies of monkeys in human shape than the serious, positive, dogmatical asseverations of a being who dignifies himself with the name of rational.

'Generally speaking,' he wrote in the *Treatise Concerning Human Nature*, 'the errors in religion are dangerous; those in philosophy only ridiculous.'[95] And they were never more dangerous than when near the throne. Priestly government, he wrote in his 1741 essay 'Of Parties in General' has 'engendered a spirit of persecution, which has ever since been the poison of human society'. At the heart of his anti-Christianity there burned a moral critique, an indignation at the hypocrisy of the pious, that could match anything around D'Holbach's table. 'What so pure as some of the morals included in some theological systems? What so corrupt as some of the practices to which these systems give rise?'[96]

Hume, then, would have sat comfortably at D'Holbach's table, their respect appreciated, wit enjoyed and atheistic sentiments a most agreeable conversation. Yet, he never became an British *philosophe* and it is worth examining briefly why.

There is, in the first instance, the sense that he was never entirely convinced by atheistic arguments. His hesitation, if it is his, at the end of the *Dialogues* seems to signify a qualification, albeit a heavy one, of some kind of deistic belief. Even if this is the right reading of Hume's beliefs, however, it is unlikely to have made much of a difference. Diderot also vacillated over the existence of a designer God, and his indecision had a sense of wistful regret that was entirely absent from Hume, yet this did not prevent him from being the archetypal atheistic *philosophe*.

More importantly, for the cast of Hume's mind and his role in the development of British atheism, was his omni-scepticism, deployed towards philosophical reasoning as much as rational religion. Philosophical reasoning was important – Hume spent many years engaged in it – but it could not offer the secure metaphysical or moral foundations that some claimed for it. Habit, experience and custom, not reason, governed humans' understanding of the world, themselves and the way they should live. 'Since morals ... have an influence on the actions and affections, it follows, that they cannot be derived from reason'.[97] Such scepticism would not allow him simply to replace theology with philosophy, revelation with reason, or religion with science in the way that many in D'Holbach's coterie did.

A third and equally significant difference between Hume and the French *philosophes* was the social and political context in which each lived. Hume had lifelong battles with clergy, dissembled, self-censored, delayed publication, and was still denied the chairs of Moral Philosophy in Edinburgh and Glasgow. But when he was charged with heresy, he was defended by friends, including clergy, on grounds that as a non-believer he lay outside church jurisdiction. It was something for which he was always grateful, writing once that 'these illustrious examples [of moderate clergy] ... must make the infidel abashed of his vain cavails, and put a stop to that torrent of vice, profanities, and immorality, by which the age is so unhappily corrupted'.[98]

He was also aware, as he wrote in his *History of England*, that the time in which he lived was characterized in Britain by a particular religious moderation – for which read lethargy – which marked it as distinct from previous ages and other nations. The country's 'spiritual guides' had been 'bribe[d]' into 'indolence', by 'assigning stated salaries to their profession', and 'rendering it superfluous for them to be further active than merely to prevent their flock from straying in quest of new pastures'.[99]

Hume, then, was too sceptical to be a systemizer in the manner of his French friends and lived too comfortably in mid-eighteenth-century Britain to feel the need to bring about a new system. None of this blunted his critique but it does help explain why atheism looked and felt different in mid-century Britain to France.

'The inevitable mixture of error and corruption': Gibbon's history
Hume was not the only British historian to sit around D'Holbach's table. Edward Gibbon's reputation as a historian would eclipse

Hume's but at the time he enjoyed the baron's hospitality he was
an unknown, yet to embark on the work that would make his
name. Failing to impress his hosts, he was not impressed by them,
writing later of their 'intolerant zeal', and how they had 'laughed at
the scepticism of Hume, preached the tenets of Atheism with the
bigotry of dogmatists, and damned all believers with ridicule and
contempt'.[100]

Gibbon had had a conventional Anglican upbringing, until
he took refuge from his adolescent doubts in Catholicism, from
which he then apostatized. This meant that, like Bayle, he had
seen Christianity from both sides of the denominational fault line,
and like him his subsequent religious beliefs were opaque in the
extreme, with critics accusing him of Arianism, Socinianism and
worse. It was not his personal religious views that were judged
influential, however, but rather his historical ones, in the form of his
monumental retelling of the decline and fall of the Roman Empire.

This enterprise was influenced by Hume, from whom Gibbon
took his mistrust of metaphysics, his understanding of history as
an arena of human rather than divine intent, and whose praise
Gibbon most appreciated. 'The theologian may indulge the pleasing
task of describing Religion as she descended from Heaven, arrayed
in her native purity,' he wrote witheringly in the introduction to
the controversial fifteenth chapter of *Decline and Fall* outlining
the 'progress' of the Christian religion. 'A more melancholy duty
is imposed on the historian,' he explained, as it falls to him to
discover 'the inevitable mixture of error and corruption, which
she contracted in a long residence upon earth, among a weak and
degenerate race of beings.' Error and corruption there were aplenty.

It was philosophic history of this nature, in which cause and
effect were demonstrably determined by human agency, or accident,
rather than divine providence or intent that animated Gibbon's
masterwork. Thus, the fact that Britain was and long had been so
thoroughly Christian might not actually be the Lord's work. In
the eighth century armies of Islam had advanced over 1,000 miles

from Gibraltar to the Loire, he explained, the repetition of which would have carried them to the Highlands of Scotland. The Arabian fleet, he mused, 'might have sailed without a naval combat into the mouth of the Thames. Perhaps the interpretation of the Koran would now be taught in the schools of Oxford, and her pulpits might demonstrate to a circumcised people the sanctity and truth of the revelation of Mahomet'.[101] History was all humanity and accident and irony. Attila the Hun might have been a 'savage destroyer' but he nonetheless 'undesignedly laid the foundation of a republic, which revived ... the art and spirit of commercial industry'.[102] God's plans were not so much inscrutable as immaterial, it seemed.

This might have been tolerable for secular history but it was an extremely tendentious and provocative claim to make of Christian history. The spread of Christianity, which conquered the empire in three centuries without ever picking up the sword, was deemed by contemporaries to be a miracle, a phenomenon so extraordinary as to defy natural explanation. Indeed, this was a view that Gibbon himself held in his first published work, *Essai sur l'étude de la Littérature*, which he began writing in 1758. It was not to remain so.

Christianity for Gibbon became a historical phenomenon to be studied like any other, which he did, to wide public consternation, in Chapters 15 and 16 of *The Decline*. Gibbon undermined the authority of the miracles and beliefs through which Christianity had spread in a way that *sounded* much like the traditional Protestant attack on Catholicism: 'The sublime and simple theology of the primitive Christians was gradually corrupted; and the Monarchy of heaven, already clouded by metaphysical subtleties, was degraded by the introduction of a popular mythology, which tended to restore the reign of polytheism'.[103]

More dangerously, he took his criticism closer to the origins of Christianity than was comfortable for any orthodox Protestant, such as when he explored the miraculous events around Christ's death. 'Under the reign of Tiberius,' he wrote, 'the whole earth, or at least a celebrated province of the Roman empire, was involved in a preternatural darkness of three hours. Even this miraculous event, which ought to have excited the wonder, the curiosity, and the devotion of mankind, passed without notice in an age of science and history.' Both Seneca and Pliny the Elder, each of whom 'recorded all the great phenomena of Nature' 'omitted' to mention this 'greatest phenomenon to which the mortal eye has been witness', despite Pliny recording a similar event following 'the murder of Cæsar'.[104] Let the reader take note.

It was the same with the death of the martyrs, whose blood was supposed to be the seed of the church. A careful reading of the early church historian Eusebius showed that 'only nine bishops were punished with death' and 'no more than 92 Christians' were martyred in Palestine. Altogether, the total number of Christians in the Roman Empire 'on whom a capital punishment was inflicted by a judicial, sentence, will be reduced to somewhat less than two thousand persons'. As if the point were not clear, Gibbon then pointedly remarked, 'Christians, in the course of their intestine dissensions, have inflicted far greater severities on each other, than they had experienced from the zeal of infidels.' Indeed, if we are to believe Grotius, 'the number of Protestants, who were executed in a single province and a single reign, far exceeded that of the primitive martyrs in the space of three centuries, and of the Roman empire'.[105] The point was clearly not simply that ancient sources concerning martyrdom were to be taken with a pinch of salt but that Christian society was itself far more bloody and oppressive than the pagan world it has supposedly conquered in peace. This was provocative stuff. It is no wonder that Chapters 15 and 16 were more revised than any others Gibbon wrote.

If the origins of Christianity could be gently undermined, its establishment was a sitting target. Constantine's conversion was self-interested and hypocritical. 'The same motives of temporal advantage which might influence [his] public conduct and professions ... would insensibly dispose his mind to embrace a religion so propitious to his fame and fortunes'.[106] Christianity did not morally improve his reign: quite the opposite in fact. 'As he gradually advanced in the knowledge of truth, he proportionally declined in the practice of virtue'.[107] It was marked by despotism rather than civic virtue – indeed, it corroded the empire's culture of civic virtue – and could be a great deal more barbaric than the barbarians. 'The ravages of the Barbarians, whom Alaric had led from the banks of the Danube, were less destructive than the hostilities exercised by the troops of Charles the Fifth, a Catholic prince, who styled himself Emperor of the Romans'.[108] And, as we have noted, it was a good deal more superstitious, at least in its institutional form, than Islam. 'More liberal than the law of Moses, the religion of Mahomet might seem less inconsistent with reason than the creed of mystery and superstition, which, in the seventh century, disgraced the simplicity of the gospel.'[109]

Gibbon was too good a historian to do a mere hatchet job on Christianity. Julian the Apostate, the fourth-century emperor who sought to revert the empire to paganism, had been a hero of earlier French writers, some of whom had influenced Gibbon. Gibbon was not so impressed. Julian's paganism was not the easy-going, tolerant sort of earlier empire that Gibbon admired, but an 'unnatural alliance of philosophy and superstition', his persecution of Christianity a sign of his own intolerance and fanaticism.[110] The barbarian tribes' embracing of Trinitarianism, for all its incomprehensibility, 'broke the violence of the [empire's] fall, and mollified the ferocious temper of the conquerors'.[111] Some popes, in particular Gregory I, were genuinely admirable.

Such honesty notwithstanding, the overall impact of Gibbon's Christian history was deflating, made all the more so by his practised wit and irony, his ridicule and innuendo. This was best seen in his notorious footnote on Apollonius, the first-century philosopher whose life Charles Blount had translated a century earlier. Apollonius 'was born about the same time as Jesus Christ', Gibbon noted. 'His life (that of the former) is related in so fabulous a manner by his disciples, that we are at a loss to discover whether he was a sage, an impostor, or a fanatic'. The parenthesis was sharp enough to be noteworthy, and itself well parodied by John Ogilvie in his *An inquiry into the causes of the infidelity and scepticism of the times*. 'The German Geistlicherlichus was born about the same time as Gibbon the Englishman. His life, that of the former, is so variously related by his contemporaries, that we are at a loss to discover whether he was a materialist, a professor of philosophical theism, or a Socinian'.[112]

Such wit was latterly often called 'Voltairean', as was Gibbon's supposed irreligiosity. In fact, Gibbon had reservations about Voltaire, describing him as 'an intolerant bigot' in a footnote in Chapter 67 of *Decline and Fall*,[113] and even more reservations about the radical *philosophes* in whom he detected considerable intellectual arrogance. He recognized that bigotry was not the preserve of the religious. Indeed, he rather admired the Latitudinarianism that dominated the established church at the time he wrote, concluding Chapter 54 of *Decline and Fall* in double-edged praise of the laxity of modern Christianity. 'The volumes of controversy are overspread with cobwebs: the doctrine of a Protestant church is far removed from the knowledge or belief of its private members; and the forms of orthodoxy, the articles of faith, are subscribed with a sigh, or a smile, by the modern clergy'. Like Hume, he appreciated 'the modern times of religious indifference'.[114]

Interestingly, around the time that Gibbon had been in Paris in 1763, the *philosophes* mooted the idea of developing an atheistic, or philosophical, civil religion, for which a properly destructive ecclesiastical history was thought necessary. Gibbon was an unknown at the time and was not approached. Had he been of such radical bent, the *Decline and Fall* might have become just the project they sought. But he was not and it did not. As historian John Pocock has perceptively commented, 'Neither Gibbon nor even Hume had reason to take part in devising a civil religion and an ecclesiastical history around which *philosophes* might rally on a ground structurally opposed to Christianity. In Erastian Protestant cultures

– part-Latitudinarian England, part-Moderate Scotland – it was easier to leave Christianity to liberalise itself'.[115] What might, in another, more authoritarian religious context, have sprung into full, vigorous atheistic bloom remained in Britain paler, more reserved, more generous and more tolerant.

American silence

If it was the oppressive theo-political culture that drew out the pioneering atheistic movement in eighteenth-century France, and the comparative religious and intellectual generosity on show in eighteenth-century Britain and Germany that tamed it there, what happened in America at the end of the century was revolutionary in more ways than the obvious one.

The British colonies that had spread across the east coast were all deeply Christian, although in markedly different ways. The First Great Awakening revivified much of their Protestant culture in the 1740s, and although there were signs of deism in the colonies, they were rare. The same intellectual influences that had redirected deist scepticism from outright atheism and towards tolerable orthodoxy in the mother country were influential in the colonies. The prolific and prominent New England Puritan minister Cotton Mather, influenced by Robert Boyle's *The Christian Virtuoso*, published *The Christian Philosopher* in 1721, which was the first significant attempt to reconcile Newtonian science and biblical revelation in America – although the fact that he also played a lead role in the Salem Witch Trials reminds us that progress is rarely linear.

In the face of such orthodoxy, deism, of the kind that so worried English divines in the early part of the century, was almost invisible in America in the eighteenth century. Ethan Allen published *Reason the Only Oracle of Man* in 1784 but the book was a financial and critical disaster. Elihu Palmer, a former Presbyterian minister, founded the Deistical Society of New York in 1796 and established the newspaper *Temple of Reason* shortly after that. Neither was influential. Only with Thomas Paine did the attack on organized and revealed religion emerge with any vigour, and even then his argument was as hostile to atheism as it was orthodoxy.

The early (and ongoing) weakness of atheism in America was not simply down to the intellectual climate, however. Indeed, here more than anywhere else the political context informed the debate. Many American clergy enthusiastically supported the revolution. They described it as a just war, blessed the revolutionaries' endeavours, and preached of God's favour on their cause, doing all in confidently biblical terms. Christianity became associated with the people's political emancipation, in a way that it did only partially in Britain, and not at all in France.

Equally important, though far more ambiguous, was the 'faith' of the Founding Fathers. Contemporary America enjoys a lively debate on the religious beliefs, commitments and intentions of their Fathers. Some, such as John Witherspoon, a signatory of the Declaration of Independence; John Jay, the first Chief Justice; and Samuel Adams, memorably described as the 'American revolutionaries' American revolutionary'[116] were orthodox in their faith. Others were not. George Washington was reticent about his beliefs but was convinced that God could and did intervene in human affairs. Thomas Jefferson rejected many core Christian doctrines, and indeed any religious teaching that did not conform to his concept of reason, and could be vehemently anti-clerical; but he was fascinated by religion and, in particular, the life and teachings of Christ, about which he wrote, and professed to follow keenly. Benjamin Franklin became a deist when young (ironically after reading Robert Boyle's refutation of deism) but he drifted from this later in life and professed a belief in the power of prayer, the necessity of worship, and in God's active superintendence of human life.

Such beliefs were clearly on, or beyond, the periphery of Christian orthodoxy, but the Founding Fathers were all in agreement about some fundamental issues that were to prove vital for the non-development of atheism in America. They recognized that a republic demanded a virtuous citizenry and felt strongly that religion, at least in the form visible in the New Testament, was the best, perhaps the only sufficient, source of such virtue. 'Let us with caution indulge the supposition that morality can be maintained without religion,' George Washington said in his Farewell Address of September 1796. 'Whatever may be conceded to the influence of refined education on minds of peculiar structure, reason and experience both forbid us to expect that national morality can prevail in exclusion of religious principle.'[117]

Moreover, the Fathers were all also marked by a deep sense of providentialism, which became written (or, perhaps more accurately, rewritten) into the nation's DNA. Such a belief, that God was just and would look after the righteous and punish the wicked, was not *necessarily* Christian, but it was hard to sustain outside a theistic framework. This loaded the cultural dice in favour of belief in God, in however vague an incarnation. It might have fostered atheist resentment in the long run had it also been built into the new nation's political structures, but it was not.

If the American debate about the Founding Fathers' faith is lively, that about the religious intent of the Constitution makes it look tranquil. However one interprets this document – was it intended to prevent the establishment of any religion or to preclude the presence of religion in public life in any form? – the fact remains that it does not refer to God,[118] precludes any religious test from becoming a requirement for office, and, most famously, in its first Amendment, legislates against Congress making any law 'respecting an establishment of religion, or prohibiting the free exercise thereof'. This did not prevent individual states from legislating about religion and many retained established churches well into the nineteenth century. Nevertheless, there could be no formal national endorsement of Christianity and this invariably provoked accusations of godlessness.

William Linn, a Dutch Reformed minister from New York, was among the many who opposed Thomas Jefferson's presidential candidacy in 1800 on the basis that his personal beliefs, combined with his efforts to establish religious freedom in Virginia, if transported to the presidency, would turn America into a 'nation of atheists'.[119] Southern clergy were particularly energetic in condemning the 'perilous atheism' of the Constitution[120] and there were repeated attempts to make explicitly theistic, even Christian, amendments to the Constitution. The short-lived Constitution of the Confederate States of America inserted the phrase 'invoking the favour and guidance of Almighty God' in the Preamble, and this prompted the National Reform Association, a group of northern ministers, to campaign for a similar amendment to the Constitution after the Civil War, as did the National Association of Evangelicals a century later.

All were unsuccessful, their failure leaving intact America's greatest bulwark against atheism. Christianity was not embedded in the nation's federal structure, and although it remained so in many states for some years, religion was, in effect, prevented from using coercion or becoming associated with coercive measures as it had fatally in the Old World.

Associated with liberty, providence and the virtue necessary to sustain a republic, American Christianity was also denied official access to power. It was a remarkable recipe. 'In France I had almost always seen the spirit of religion and the spirit of freedom marching in opposite directions,' wrote the astonished Alexis de Tocqueville in the 1830s. 'But in America I found they were intimately united and that they reigned in common over the same country.'[121] If there is a reason why atheism long remained such a meek and docile beast in this most educated, technologically sophisticated and *modern* of Western nations, it surely lies here.

Promises

The road from revolution

"Tis with yourself you must be solely concerned': Liberty and libertines

The Baroque Church of Saint-Roch stands in the rue Saint-Honoré in the 1st arrondissement of Paris. Built in fits and starts between the mid-seventeenth and mid-eighteenth centuries, it was the church in which the Marquis de Sade was married in 1763, and in which Helvétius, Diderot and D'Holbach were buried, in 1771, 1784 and 1789 respectively. A few years after the baron's entombment, the church was wrecked during the revolution, its treasures and paintings stolen, its crypt, in which the *philosophes* rested, torn up. Such a combination of anti-Christian violence and disrespect towards the nation's greatest atheists points to the ambiguous legacy of the French Revolution on the course of European atheism.

There was a violent anti-Catholic element to the Revolution from the outset. The Church's right to impose tithes was abolished almost instantly, and was soon followed by the expropriation of church land and property, and the abolition of religious orders. Clergy were made employees of the state, to which they were forced to swear allegiance. Papal denunciation of this confirmed suspicions that, whatever they said, clerics were merely a treacherous, counter-revolutionary force. By 1792, mobs were lynching priests in Paris and, the following year, the violence was nationwide, if not exactly systematic. Churches were pulled down, their statues desecrated, their paintings stolen, their plate sold off. Those priests unwilling to swear the oath were sentenced to death, as was anyone found harbouring them. A counter-revolt in the Vendée in early 1793, hardly peaceable itself, was put down with epic brutality, with tens of thousands, priests prominent among them, committed to the guillotine, canon, musket, sword, and Loire.

At the same time as they attempted to destroy one religion, however, rebels sought to construct another. Streets and towns were renamed, Christian associations dropped in favour of more appropriate titles. Christian holidays were banned and Christian rituals forbidden. In their place, the Cult and festivals of Reason and of the Supreme Being were established. A new revolutionary calendar replaced the Gregorian one, dating recommenced, and Notre Dame turned into a Temple of Reason.

For all that Diderot, D'Holbach and his coterie would have approved of this de-Christianization, the revolutionaries sailed under the flag of Reason rather than atheism. Voltaire once opined that 'almost everything that goes beyond the adoration of a Supreme Being and of submitting one's heart to his external orders is superstition',[1] and it was this idea that served as the revolutionary lodestar. Voltaire, whose remains were transferred into the Panthéon in 1791, and Rousseau, whose ideas inspired Maximilien Robespierre, became the Revolution's secular saints. 'Helvétius was a schemer ... an immoral being, one of the cruel persecutors of that good J. J. Rousseau,' Robespierre observed, when the *philosophe*'s bust was shattered in the Jacobin Club in December 1792.[2]

This is not to say that atheistic creeds were entirely absent during the turbulent 1790s. Jacques Hébert, the radical journalist who became chief spokesman for the Parisian *sans-culottes*; Pierre Gaspard Chaumette, medic turned Jacobin; and Joseph Fouché, famed for having the words 'Death is an eternal sleep' inscribed over cemetery gates, were all firmly godless, children of Diderot and D'Holbach rather than Voltaire and Rousseau, and among the most violent de-Christianizers.

Their influence was circumscribed, however, and their position made vulnerable by Robespierre's preoccupation with Rousseau and reason. When Chaumette, for example, began to question the existence of a Supreme Being, and adopted the name Anaxagoras, in honour of the pre-Socratic philosopher who, according to some accounts, was put on trial for his impiety, he was venturing on to thin ice. It turned out to be a prescient name change, as Chaumette was eventually guillotined in April 1793, one of his crimes being 'seeking to destroy all morality, efface any idea of the divine, and founding the government of France on the principles of atheism'.[3]

Atheism, then, could be judged as much of a threat to morality by those who worshipped Reason as by those who worshipped God. We should not, however, exaggerate the threat. Chaumette was executed not so much for his atheism as for his extreme radicalism. Moreover, the revolutionaries had shown themselves quite able to cope with public godlessness when it had released the Bastille's most famous prisoners nearly four years earlier.

Donatien Alphonse François, the Marquis de Sade, was nearly 50 years old when the Revolution broke out, having spent the last 13 years in prison, five in the Bastille, for sexual misconduct and poisoning. A child of privilege and libertinism, de Sade spent most of his life in and out of jail, frequently imprisoned for debauchery and brutality borne of his insatiable obsession for sodomy, flagellation, coprophilia and the abuse of women. Although prison turned, in his final years, into an asylum, he was perfectly coherent and, considering himself something of a creative philosopher, wrote at length about his beliefs and opinions.

These were defiantly and cogently atheistic. 'When atheism wants martyrs,' challenged one of his characters, 'my blood is ready.'[4] De Sade was influenced by D'Holbach's atheism – he called the Baron's *Systeme*, from which he lifted whole passages for his novels, 'indubitably the basis of my philosophy',[5] – but also, more obviously, by La Mettrie's denial of God. In many ways, the Marquis' whole philosophy can be read as the logical conclusion of La Mettrie's libertine atheism.

De Sade was anti-Christian with an intensity and bitterness that could compete with D'Holbach. His *Dialogue between a Priest and a Dying Man*, written in Bastille in 1782, vigorously attacked a whole range of Christian ideas – creation, mystery, miracles, God's existence – with ideas borrowed from his intellectual heroes, and ends with the dying libertine converting the priest. He was as anti-theistic as he was anti-Christian, however, writing to his wife shortly after completing the novel, 'if the people who make up this universe had the slightest idea of what constitutes their true happiness and tranquillity … theism cannot for a minute stand up to the slightest scrutiny'.[6]

Were this all he did, de Sade would be as well-known as, say, Naigeon. The Marquis' notoriety came from his particular pleasure in being as offensive as possible. At the height of their sexual excitement, many of his libertine characters would taunt God with obscenities and blasphemy, using sacred furniture of Catholicism for their pleasure. The author himself had scared prostitutes in his younger days by masturbating into chalices, or inserting the consecrated host into their vaginas. This was atheism as offence rather than as simple atheistic libertinism.

Which is not to say it was devoid of logic: de Sade believed that humans were alone in a universe that was without objective moral order. The only moral laws to speak of were those seen in nature, whereby the strong held power over the weak, and vice over virtue. All attempts to reverse this, or to protect the weak, simply went against Nature's plan. Nature undermined morality or, at least, Christian morality.

The same went for reason. Just as in a godless universe morality was subject to nature, so, he believed, was reason. How humans think was as subject to desire as how they behave, and given de Sade's unquenchable and violent sexual appetite, this meant that it was reasonable, as well as moral, to conclude that 'there is no more selfish passion than lust … 'tis with yourself you must be solely concerned'.[7]

The 'literary' nature of de Sade's publications placed them differently to, say, La Mettrie's more earnest philosophical tracts.

Nevertheless, no one doubted the Marquis' atheism, or his libertinism, or his sincerity, even if some doubted his sanity. He managed to survive the Terror, his political pliability helping his cause, but spent the final years of his life back in prison and asylum.

'Catholicism minus Christianity': Ritual atheism

The French Revolution stands at the head of all nineteenth-century European atheism. Just as the complex and shifting confessional allegiances of the previous age could be lumped together as wars of 'religion', so the nineteenth century was often blind to the sceptical differences between revolutionaries, preferring to see the whole bloody affair as an indictment of impiety. The fact that different radicals rejected and replaced the Christian God in different ways was lost in a blur of fear and fury. In spite of this, however, different forms of rejection and replacement persisted into the century, perpetuating the different atheisms that had first emerged in the pre-Revolutionary decades.

Post-Napoleonic France rejected the *philosophes*, not only the outright atheism of Diderot's circle but also the deification of reason so prominent during the Terror. Scepticism was felt to be shallow, desiccated, desolating. There was a sense, even among the sceptically minded, that religiosity was not as malignant, still less as eradicable, as the previous century had imagined. Many may have had hardly more religious faith than their philosophical predecessors, but they viewed atheism from the other side of a revolution that warned them against the horrors of irreligion.

That recognized, few of the old questions had been satisfactorily answered and a renewed appreciation of religion did not necessarily translate into conventional faith. French intellectuals in the early nineteenth century may have taken a less simplistic (and less optimistic) view of what reason and education and legislation could achieve, but material, moral and philosophical doubts remained.

This was an unusual and uncomfortable position to be in and it was not made easier by a resurgent and triumphant Catholicism.

Following the horrors of the Revolution and the uncertainties of Napoleonic wars, church lands were restored, divorce abolished, Sabbath observance enforced, and the universities brought under control of Gallican bishops, despite their not being renowned for overwhelming intellectual superiority. There were liberal Catholics in nineteenth-century France but they were a minority, viewed with ambiguity that bordered on outright mistrust, as were French Protestants. In spite of everything that had gone before, it still felt that a workable compromise between free thought and Christianity remained problematic.

Forced to choose between the unpalatable and incredible, some French freethinkers developed a third way: religiosity shorn of God. The nineteenth century became the great age of credulity in France, with a relentless fascination for non-Christian and often non-theistic religious beliefs and phenomena. Neo-Platonists, gnostics, cabbalists, mystics, Rosicrucians, Swedenborgians, illuminists, freemasons, Essenes and spiritualists multiplied, as did interest in eastern religions, and a fascination with table-turning, automatic writing, séances, magic, the paranormal, phrenology, thaumaturgy, mesmerism, somnambulism, chiromancy and cartomancy, to name only the saner phenomena.

Rising above these were great systems in which God, or at very least the Christian God, was replaced by humanity, or morality, or science, or progress, or some other ethereal absolute that, despite often being dressed in the fripperies of Catholicism, promised more and demanded less of those in search of certainty.

Crucial to these systems was a dogmatic belief in science and its ability to save. The doctrine of scientific infallibility may not have been as dogmatic as its papal counterpart, but it was nonetheless an article of faith sincerely held by many intelligent men. Positivism – the idea that experimental science was the only way to truth and that all knowledge must therefore be scientific knowledge – gripped the imagination, carrying with it the conviction that all religious and metaphysical claims were nonsense, an idea that would reach its hubristic conclusion early the following century.

This was not altogether different from the faith of many *philosophes*, the difference this time being that the industrial revolution had popularized such beliefs. Science, partially understood and vaguely defined, could, it seemed, achieve anything, refashioning man's moral and social nature, just as it had the world in which he lived. The human lot could be perfected. Eden, albeit one with more railways and hospitals, lay in the future not the past. Atheistic religions grew around scientific idolatry and its material utopianism, evolving beyond God and offering the potential for a new humanity that had previously been confined, in the Christian story, to another world.

The name most commonly associated with this kind of positivism was Auguste Comte. Comte, however, was an intellectual child of the more original Henri de Saint-Simon. Having enjoyed a career as soldier and financial speculator, Saint-Simon turned to philosophy in middle age. Although largely an autodidact, he had once been a pupil of D'Alembert and had met some of the late *philosophes*, and developed some of their scientific enthusiasm. Morality, politics, philosophy: all were, or at least could be, based on science.

Saint-Simon posited a three-stage process – religious, metaphysical and finally scientific – through which society passed as knowledge became more assured. Ultimately ethics itself would become a science, to be calculated and defined with precision and certainty, in the process banishing conflict to the history books. For all his uncritical worship of science, however, Saint-Simon recognized that dry rationality alone would not suffice and that people needed emotions and feelings in their life. Accordingly, rather than crush Christianity, he sought to replace it within a different system, even to the extent of writing a book entitled *Nouveau Christianisme* in 1825. He replaced deity with humanity, clergy with scientists, faith with scientific knowledge, and proposed a social reorganization centred on a cult of Newton.

Saint-Simon could verge on the mad but he was also genuinely original, his religion of scientific atheism forming the mould from which many others would take their shape. He was taken seriously by some of the nineteenth century's finest minds, including John Stuart Mill, Thomas Carlyle, Karl Marx and Friedrich Engels. In France, a number of disciples such as Prosper Enfantin and Saint-Armand Bazard took on his ideas and formed a Saint-Simonian sect, which managed to remain together for two whole years and became a favourite weekend outing for curious Parisians.

Saint-Simon also epitomizes the problem there is in defining the boundaries of atheism. Not especially hostile to religion or as violently anti-clerical as those at whose feet he once sat, he had no belief in God in any recognizable or conventional sense. Yet, his determined use of religious language, imagery, ideas and structures, and his conviction that man lived by more than rationality alone, gave him a distinctly pantheistic tone. However clear it is that Saint-Simon did not believe in God, he sits uneasily within the pantheon of Western atheists.

A similar point can be made of his most prominent disciple, Auguste Comte. A brilliant, scientifically minded young man, albeit one of questionable mental stability, he fell under Saint-Simon's spell, developing a total faith in the power of science and social engineering, but then fell out with his master on account of the latter's quasi-religious turn of thought, which was somewhat ironic given where Comte's own atheism would lead him.

Having broken acrimoniously with his first wife, Comte fell in love with the married, but at the time abandoned, Clothilde de Vaux. They formed an intense relationship that was never consummated and which ended early, in 1846, with Clothilde's death. The affair scarred Comte, turning his positivism into a fully fledged Religion of Humanity which made Saint-Simon's seem like a restrained Protestantism by comparison.

Comte devised the ritual and order of this new atheistic religion in excruciating detail. Positivists should pray three times a day, once to each of his household goddesses: mother, wife and daughter.

He was to cross himself by tapping his head with his finger three times in the place where, according to phrenology, the impulses of benevolence, order and progress were to be found. The religion had nine sacraments, beginning with presentation (a form of baptism), and going through initiation, admission, destination, marriage (at a specified age), maturity, retirement, transformation, and then, seven years after death, incorporation.

He set out a new calendar, with months named after great men like Aristotle and Archimedes, and new festivals, celebrating fundamental social relations. He specified the duties of various, ranked, positivist clergy, their stipends rising in neat mathematical progression. He ordered new hymns, celebrating holy Humanity and commemorating in George Eliot's words 'the choir invisible / Of those immortal dead who live again / In minds made better by their presence'. He designed new clothing, such as waistcoats that buttoned only at the back and could thus only be put on and removed with others' help (thereby inculcating mutual inter-dependence). As the Grand Pontiff, Comte regulated all this piety, elevating Clothilde as a kind Virgin Mary, and Humanity in place of God. Not without reason did Darwin's bulldog Thomas Huxley call it 'Catholicism minus Christianity'.

Comte himself disliked the label of atheism, as well as materialism and fatalism, not so much because he believed in God – like his friend John Stuart Mill he was willing to countenance the vague possibility of an intelligent mind behind the universe – but partly because it brought social opprobrium and partly because he thought atheism, like Christianity, was a metaphysical doctrine, unverifiable by scientific means and therefore untenable. It was far better to believe in humanity, which clearly existed, rather than God, who was probably a delusion.

The road to revolution (part 1)

'Without a world invisible to us': Kant's critique of dogmatic atheism
The French revolution shaped the course of atheism in the German
territories as it did in France (and, as we shall see, Britain) but in a
somewhat different way.

The alliance between throne and altar had been as important to
the Holy Roman Empire as it had been in pre-Revolutionary France.
There were important differences, however. The imperial lands were
more fragmented and diverse than France had been. Moreover,
German Christianity had been deeply coloured by Pietism, a
movement that had developed in response to the Thirty Years War
and the sense of moral laxity that had infected the Lutheran church,
and which placed a premium on simplicity and piety in church, and
frugality, modesty, duty and charity outside it.

Pietism shaped the culture from which most prominent German
thinkers emerged, not least Immanuel Kant, who grew up in a
devout household, church and school, which left him with a deep
appreciation for inward, morally grounded faith, over and against
any more demonstrative or ritual practice.

Kant, under the influence of Hume, whom he credited for
awakening him from 'dogmatic slumber', rejected speculative
arguments for the existence of God.[8] His *Critique of Pure Reason*
confronted the ontological, cosmological and teleological proofs for
God's existence that had dominated so much theological argument
in the eighteenth century.[9] As far as he was concerned, *knowledge*
of God – meaning, specifically, holding something to be true on
grounds that are both subjectively and objectively sufficient – was
not possible.

If knowledge of God was impossible, however, *belief* in him
– meaning, again specifically, holding something to be true on
grounds that are subjectively sufficient but objectively insufficient
– *was* justified. Those subjective grounds were moral and God
thereby became 'a postulate of pure practical reason'.[10] Writing in

the eighteenth-century intellectual milieu that sought to establish the existence of (the Christian) God on irrefutable and objective grounds, this could have been something of a threat, but Kant himself claimed that belief in God that was grounded in this sort of moral argument was uniquely solid.

This belief shaped Kant's attitude to atheism in an important way. Kant saw in God the highest good and although he argued moral duties were not dependent on God's commands but were in fact based and justified by the moral law, he also contended that it was only the existence of God that allowed humans to retain the belief that the highest good was possible. Because humans are frail and finite creatures, and virtue and happiness are not necessarily connected in this world, belief in this reality of the highest good is necessary in order to encourage and supplement our limited and fallible moral endeavours. In this way, morality leads inevitably to religion.

This invariably provoked worries about, and moral criticism of, atheism: four, to be precise.[11] First, atheism deprives the atheist of incentives to morality. God may not be *necessary* for morality, but to deny the highest good inherent in God is to close down a vital resource for living up to demanding moral duties. 'Without a God and without a world invisible to us now but hoped for, the glorious ideas of morality are indeed objects of approval and admiration, but not springs of purpose and action.'[12]

Second, atheism leads to despair. Denying the reality of the highest good also means denying any justification for the belief that virtue will be rewarded with happiness. 'While [the atheist] can expect that nature will now and then cooperate contingently with the purpose of his that he feels so obligated and impelled to achieve, he can never expect nature to harmonise with it in a way governed by laws and permanent rules ... Deceit, violence, and envy will always be rife around him, even though he himself is honest, peaceable, and benevolent.'[13]

Third, atheism erodes virtue and leads to vice. Following on from the previous two points, Kant argues that even a good person, faced with motivation diminished and despair aggravated by a godless reality, is liable to have his respect for the moral law damaged, with 'such weakening of his respect ... inevitably impair[ing] his moral attitude'.[14] Finally, the atheist has a pernicious influence on his society. Tempted to libertinism and without defence against despair, he risks undermining the moral motivations and commitments of fellow citizens, 'cannot be regarded as a good citizen, and damages the obligating power of the laws'.[15]

Kant is clear that these reasons constitute less of an attack on 'sceptical atheists', for whom speculative arguments cannot establish the existence or the non-existence of God (those we might today call agnostics), than it had on dogmatic atheists, who straightforwardly denied the existence of God. Coming from Kant, not only the pre-eminent German philosopher of later eighteenth century, but also evidently neither an apologist for Christianity, nor a man given to cheap polemics, and someone who was quite insistent that there were 'righteous' atheists (citing Spinoza as an example), this was a powerful critique.

'The solemn unveiling of man's hidden treasures': Progress and myth
Powerful maybe, but Kant's religious writing, especially his *Religion within the Bounds of Reason*, still landed him in trouble, and enforced a (temporary) silence on religious topics. Germany, like other European countries, was traumatized by the events in France and censured, and censored, those whose thinking combined intellectual prominence and questionable orthodoxy.

Such was also the fate of Johann Gottlieb Fichte, Kant's protégé, whose first publication, the anonymous *Critique of All Revelation*, was so like his master's that it was widely mistaken for Kant's. Fichte took up the chair of Critical Philosophy at the University of Jena in 1794 but lost it five years later when his essay 'On the Basis of Our Belief in a Divine Governance of the World' provoked accusations of atheism and nihilism, which escalated into a major political crisis as various German princes threatened to forbid their students from going to Jena. In reality, Fichte's views were not so different from Kant's. His beliefs were far closer to pantheism than outright atheism, but he handled the so-called 'atheist controversy' intemperately, and it didn't help that a few years earlier he had published, albeit again anonymously, two tracts entitled *Reclamation of the Freedom of Thought from the Princes of Europe, who have hitherto Suppressed it* and *Contribution to the Rectification of the Public's Judgment of the French Revolution*, the second of which defended the principles, if not the practice, of the revolutionaries.

Fichte's political philosophy took an authoritarian turn in his later years, part of the emergence of German national feeling as it reacted against the French culture, French philosophy and French armies. Henceforth, political, social and philosophical values were to be rooted in the genius of the nation, the German genius being both ancient and free of the corruption that had infected the French. National sentiment was set against French universalism, and German idealism against French materialism. Fichte was instrumental in this but not as much as his contemporary Georg Wilhelm Friedrich Hegel, with his lengthy and dense definition of the 'Idea' or 'Spirit'. Hegel's articulation of the Spirit – of a nation, of an age, ultimately of the world – envisioned an idea of progress, albeit one punctuated with repeated, necessary conflicts, which became almost national doctrine.

His philosophy was steeped in Christian language, ideas and structures. He was convinced that he had moved beyond the anti-Christian polemic of Enlightenment *philosophes*, to the point at which religion – through image and worship – and philosophy – through thought and critical reflection – could bring mankind to the same point of Truth. He also insisted that his philosophy rendered Christianity true, rather than superfluous, and thought himself a faithful Lutheran. Overall, his attitude to Christian doctrine was, in Antony Kenny's felicitous words, one of 'sympathetic condescension'.[16]

For all of this sympathy and alleged, if somewhat contrived, fidelity, Hegelianism became the key in which much nineteenth-century German atheism was played. The way that philosophical thought renders theology redundant (in spite of his protestations to the contrary); progress becomes all but inevitable; history replaces theodicy as an explanation for evil; and the Absolute or creative principle is identified with the universe rather than anything beyond it: such factors left Hegel's philosophy open to non- and then anti-Christian interpretations, which was precisely where a coterie of his followers took it.

These 'Young Hegelians' began their academic life in the master's slipstream but thereafter went their own radical ways. In the 1830s, two out of every five graduates from German universities studied theology. Unfortunately, the number of ecclesiastical roles was declining, and those available were open only to graduates of conservative theological and political opinion and/or from the aristocracy. With political pamphleteering forbidden, theology came to serve as a substitute for radical discourse and there emerged a kind of 'intellectual proletariat', theologically literate, ecclesiastically alienated, and disaffected with the civil and religious establishment.[17]

For a few years after Hegel's sudden death in 1831, his disaffected younger disciples were neither especially controversial nor a group. By the end of the decade, however, their departure from Hegel's dubious Christian sympathies was public and provocative. For all they preserved his dialectical method as a means of understanding, criticizing and reforming society, they became a new, distinct and threatening philosophical movement, orienting his thought away from the past and firmly towards the future, and seeing the philosopher's duty to promote intellectual warfare and revolution.

Friedrich Engels, one of their younger members, described the process in 1843 in his *Progress of Social Reform On the Continent*. Notwithstanding Hegel's 'enormous learning and his deep thought', he wrote, the great philosopher was 'so much occupied with abstract questions that he neglected to free himself from the prejudices of his age – an age of restoration for old systems of government and religion'. His disciples rectified this and by 1837 they were being grouped together and denounced as atheists.

At first, they naturally denied that charge. 'At that time, [they] were so little conscious of the consequences of their own reasoning, that they all denied the charge of Atheism, and called themselves Christians and Protestants, although they denied the existence of a God who was not man, and declared the history of the gospels to be a pure mythology.' However, Engels went on, last year, in 1842, 'in a pamphlet, by the writer of these lines, the charge of Atheism was allowed to be just'.[18]

The pamphlet in question was Engel's *Schelling and Revelation*, although the author's chronology appears to have been a bit self-serving. If any one individual led the movement and steered it towards atheism it was Bruno Bauer. Bauer had studied under Hegel in Berlin and lectured on theology there, and then at Bonn, but had drifted from his teacher's rationalized religion. His first public controversy was with David Strauss. At a mere 27, Strauss had published two long, dense volumes, entitled, in George Eliot's translation a decade later, *The Life of Jesus, Critically Examined*, in which he demythologized Christ and repositioned early Christian beliefs as a stage in mankind's self-awareness, in the process shocking many contemporaries.

Bauer was called upon by his peers to refute the book, not for its radicalism but its timidity and willingness to credit Christianity and Jesus with any historical merit at all. The argument between the two scholars was bitter and long-lasting, and Bauer himself went on to publish still more sceptical works, initially on the Old Testament and then the New, in which he described religious experience as a form of self-consciousness and attacked the reliability of the gospels, the historicity of early Christianity and the existence of Christ.

In doing so he was, quite deliberately, also attacking the Prussian monarch. Friedrich Wilhelm IV had come to power in 1840 with promises of reform that came to nothing. Official censorship remained, growing more efficient and ubiquitous, and fed Bauer's atheism. If unhampered self-consciousness and autonomy were the goal towards which history was lurching, the unholy union between Prussian state and the church that sanctified it was nothing more than an obstacle to progress. Christianity, whatever its merits might once have been, must now be transcended in the quest for genuine freedom and whereas prior to Wilhelm's accession that progress might have involved the present Prussian state, afterwards it could not.

Such powerful political and philosophical motives were soon joined by personal ones, when Bauer and his (then) friend Karl Marx penned several works purportedly by a pious Lutheran critic of Hegel but in fact bitterly and ironically atheistic, for which pains (along with other slights) Bauer was removed from his post by direct order of the king. The experience didn't cure him of his atheism and his subsequent, prolific biblical criticism and political journalism converged on a visceral loathing of God and King.

Bauer was the *de facto* leader of the Young Hegelians in the early 1840s but their holy text was Ludwig Feuerbach's *The Essence of Christianity*. Feuerbach had studied theology at Heidelberg and then in Berlin, where he came under Hegel's spell. Like his peers, he soon passed from this shadow, developing a philosophy in which he argued that men ate before they thought. Ideas rested ultimately upon matter, and the driving force of history was mankind's material conditions, not his spiritual or philosophical ideas.

Feuerbach's early and anonymous publication *Thoughts on Death and Immortality* argued that Christianity's teaching on immortality was inconsistent and impoverished life here and now, resting as it did on an imaginary, immaterial compensation in heaven for very real, material unhappiness on earth. The argument helped destroy his academic career but not his writing, and he went on to publish, among other things, a biography of Pierre Bayle, and then his seminal *Essence* in 1841.

The book's key idea was that God was a creation of the human imagination and needs, and although this was hardly a new observation, Feuerbach elaborated upon it in detail, applying it systematically and specifically to Christianity. God, he argued, was the infinite projection of man's finite nature. Frustrated by his inability to realize his needs and hopes and dreams on earth, mankind projected them onto the canvas of eternity, inventing a higher being through whom they would all, one day, be fulfilled. God was human wish-fulfilment, 'the manifested inward nature, the expressed self of man, – religion the solemn unveiling of his intimate thoughts, the revelation of his innermost thoughts, the open confession of his love secrets'.[19] Hegel had seen overcoming alienation as central to his theory of progress. Feuerbach had put religion as the source of that alienation, the symbol of man's division from the real world.

Such ideas became more credible in the hungry and angry Germany of the 1840s, although Feuerbach himself was neither hungry nor particularly angry, marriage to an extremely wealthy heiress in 1837 softening the blow of academic rejection. Although the *Essence* presupposed atheism rather than attempt to prove it, the manner in which the church had allied itself to a reactionary establishment that was blind and indifferent to urban poverty lent his presuppositions considerable weight. It was to have lasting influence and not just among his German peers. George Eliot wept with grief as she translated it. The Russian socialist Alexander Herzen wept with joy, recalling in his *My Past and Thoughts* how he 'leapt with joy. Down with the masquerade costume, away with insinuation and allegories; we are free people … we do not need to drape the truth in myths'.[20]

'The heart of a heartless world': Karl Marx

The most famous and influential of the Young Hegelians was, of course, Karl Marx. Like his loyal, principled and generous friend Engels, Marx was a junior member of the group, if only chronologically.

Marx was heir to a long line of rabbis, although his father had converted to Christianity to circumvent anti-Semitic laws. Attending first Bonn and then Berlin Universities, Marx initially wrote romantic poetry and studied law until he too was drawn into a Hegelian orbit. Whatever his adolescent faith had been, it was gone by the later 1830s when he wrote his doctoral thesis, examining the difference between the Democritean and Epicurean philosophy of nature, in which he celebrated the liberating materialism of Lucretius. 'As long as philosophy still has a drop of blood left in its world-conquering, absolutely free heart,' he wrote in its introduction, 'it will not cease to call to its opponents ... "Not he who rejects the gods of the crowd is impious, but he who embraces the crowd's opinion of the gods."'[21]

Under the influence of Feuerbach and Bauer, with whom he would unsuccessfully plan to edit a journal entitled *Archives of Atheism*, Marx soon took leave of Hegelian idealism, dismissing Hegel for his mystification, and embraced the materialism that would underpin his mature thought, in the process articulating a criticism of religion that, while less original than that of his fellow Young Hegelians, would become somewhat more influential.

For all that atheism owes to Marx, at least in the popular mind, he wrote surprisingly little on the subject. At the heart of his criticism was the idea of alienation, common among the Young Hegelians. Society was alienated, men stratified into competing classes, mankind estranged from his true nature. God and religion were human inventions, created to compensate for this intolerable reality. Although not necessarily the cause of alienation, religion had become its keystone by legitimizing and consecrating it, ameliorating its worst excesses and ascribing to it an entirely illusory permanence. By proffering divine justification for social evil, and substituting imaginary, *post mortem* judgement for real, concrete earthly justice, it had become the problem. In a society cured of alienation, no one will want religion. It would disappear naturally. Yet, because it had become the load-bearing pillar of social evil it still needed demolition.

Marx began the Introduction to his 1843 *Critique of Hegel's Philosophy of Law* by claiming that criticism of religion is the premise of all criticism. Man made religion, he explained. He sought a superman in the fantastic reality of heaven but found no more than a reflection of himself. The search was a perfectly natural endeavour for alienated mankind, but now the true cause of alienation was unmasked, it was no longer necessary. 'The abolition of religion as the illusory happiness of the people is required for their real happiness,' Marx reasoned, which was why criticism of religion is 'in embryo the criticism of the vale of woe, the halo of which is religion.' Hence, religion's ambiguous role: both wound and bandage, pain and salve. 'Religious suffering is, at one and the same time, the expression of real suffering and a protest against real suffering. Religion is the sigh of the oppressed creature, the heart of a heartless world, and the soul of soulless conditions. It is the opium of the people.'[22] This famous metaphor had been used before Marx, by Bauer and Moses Hess, another contemporary radical philosopher and early socialist, who introduced Marx to workers' associations and unions in 1843.[23] But it was Marx with whom it would become associated.

Marx may have lacked originality in this attack but that did not mean his contribution was entirely derivative. His skills as a wordsmith and polemicist were unparalleled. He also had a genius for losing friends and alienating people. Fellow revolutionary Michael Bukunin once memorably described him as 'immensely malicious, vain, quarrelsome, as intolerant and autocratic as Jehovah, the God of his fathers, and like Him, insanely vindictive'. Marx's opinion of Bakunin was, if anything, lower.

His contribution to the course of atheism is marked by two other, more material factors, however. First was his decisive shift in focus from criticism of religion-as-untrue to religion-as-anti-social. The two had, of course, been long linked in atheists' minds but remained distinct in as far as the former demanded attack by rational means, whereas the latter necessitated other tactics. Just as in the seventeenth century atheism had been seen as a moral evil even before it was intellectual folly, so religion was now primarily a social evil before an intellectual one. 'The social principles of Christianity,' Marx thundered in 1847, 'preach cowardice, self-contempt, abasement, submission, dejection, in a word all the qualities of the *canaille*; and the proletariat, not wishing to be treated as *canaille*, needs its courage, its self-reliance, its pride and its sense of independence more than its bread. The social principles of Christianity are sneakish and the proletariat is revolutionary.'[24]

The second factor was the way in which Marx's atheism took its place in, and power from, his wider systematic analysis. Marx's materialism bears comparison with that of the *philosophes*. An omnivorous reader, he had consumed both D'Holbach and Helvétius and although critical of both (as he was of pretty much every thinker but himself), he also judged their materialism to be 'the social basis of communism'. Yet, for all these *philosophes* could match Marx's own anti-theistic contempt and self-righteous anger, none placed their atheism in a comparable system.

Marx's materialism demonstrated how morality, religion, metaphysics and ideology were not independent forces shaping history, but parasitic on material reality. Accordingly, because 'intellectual production changes its character in proportion as material production is changed',[25] and 'the religious world is but the reflex of the real world',[26] Marx offered not only an explanation for religion but also the means and promise of its abolition.

As with Feuerbach, Marx's atheism was presupposed rather than proven, but it lost none of its power for that. Because he could place belief in God within a system, he could do away with the vague demands for education or good government which had been the *philosophes*' best (and often only) solution. Marx's atheism was harder-edged, and had no time for amelioration or accommodation. 'Christian Socialism is but the holy water with which the priest consecrates the heart-burnings of the aristocrat,' he famously wrote in the *Communist Manifesto*.[27] Economic alienation was at the heart of religion, so economic revolution, which would necessarily be violent, would be its demise.

And yet, for all Marx's careful, detailed and precise systematization, and his scientific analysis of the economic causes and cures for belief in God, his own atheism was not entirely free of personal sentiment. Already resentful, he developed a passionate animus against the Prussian state which had ended his academic future with Bauer's. Censors then crawled all over *Rheinische Zeitung*, the newspaper he edited in Cologne, until the Prussian government closed it down at the request of Tsar Nicholas I whom it had criticized. Marx then moved to comparatively tolerant France where the French government closed down his next radical publishing venture, again at Prussian request, expelling Marx in the process. Thereafter, he was expelled from Belgium shortly after publishing *The Communist Manifesto*, Germany (again) and Paris (again). His life remained peripatetic, vulnerable and poor until he finally found refuge in London 1849, where it just became poor.

Marx's treatment was, in reality, no worse than that of thousands of radicals and socialists who plotted revolution in mid-century Europe. However, the fact that he was, in effect, made a lifelong exile by a self-consciously self-righteous Christian state marked his atheism.

The road to revolution (part 2)

'Orthodoxy, Autocracy, Nationality': The conditions for Russian atheism
Marx's ideas would transform Russian society far more than any in which he actually lived, but that was many years in the future. At the time, Russian atheism faced more determined opposition than anywhere else in Europe.

Atheism had been known in Russia since the 1770s when Diderot had been invited to St Petersburg by Catherine the Great, provoking indignation and sermonizing among many Orthodox clergy. In spite of Diderot's atheistic zealotry, however, the orthodox were chasing shadows, albeit shadows painted in lurid colours. 'The essence of [the atheists'] actions are clear,' cried one indignant cleric. 'They are blasphemy, trampling on faith and doctrine, lack of submission to God, parents and authorities, adultery, debauchery, greed, enmity, jealousy, murder, drunkenness, disregard for future divine judgement, carelessness, despair, suicide, and so on.'[28] Nicholas Breton couldn't have put it better.

It was not until the French Revolution and its grisly wake that atheism became a genuinely live possibility in Russia and here, as elsewhere, the engine was not science but a combination of philosophy and politics. In the 1820s, a circle of Russian intellectuals, called the Society for the Love of Wisdom, began to meet in St Petersburg. They were elite and elitist, upper class, highly educated, and had little desire to reach or convert a wide audience. Influenced by romanticism and German idealism, they sought to reconcile the divine and the material, perceiving the former within the latter in a kind of pantheistic synthesis that was in a state of permanent flux. Theirs was the task of grasping this mutable reality, for which doubt and scepticism were essential tools.

If not a threat to theism, this was undoubtedly a challenge to Orthodoxy, which was then being reasserted as central to Russian social, political and cultural stability. Following the Napoleonic wars, and a sense that the nobility had become corrupt under Catherine II, Tsar Alexander I set about a programme of reform, including the banning of all secret societies, which his successor, the temperamentally suspicious (even by the standards of Tsars) Nicholas I continued. Nicholas tackled bureaucratic corruption and sought to foster a sense of noble responsibility towards Russian people. He also nurtured an official cult of the pious Tsar, promoting religious morality and looking out for the spiritual health of his subjects.

Russian education had always been deeply suspicious of philosophy. The country had been without a university until 1755 and even thereafter had retained a singular emphasis on the Church Fathers over any later theologians, let alone philosophers. Voltaire's library, brought to St Petersburg by Catherine the Great after his death, was locked safely away in the basement of the Hermitage. The Ministry of Spiritual Affairs and Public Enlightenment reported in 1822 that idealism was 'a perverse system of doubting the authenticity of divine revelation', which it sought to replace 'with the false reasoning and insolent conjectures of alleged scholars and philosophers'.[29] Soon after Tsar Nicholas I ascended to the throne in 1825, courses in 'moral and dogmatic theology' became mandatory for all Moscow University students. Even the Bible, some of which had been recently translated into Russian by the newly formed Russian Bible Society, was condemned and burned for encouraging freethinking.

All of this was supported and encouraged by the Orthodox Church, which was woven into the identity and culture of the country in a way that was hard to conceive even among French Catholics. The relationship was perfectly symbiotic: the state preserved Orthodoxy as it was only Orthodoxy that could preserve the state. Confession and communion had been made a legal requirement for all Orthodox Christians since 1716. Laws on blasphemy and heresy were severe. The Russian Orthodox clergy were effectively a superior, hereditary caste, comprising about one per cent of the total population. 'Orthodoxy, Autocracy, Nationality', long the country's rallying cry, was heard with particular clarity and determination in the early decades of the century.

The Wisdom Lovers were more of a literary than a philosophical society. They were by no means hostile to Orthodoxy, and many turned towards conservative Orthodoxy in their later years. And they had little to do with more radical groups, such as the Decembrists, who rebelled against Nicholas I's ascension in 1825. However, they were repelled by the rigidity and intrusiveness of Nicholas I's aggressive reassertion of Orthodox autocracy and as such set the tone for Russian atheism for much of the rest of the century. Because God was the basis of all hierarchy in Russia, whether moral, political or epistemological, and because that hierarchy was so aggressively enforced, Russian atheism took upon itself a moral and political anger that was akin to that of the French *philosophes* but rarely seen in Britain, Germany or America.

'What is to be Done?': The emergence of Russian atheism

The Wisdom Lovers championed doubt but never strayed far from God. They did, however, influence a younger generation of writers, including Alexander Herzen, the so-called father of Russian socialism, and his friend the poet Nikolai Ogarev, both of whom were more steeped in German idealism than their forbears. Hegel was pictured by the conservative Russian press at the time as an atheist who encouraged political free thought and, misleading as that was, the left Hegelian path that these Russian thinkers trod did cast doubts on some fundamental spiritual ideas, such as immortality and the soul.

Like their predecessors, however, Herzen, Ogarev and their peers were not, at least at first, a deliberately antagonistic movement. Excited by early French Socialism, especially the ideas of Saint-Simon's new Christianity, which they discovered in 1830s, they initially adopted a more straightforward reformist message, advocating a return to the simplicity of the gospel, away from the corrupting theological accretions of Orthodoxy.

Even this, however, was deemed a threat. Herzen and others came from lower social positions than the Wisdom Lovers and were more peripheral to the autocratic state. Moreover, in the early 1830s, in the wake of revolutions in France, Belgium and Poland, the Russian authorities were especially vigilant. Herzen was arrested in 1834 and exiled for five years, the experience of which, combined with a subsequent immersion in Feuerbach, radicalized him, politically and theologically.

It was not until the end of the 1840s that any young Russians became explicit about their atheism. Petr Shaposhnikov, Aleksei Tolstov and Vasilii Katenev appear to have been the first to do so, although their precise intellectual journey is not easy to follow as many of them destroyed their papers. Again, the Young Hegelians were influential. The Russians owned various atheistic tracts, including Friedrich Feuerbach's *The Religion of the Future* written to spread his brother's ideas. According to these, Jesus was simply 'an intelligent man who, having learned from the Chaldeans, worked a variety of wonder just like Mohamed and others'.[30] Faith in God was a sign of stupidity, or at least lack of education (intelligence, by contrast, could be measured by radicalism). Christianity was at best unnecessary. Human beings were independent, owing nothing to any higher power. Salvation depended on humans alone. Reason and instinct were the only justifiable bases for action but as humanity's natural inclination was to happiness, humans could, and would, establish salvation. The Athenian Republic, after all, had flourished quite well without faith in one, true God.

At the same time as these atheistic ideas were making inroads among the Russian intelligentsia, the aged Nicholas I was grappling with the slow industrialization and urbanization of his country. The European-wide revolutions of 1848 induced panic at home and confirmed the dangers inherent in Westernization. Archimandrite Ignatii Brianchaninov blamed revolutions on 'rationalism'[31] and demanded an immediate religious response. Nicholas I hardly needed convincing, believing, as he did, that the rebellions were caused by impiety. He issued a manifesto in March 1849 in which he said that although other nations had been possessed by chaos and anarchy, God would save Holy Russia. Censorship, hardly lax, was tightened, plots discovered and plotters executed or exiled to hard labour in Siberia.

The transition from the sceptical literary pantheism of the 1820s to the harder, political atheism of the second half of the century was thereby made complete. Katenev and his fellows were motivated by a loathing of Nicholas and his reactionary Orthodox politics, and exchanged drunken lyrics about the tsar's corpse dangling from a lamppost. Given that the authority of Tsar and Orthodoxy rested on God alone, atheism was not only a profound but, to borrow from Shelley, *necessary* stance for radicals. In Frede's words, 'the atheism of the[se] men ... centred on the problem of authority ... It was a denial of God's right or ability to set laws for human behaviour, and it was an assertion of the rights and ability of 'intelligent men' to think and act as they saw fit'.[32]

This combination of theo-political oppression and the assertion of human autonomy and capacity gave early Russian atheism an anger unmatched even in France. From as early as mid-century, some atheists, such as Nikolai Speshev, associated denial of God with revolutionary violence: 'I intend ... to disseminate socialism, atheism, terrorism, everything, everything good in this world'.[33] Such sentiments were exceptional at the time. Nevertheless, there soon emerged a programmatic sense to Russian atheism, in which the corrupt authority of God and Tsar were to be replaced by not only a new social and political system, but a whole new concept of mankind. In this Russian atheists borrowed liberally from the Christian worldview.

Two young men, Nikolai Chernyshevsky and Nikolai Dobroliubov, were particularly important in developing this thinking in the 1850s. Both were the sons of priests. (It is striking how many atheists came from ordained families, in Russia and beyond, a fact that is only partly explained by the educational advantages of such an upbringing. There seems to be something of the filial rebellion in atheism.) Both received a theological training, and both underwent spiritual crises after reading Feuerbach and Strauss in the early 1850s,[34] thereafter becoming journalists who denied God while seeking to construct a non-Christian system of ethics that would undermine atheism's negative moral associations.

Chernyshevsky and Dobroliubov inherited but hardened the nascent atheism of the time, explicitly equating loss of faith with intellectual maturation. Orthodoxy was intellectually and politically stagnant. Doubt, once favoured by Russian freethinkers, was inadequate for the scale of the challenge facing the nation. Chernyshevsky and Dobroliubov argued that outright and total unbelief alone was needed to make Russia new.

Newness was central to their philosophy, but it was also in the cultural air at the time. Following Nicholas I's death in 1855, and amid the ongoing humiliation of the Crimean War, his son Alexander II engaged in a program of military, administrative and economic reform, including, most significantly, the emancipation of Russia's 20 million or so peasants. This helped ease tension but was too little too late for Russia's atheistic radicals, who saw the act as mere palliation, its terms insufficiently generous and its processes unduly brutal.

Chernyshevsky and Dobroliubov were lead voices in this rejection, transforming the journal *Contemporary* into a popular vehicle for radical socialism and agitating readers into a conscious, active political force, for whom atheism was the necessary predicate for true emancipation.

They suffered accordingly. Chernyshevsky was arrested and imprisoned on suspicion of revolutionary conspiracy in 1862, and was held for two years during which time he wrote *What is to be Done?: Tales of the New People*. This novel depicted the 'new people' of Russia's future, liberated from the intellectual torpor of faith and recreated as fighters for the radical cause, unperturbed by doubt, immune from uncertainty.

Like much else in Russian atheism of the time, it adopted and refashioned Christian ideas for materialist and socialist ends, the title of the book itself being derived from the story in Luke Chapter 3 in which the crowd come to John for the baptism, itself a form of rebirth, and asked him 'What shall we do?' Chernyshevsky's answer was somewhat different to the Baptist's, though it maintained the idea of 'new birth' that was central to the gospel. Provoking critical

responses from Dostoevsky and Tolstoy, the novel proved an inspiration to, among other revolutionaries, Peter Kropotkin, Rosa
Luxemburg and Vladimir Lenin, who wrote his own pamphlet under
the same title 40 years later. Chernyshevsky himself was pilloried
in Mytinskaia Square two years after his arrest, a punishment
considered by his contemporaries to be a 'mock crucifixion', after
which he was sentenced to exile in Siberia, which killed him.

His cause did not die with him, however, and younger writers
took inspiration from his life and teachings. Enthused by a massive
uprising in Poland in 1863, and again in direct imitation of early
Christian activity, enthusiastic radicals determined to take their
message of atheism and revolution into the countryside, where it
was still largely absent. These student apostles preached the merits
of unbelief to, and attempted to co-ordinate rebellion among,
the peasantry. Their audience was not impressed and the atheist
evangelists met with paltry success. The doctrine of earthly apocalypse, in which Russia would be transformed and made new by
human hands, remained an article of faith confined to an educated
urban elite.

The reaction to reaction

'Atheists are not our preachers': How not to be French
Britain avoided the atheistic excess of the French *philosophes* in
the eighteenth century not because it was any less scientifically or
philosophically advanced but because it had a measure of religious
and political tolerance built into its system. British atheists had less
to upset them.

That recognized, it would not do to draw differences too strongly.
William Blackstone's seminal *Commentaries on the Law of England*
baldly stated that 'Christianity is part of the laws of England'.
Around the same time Peter Annet, a freethinking deist, was
pilloried and sentenced to a year's hard labour, at nearly 70, for
denying divine inspiration of the Pentateuch. British atheism was

not totally unheard of before the French revolution, the first openly atheistic text, the anonymous *Answer to Dr Priestley's Letters to a Philosophical Unbeliever*, appearing in 1782. Usually attributed to Matthew Turner, a Liverpudlian physician, it was a response to the Unitarian chemist, Joseph Priestley, who had sought to combat the philosophical unbelief of D'Holbach's circle, whom he had met in France, by defending God on philosophical grounds. Turner's response was admirably clear.

> As to the question whether there is such an existent Being as an atheist, to put that out of all manner of doubt, I do declare upon my honour that I am one. Be it therefore for the future remembered, that in London in the kingdom of England, in the year of our Lord one thousand seven hundred and 81, a man has publickly declared himself an atheist.[35]

The author went on to claim that 'modern philosophers are nearly all atheists', citing Helvétius, Diderot and D'Alembert as his prime examples. D'Holbach's *System of Nature* had only been in print for a decade or so and was yet to be translated into English but it was widely quoted in the *Answer*, which spoke breathlessly of fossils, and materialism, and Lucretian atoms, and redundant revelation, and against the wickedness of human exceptionalism and self-aggrandizement.

Britain was not, then, entirely isolated from French atheism. But it was, nonetheless, on the other side of an ideological channel that grew much wider in the 1790s. Atheism, long felt to be a vaguely and disreputably French dogma, became much more so with the Revolution.

The tangled and messy relationship between atheism and deism, scepticism and reason, reform and revolution in France was largely lost on the British. Books like William Richards' *Reflections on French Atheism and on English Christianity* and John Estlin's *The Nature and Cause of Atheism* demonstrated the logical and necessary connection between infidelity and

Terror. When the infidels in Augustin Barruel's popular *History of Jacobinism* exhorted one another to 'Crush Christ, crush the religion of Christ', it didn't really matter whether they did so in the name of atheism or reason.[36] People got the message. Burke spoke for a generation when he denounced 'the spirit of atheistical fanaticism' that had been 'inspired by a multitude of writings'.[37] To be British was not to be French, and as the most notorious Frenchmen were infidels, it therefore also meant being religious. 'We are not the converts of Rousseau; we are not the disciples of Voltaire; Helvétius has made no progress amongst us. Atheists are not our preachers; madmen are not our lawgivers.' Rousseau, Voltaire, Helvétius, D'Holbach were all heads of one great hideous freethinking hydra.

The irony in the British story is that it was largely this political response to French infidelity, rather than the infidelity itself, that would kick-start the atheist tradition in Britain and help mark it out, for the next century or so, as a predominantly working-class phenomenon. In response to Revolution, Terror and the threat of invasion, political controls were tightened considerably in the 1790s, and remained tight for a generation. Printers, street preachers, reformers and radicals came under extreme pressure. Those renowned as, or at least reputed to be, atheists were condemned and even tried in the effort to root out Jacobinism, the revolutionary movement that so panicked the British in the early 1790s.

A neat example of the difference between Britain and France or, more precisely, of the difference between how the British saw Britain and the British saw France is captured by their respective encyclopedias. Everyone knew the *Encyclopédie* and everyone knew it was the fertilizer spread on the fields in which atheism grew. Not so the resolutely British *Encyclopaedia Britannica*, first conceived as a reputable riposte to French efforts. By the turn of the century, this was in its third edition, with a supplement published in 1801, to which the editors wrote, in dedication to king:

The French Encyclopédie has been accused, and justly accused, of having disseminated far and wide the seeds of anarchy and atheism. If the Encyclopaedia Britannica shall in any degree counteract the tendency of that pestiferous work, even these two volumes will not be wholly unworthy of your Majesty's patronage.[38]

Knowledge was armed and sent forth in the cause of godly order.

'I will stab the wretch in secret': The necessity of atheism

It was in this context that the most famous atheist book to be published in Britain, at least until recent years, was printed, coming from the pen, not of a working-class radical, but of a very angry young man.

Percy Bysshe Shelley had arrived at University College, Oxford, in 1810. The college was a fortress of Anglican and royalist tradition, even by Oxford's standards. Already absorbed by science, the teenage Shelley's surviving letters show him a thoroughly modern man, immersed in Hume and Gibbon, Voltaire and Condorcet, Paine and Benjamin Franklin. As if these weren't enough, the ancient world also provoked doubts. 'The first doubts which arise in boyish minds concerning the genuineness of the Christian religion, as a revelation from the divinity,' he wrote to William Godwin in June 1812, 'are often excited by a contemplation of the virtues and genius of Greece and Rome. Shall Socrates and Cicero perish, whilst the meanest hind of modern England inherits eternal life?'[39]

He was further radicalized in his first term at Oxford by his new friend Thomas Jefferson Hogg, whose sceptical deism drew the impetuous young poet further down the road of outright infidelity. In reality, Shelley needed little encouragement, as personal reasons had already dragged him a long way. Having hoped to marry his cousin, Harriet Grove, Shelley had been rejected on account, he believed, of his religious unbelief. 'O! I burn with impatience for the moment of Christianity's dissolution,' he wrote to Hogg during their first vacation.[40] 'It has injured me; I swear on the altar of perjured love to revenge myself on the hated cause … I will stab the wretch in secret'.[41] '*Écrasez l'infâme, écrasez l'impie*' he ended, with a Voltairean flourish.

The Christmas festivities did not dampen his ardour. 'Here I swear, and as I break my oath may Infinity Eternity blast me, here I swear I will never forgive Christianity!' he told Hogg in early January. 'Oh how I wish I *were* the Antichrist, that it were mine to crush the Demon, to hurl him to his native Hell never to rise again'. Hogg sent him back an argument, adapted from John Locke's *Essay Concerning Human Understanding*, which provided a supposedly watertight case against God, which delighted Shelley ('Your systematic cudgel for Xtianity is excellent'[42]) but which frustratingly failed to work when he used it on his father.

This angered him further and Shelley returned to Oxford seething, haranguing his father in a letter of 6 February. Reasonable people did not require religious belief to behave morally. Christianity was unreasonable and incredible. Irreligious periods in world history were the most peaceful. 'Religion fetters a reasoning mind with the very bonds which restrain the unthinking one from mischief'.[43] Shelley Snr remained unmoved.

The pair did at least agree that the son should not disgrace the father by making his sceptical rage public. It was, alas, a vain hope. Drawing on Hogg's Lockean arguments and his own boundless passion, Shelley wrote a short pamphlet, hardly more than 1,000 words in its first edition, which was entitled *The Necessity of Atheism*. The pamphlet proposed 'impartially' to examine the proofs of God's existence, of which the author isolated three: the senses, followed by reason and lastly testimony. Each was perfunctorily examined and dismissed. The conclusion was unavoidable – 'Every reflecting mind must allow that there is no proof of the existence of a Deity. Q.E.D.' – as, importantly, were its political implications: 'as belief is a passion of the mind, no degree of criminality can be attached to disbelief'. Atheists were not socially harmful. Indeed, as atheism was true and 'truth has always been found to promote the best interests of mankind', atheism was not only necessary but commendable.

When Shelley extended and reprinted the essay two years later, he headed it up with a statement in which he hedged his bets and left open a pantheistic option, which seems to have been closer to his eventual position. 'I have lately had some conversation with Southey which has elicited my true opinions of God,' he wrote to Elizabeth Hitchner in January 1812. 'He says I ought not to call myself an Atheist, since in reality I believe that the Universe is God. I tell him I believe that God is another signification for the universe.'[44]

Such subtlety would not have impressed the masters of University College, however, even had they been inclined towards lenience with their young Turk, which they weren't. Shelley was expelled, although his eventual departure was less for his pamphlet or its atheism than for the way he dealt with the fallout. Having had the volume printed anonymously, Shelley sent copies to all the bishops and university college heads. His authorship was soon revealed but he continued to deny it, even when it had become obvious. In the words of his biographer, Richard Holmes, 'he either lost his temper or his nerve'.[45] It cost him his place. Had he acknowledged guilt and repented before the authorities, he might have saved his Oxford career. But then, Shelley did not like authority, whether paternal, academic or divine, and he was not a man given to apologize.

'Take up my book and follow me': The utility of atheism
Shelley's atheism was something of a sideshow, a brief, upper-class, sceptical supernova in a sky that was slowly being dotted with fainter and slower-burning marks of working-class infidelity.

For all his loathing of the government of what he would later call 'an old, mad, blind, despised, and dying king', Shelley had as much contempt for the working classes as the French sceptics before him. He was happy for the peasants to stay religious. 'Let this horrid Galilean rule the Canaille,' he wrote to Hogg shortly after being expelled. 'The reflecting part of the community, that part in whose happiness we have so strong an interest, certainly do not require his [Christ's] morality which when there is no vice fetters virtue.'[46] Unlike their inferiors, the philosophically minded did not need God.

If the working classes did need God to moralize them, many weren't getting him. Industrialization had torn up vast tracts of life and, with them, religion, and there was considerable working-class indifference to Christianity. In one early factory in Lambeth with over 1,000 employees, it was discovered that only 33 attended public worship. This was extreme but indicative of a trend. A few years later, Engels observed that, 'among the masses there prevails almost universally a total indifference to religion, or at the utmost, some trace of deism too undeveloped to amount to more than mere words'.

These working men might have been anti-clerical – 'the clergy of all sects is in very bad odour' – but they were certainly not atheist, having 'a vague dread of the words infidel, atheist, etc.'[47] In actual fact, the picture was not quite as anti-religious as Engels imagined. Working-class Christianity remained a reality, most notable among Roman Catholic immigrants and urban noncon-formists. 'Young men generally either attend church, or do not care about religion,' noted secularist leader Christopher Charles Cattell.[48] Nevertheless, indifference mixed with anti-clericalism – a hatred of tithes, churches rates, clerical magistrates and evangelicals – was widespread and became the soil in which infidelity grew.

This infidelity was steered away from outright atheism, at least at first, by Thomas Paine, the inspiration of the British radical movement. Paine was fiercely anti-clerical and anti-Christian, but equally fiercely deistic, writing (the first part of) his *Age of Reason* in 1794 to prevent France from rushing into atheism, 'lest,' as he told Samuel Adams, 'in the general wreck of superstition ... and false theology, we lose sight of morality, of humanity, and of the theology that is true.'[49] He opened up a Temple of Reason as a home for his new religion of Theophilanthropy when in Paris in 1796 at which people sang humanitarian hymns and read ethical texts from various sacred books, and then another in London the following year, and although his religion of reason never took off, his influence on the radical movement tempered its most aggressive atheistic tendencies.

There were good grounds for those tendencies, economic as well as political. Not only did the established church throw its weight behind the repressive politics of the post-Napoleonic era, but a number of its more prominent figures justified the economic severity of the times, often on explicitly religious grounds. Self-consciously Christian thinkers, most famously Thomas Malthus, explained how the harsh reality of a merciless political economy – competition, inequality, poverty and misery – was not simply an acceptable part of the natural order but part of God's good plan. To interfere with them was to deny him. Small wonder early radical thought tended towards anti-clericalism and then atheism.

Even here, however, the picture is more complex, as one of the main architects of the New Poor Law that so brutalized working men was himself an atheist, if not a very public one, who worked, in exhausting detail, from atheistic principles. Jeremy Bentham had been brought up by pious grandmothers but lost whatever Christian faith he had early on. He went to Queen's College, Oxford, aged 12, but had great difficulty swearing the required statements of Anglican faith when he graduated four years later. He never publicly avowed his atheism although that was simply for reasons of caution. His friends knew otherwise. 'The general tenor of his observations … was to discredit all religion,' wrote John Quincy Adams, 'and he intimated doubts of the existence of a God.'[50]

What precipitated Bentham's early religious scepticism is unclear, but he seems to have been temperamentally ill-disposed to faith. In his essay 'Of Ontology' he directly discusses the existence of God within the wider context of logic and language, separating out the categories of fictitious and real entities, and then subdividing the latter into perceptible real entities and inferential real entities. In as far as God could to be said to be real at all, he was inferentially real, and all inferential knowledge, he reasoned, was imperfect and uncertain. Moreover, as there was nothing to be lost from not inferring this divine reality, Bentham thought, God might as well not exist.

This, it is worth noting, didn't mean God definitely did not or could not exist. Rather, it meant that his existence was not sustainable within Bentham's system. As language only made sense in as far as it was rooted in the physical world, all God-talk, indeed all metaphysics, was impossible. In the words of one scholar 'Bentham did not have a theology because, according to his theory of logic and language, there was none to be had'.[51]

Bentham's positivism was the foundation of, but not the only reason for, his atheism. He wrote occasionally about the Bible, usually in order to ridicule its logical incompatibilities and historical inaccuracies. More daringly, in *Not Paul, But Jesus* published under the pseudonym Gamaliel Smith in 1823, he mocked historical Christianity and criticized Jesus. The Golden Rule, if taken seriously, would utterly subvert government, he argued. Christ's instructions to take no thought for the morrow and to give someone your coat if they ask for your shirt would result in total discord and the destruction of private property. It was just as well contemporary Christians paid no serious attention to them.

Jesus himself, he argued, had something of a messiah complex, his prophecy intended to advance his own temporal ambitions (which was why he needed both rich and poor followers, apparently: for money and muscle). His teaching on generosity meant accruing wealth for disciples and ultimately himself. All in all, if he had really wanted to promote human happiness Jesus would, by means of reason rather than revelation, have identified those evils that were legally punishable as crimes, not those that were merely moral offences, and would have evaluated which demanded what level of punishment. He would, in other words, have written *An Introduction to the Principles of Morals and Legislation* by Jeremy Bentham.[52]

As if this weren't enough, Bentham insinuated that not only was Jesus sexually active but possibly bisexual, interested not just in Mary Magdalene but also in the disciple who lay on his breast at the last supper, and the young man whom Mark's gospel describes as fleeing from Gethsemane naked having had his linen cloth torn from him. Marlowe's ghost walked again, although in less readable form.

Not surprisingly, given his positivistic mind and biblical doubts, Bentham could give no credence to (what he thought were) basic Christian creeds. A pure spiritual future life was nonsensical: how could people exist without body? 'What pleasures can it indulge, what gratifications can it propose to itself, what pursuits embark on?'[53] Alternatively, if people were to be resurrected, at what age and with what faculties? Would the blind be resurrected blind, the retarded retarded? If an infant died and was resurrected as an adult, what would happen to the missing years and identity? What about animals? Dogs, monkeys, horses and elephants all showed intellectual facilities, some more than newborn children. Why should they not have souls and eternal life? These were problems that had much exercised medieval theologians. For Bentham they were insuperable barriers.

For all these biblical, theological and philosophical problems, however, it was religion's practical implications, and in particular its contradiction of his utilitarianism, that most vexed Bentham. In an early unpublished manuscript from the 1770s, he had written that so far as religious matters were concerned he considered them 'solely in the character of the politician: not at all in that of the divine'.[54] It was these 'political' implications that concerned him.

Religion dissolved the promise of happiness in this life. In this Bentham was a child of D'Holbach's table, and, in particular, of Helvétius, who had informed his thinking, via Joseph Priestley and Cesare Beccaria. Bentham analysed the problem of religion and happiness in his late, pseudonymous *Analysis of the Influence of Natural Religion on the Temporal Happiness of Mankind*. This was originally based on a series of manuscripts entitled 'Jug. Util', which were not included in his complete works, despite his desires they would be.[55] 'Util.' stood for utility while 'jug', Bentham's nickname for religion, referred to Juggernaut, the huge processional carriage carrying an idol of Krishna under which the faithful allegedly threw themselves. The two concepts neatly summarized Bentham's attitude to religion.

Christianity, with its preference for asceticism, destroyed the possibility of earthly happiness, but the problem was more profound than that. Simple belief in an afterlife, not only in hellfire but in heaven also, caused misery, simply by focusing attention and labour on an illusory eternity. Belief in God, even without confessional details or an ecclesiastical establishment to compound the problem, would still be a curse. Bentham's atheistic world was a better one: wholly secular, structured on utilitarian principles, devoid of meaningless talk of God or the human soul, with no eternal sanction for morality, in which the only way one existed *post mortem* was in the minds of those who came after, and where the view of posterity replaced religious rewards or punishments.

There was an element of messianism in all this. If there was no God, Bentham was his prophet. The philosopher saw himself as the leader of a sect whose ideas would liberate society from irrational, religious slavery. When asked by 'a great man', presumably his then patron Lord Shelburne, what he should do in order 'to save the nation', Bentham told him to 'take up my book' – meaning his *Introduction to the Principles of Morals and Legislation* – and 'follow me'.[56] And Bentham was not known for his sense of irony.

In his later work he planned for such a religion-free world. *Swear Not At All*, from 1817, and *Church-Of-Englandism and Its Catechism Examined*, the following year, criticized organized religion and outlined plans for disestablishment. His massive and unfinished *Constitutional Code*, which offers his most exhaustive theory of constitutional democracy, hardly mentions religion at all. Chapter

14 of Book I declares that 'no power of government ought to be employed in the endeavour to establish any system or article of belief on the subject of religion', while a note in Chapter 11 of Book 2 says simply, 'for the business of religion, there is no department: there is no Minister. Of no opinion on the subject of religion, does this Constitution take any cognizance.'[57] Just as – indeed largely because – religious statements made no sense to Bentham, religious matters had no place in his utilitarian utopia. Ultimately, he sought the elimination not just of religious structures but of religious belief itself, for as long as God remained a source of human action, the rational, earthly, pursuit of self-interest would be thwarted. Utilitarianism demanded no less.

To complicate matters, however, utilitarianism also demanded that any form of charitable relief should make the conditions for the undeserving poor sufficiently atrocious as to serve as a serious deterrent. If people naturally chose the pleasurable over the painful, government needed to make the alternative to productive work so painful that it would deter any but the most work-shy. The path to the greatest happiness for the greatest number lay through fields of great unhappiness for a great number.

Through the influence of Edwin Chadwick, Bentham's friend, assistant and author of the New Poor Law, these principles assumed political form. It is doubtful whether those many working men and women who so despised the New Poor Law made the connection with Bentham's utilitarianism, still less with his logically ruthless atheism, but there was a link there nonetheless.

'If poor men cost the state as much …': Working-class atheism
It was those working men who were to form the basis of nineteenth-century British atheism. Their infidelity owed rather less to Paine's reason, Shelley's romanticism or Bentham's utility than it did to their first-hand experience of what the nation's faltering *ancien régime*, propped up by a tithe-hungry established church, was doing to its poorest, particularly urban subjects.

Richard Carlile was one of them. Born in Ashburton in Devon in 1790, he lived a precarious existence from his earliest years, when his father abandoned the family four years later. Suffering in the economic downturn after the Napoleonic wars, Carlile became involved in the radical movement, publishing and selling radical tracts. He was instinctively a deist, after Paine, but his religious beliefs varied, once remarking that 'the words Deism and Atheism, upon my view of them, differ more in sound than in meaning'.[58] His views hardened when imprisoned in Dorchester for radical activity, and he wrote defiantly in *Republican*, his radical magazine, 'there is no such a God in existence as any man had preached, nor any kind of God'. Carlile's atheism, like that of many who followed him, was not a rationalized reflection on philosophical, let alone theological, arguments, but rather a visceral reaction against the religiously justified system that so oppressed him. '[I am] quite proud of being called a Deist, Materialist, or Atheist, just as the idolaters please,' he wrote in the preface to his *The True Meaning of the System of Nature*, 'so [long] as [I am] distinguished from them.'[59]

Eliza Sharples, his common-law wife, also spoke publicly on the subject but with similar reservations. 'I am no atheist, in the vulgar sense of the word,' she said in 1832. 'I attribute every thing to God, as the first cause and universal creator.' This sounded like deism or possibly Shelley's pantheism but was in fact closer to Bentham's positivism. When we enquire what we mean by god, or first cause, or universal creation, she went on to reason, we must conclude 'that we mean nothing by them, that we know nothing by the use of such words ... they are mere covers for our ignorance'.[60] Whether or not Sharples can be definitively termed an atheist is, thus, uncertain. However, even if she, like Carlile, did vacillate, it is tempting to number her among the unbelievers, if only because atheism otherwise remains an insufferably male pastime.

Carlile was not an easy man to get on with. Even other radical booksellers, a quarrelsome bunch by nature, found him abrasive.

Yet he could form partnerships, notably with the Revd Robert Taylor, when he wanted to preach his particular gospel. Taylor was no ordinary clergyman. Trained as an Anglican minister at Cambridge, he became deist and anti-clerical on reading Paine, entering the lists against revelation. Sentenced to a year in Oakham prison, he there wrote *The Diegesis; being a Discovery of the Origin, Evidence, and Early History of Christianity*, which dismissed the New Testament as a collection of forgeries and foreign influences. This was published by Carlile with whom Taylor went to live on his release, before the pair set off on an infidel mission to the provinces.

Such radical and atheistic missionary activity was rare but not unheard of at the time. That which did take place usually did so under the name of Robert Owen, whose spirit dwelt powerfully among his godless disciples. Owen was a self-made man of seemingly undefeatable self-belief, self-confidence and energy. He began his long working life in manufacturing in Manchester and then at New Lanark Mills in Scotland, where he became manager and owner, and which he then recreated in his own image.

That image was solidly atheistic. Owen denounced religion with zeal, although also with the caution necessary at the time. 'When religion is stripped of the mysteries with which the priests of all times and countries have invested it,' he remarked in his *Second Lecture on the New Religion* in 1830, 'all its divinity vanishes; its errors become palpable; and it stands before the astonished world in all its naked deformity of vice, hypocrisy, and imbecility.'[61] His anger was palpable and personal. 'There is no sacrifice ... which I ... would not have ... willingly and joyously made to terminate the existence of religion on earth.'[62]

Owen's atheism was like Bentham's, in its utilitarian rather than positivistic guise. Religion wrecked human well-being and happiness with its gross misconception of human nature. Christianity, Owen believed, was based on the absurd notion 'that each [person] ... determined his own thoughts, will, and action, and was responsible for them to God and his fellowmen', a notion that turned man into 'a weak, imbecile animal; a furious bigot and fanatic; or a miserable hypocrite.'[63] Owen knew otherwise. Environment and education made the man. People were the product of their 'constitution or organisation at birth, and of the effects of external circumstances upon it from birth to death.'[64] A man's entire character – physical, mental and moral – was formed independently of himself. Ultimately, no one 'is responsible for his will and his own actions.'[65]

Owen's genius and claim to fame lay not so much in his atheistic ideas, many of which simmered in the British slipstream of Paine's anti-clerical deism, as in what he did with them. Not only did he debate the merits of God in public, establish socialist missionaries who proclaimed a new world order with millenarian fervour, and set up various societies and sects, such as the Universal Community Society of Rational Religionists, but he also reformed New Lanark in line with his ideas.

Owen took the question of environment, education and character seriously. Not only his mill but its village and environs were thoroughly redesigned. Accommodation, schooling, gardens, playgrounds, even the villagers' dress were planned by the manager, in the process transforming New Lanark into the best ordered and most worker-friendly mill in the country. 'Any general character, from the best to the worst, from the most ignorant to the most enlightened, may be given by the application of proper means,' Owen wrote in his 1813 *Essay on the Formation of Character*, 'which means are to a great extent at the command and under the control of those who have influence in the affairs of men.' Owen was the potter, his workers the clay. Anything was possible, 'men and women of a new race, physically, intellectually and morally; beings far superior to any yet known to have lived upon earth.'[66] This particular godless society would be a good one.

New Lanark was controversial. Owen treated his workers vastly more humanely than almost anywhere else at the time, but his view of human nature was still worrying. His moulding the lives of the lower orders was not a great problem in an age given to stressing the duties of paternalism, but his doctrine of non-responsibility was, provoking rumours of sexual freedom that scandalized respectable opinion.

It was also unsuccessful, at least in so far as it survived only through its owner's subsidies. Owen was undeterred and went on to found a second such enterprise, New Harmony, in Indiana, with another unbeliever, William Maclure. This venture made New Lanark look like a roaring success but Owen, boundless in self-conviction, tried to persuade the Mexican government to grant him Texas to repeat the experiment on a still grander scale. The authorities were not to be persuaded and Owen returned home to Britain with renewed atheistic and socialistic efforts.

These included the aforementioned Universal Community Society of Rational Religionists, soon renamed the Rational Society, which held Sunday services in 'halls of science', sang Social Hymns, published a weekly newspaper entitled *New Moral World*, paid missionaries who were known as 'socialist bishops', and even attempted to inaugurate a new calendar.

By 1840, the Rational Society had over 60 branches and attracted several thousand weekly visitors, including the young Friedrich Engels. It was not entirely on its own. Aside from failed ventures like Paine's Theophilanthropic Temples, a handful of atheistic meeting halls had sprung up in the early decades of the century. There was an atheist chapel of a kind in Stepney, a communist church at Bow Lane in Bromley, as well as several groups of self-consciously free-thinking Christians, and the John Street Literary Institution, called by some the 'palace of London socialistic atheism'.[67]

The most famous of all such meeting places was the South Place Society, which since 1795, had been home to the various liberal sects that sat at first on the edge of, and then some way beyond, the boundaries of Christian orthodoxy, before becoming an Ethical Society, and then a home to the atheistic humanist movement. A few other places, such as The Rotunda where Robert Taylor and Richard Carlile spoke, were also well known, but most were small-scale affairs, often created when dangerously radical working men were evicted from their existing religious places of meeting. The Coventry Mutual Improvement Society, for example, met in the schoolroom of an independent chapel, but when it began to hold discussions about religion, chapel elders expelled all 40 members who then went on to form a secular society.

These societies might have been able to meet without too much fear of imprisonment or provoking a riot, but they were still feared and loathed in early Victorian England, as were the few atheistic journals that emerged in the 1840s. The battle over the radical press was a bitter one in the post-Napoleonic decades and those found responsible for publications like *The Oracle of Reason* or the *Investigator* lived a precarious existence.

Charles Southwell was a social missionary, radical bookseller and anti-religious lecturer who founded the *Oracle* in 1841. He was one of the few people to think Owen a woolly-headed dreamer, and one of the even fewer to tell him so. Southwell was arrested for blasphemy, imprisoned for 12 months and fined £100 in 1842 for having called the Bible a 'revoltingly odious Jew production'. It was in his absence that George Jacob Holyoake took over the *Oracle*'s editorship and became the longest lived and, after Charles Bradlaugh, most famous Victorian infidel.

Holyoake had sincere Wesleyan origins but his younger sister died in 1829 partly as a result of the family's temporary poverty after being forced to pay church rate. It fed a nascent anti-clericalism, which in time became fully fledged atheism. At first, he avoided Owenism because of its anti-religious reputation but in time he became an Owenite missionary at Worcester where he held services of rational religion. His anti-clericalism ran deep. Britain is 'afflicted by no fewer than 23,000 clergymen', he later wrote, crippling the population's moral energies, humiliating its active spirit and diverting people 'from independence and social amelioration'.[68] Religious morality was retarded. Holyoake sought to replace it with scientific morality, and positive principles, arguing that without such principles, 'secularism will fall back into the aimlessness and chaos of old Infidelity, which never had cohesion except when persecution was present'.[69]

For all that, he was not totally indiscriminate in his condemnation, supporting the (largely religious) temperance movement and generally eschewing the deliberately provocative approach of many Owenite missionaries. When one correspondent wrote to the *Reasoner*, yet another atheistic paper, rebuking it for still using Christian dates and suggesting a secularist calendar instead, Holyoake replied that 'there is no objection to be taken to anything useful because it is Christian'.[70]

Holyoake was keen on being respectable, as well as being reasonable. He once proposed that officers of secular societies should be of good moral character and subscribe to principles of secularism. Some protested loudly. 'We have in this outline a regular sectarian church of the most objectionable kind', one secularist wrote. 'A secular order with clerical and lay brothers; a secular creed; a secular clergy – a secular episcopacy of directors – a secular convocation of delegates – a central college of secular cardinals – with the editor of the *Reasoner* as Secular Pope.'[71] There was no pleasing some secularists.

Neither Holyoake's reasonableness nor his respectability were to save him. In May 1842 he delivered a lecture on 'Home Colonisation as a means of superseding Poor Laws and Emigration' in Cheltenham, in which he carefully avoided all references to God. Towards the end, one Mr Maitland, a local teetotaller and lay preacher, stood up and complained that though he had spoken of man's duty to man, he had been silent about their duty to God. Would there be churches and chapels in his Socialist society?

Holyoake recorded the question and his answer in his autobiographical fragment *The History of the Last Trial by Jury for Atheism in England*, published eight years later. He began by pointing out that the national debt 'already hangs like a millstone round the poor man's neck' and that the established church cost around £20 million per annum. That being so, are we not too poor to have a God, he asked rhetorically. 'If poor men cost the state as much, they would be put like officers upon half-pay, and while our distress lasts I think it would be wise to do the same thing with deity.' He wasn't finished. As far as he was concerned, others could pay for all the chapels they wanted. 'Morality I regard, but I do not believe there is such a thing as a God … For myself, I flee the Bible as a viper, and revolt at the touch of a Christian.'[72]

It was too much. He was tried and convicted of blasphemy, and sentenced to six months, a period of great hardship during which time his infant daughter died. Holyoake records how he managed to save a guinea while in prison to buy her a winter cloak, but how it was eventually spent on her coffin.

Holyoake's case attracted some attention, less on account of his daughter's death, an all-too-innocuous event for the time, as for his imprisonment. The Anti-Persecution Union was formed to defend him (and Southwell). Questions were asked in Parliament and sermons even preached in his defence.

Holyoake's unbelief was such that he preferred to treat religion as irrelevant rather than wrong and was even prepared to work with Christians in promoting secular good. This angered some of his more prominent supporters who objected to Holyoake's rejection of outright atheism and started a new journal the *Investigator* in 1854 to propagate atheistic socialism.

The division was typical of those that dogged nineteenth-century British atheism. Without the all-encompassing ideas of a Saint-Simon or a Comte or a Hegel or a Marx, it was a more *ad hoc* affair, reactive, unsystematic and, more than its continental cousins, led by the working class. It was far from devoid of a sense of promise and expectation, whether through Bentham's godless utilitarian utopia or Owen's godless socialist one. But the absence of a systematic vision meant that it was never clear whether it was atheistic or pantheistic or socialist or secularist or merely anti-clerical.

Moreover, although the establishment fear and indifference that jailed Holyoake and killed his daughter gave the atheists something to hate, British Christianity was too socially complex to permit straightforward, uncomplicated loathing. There were plenty of sincere nonconformists among the early socialist and trades union movement.[73] When asked for his religion on admittance to prison, Chartist leader William Lovett said he was 'of that religion which Christ taught, and which very few in authority practise'.[74] Chartism was, in the words of Michael Burleigh, 'little more than a secularised form of Methodism'.[75] In such a context, comprehensive, morally furious atheism became harder to sustain than in Russia, Germany or France.

Chartism collapsed in failure in 1848. Britain soon passed into nearly a decade of economic growth, and the socialist cause faltered. The socialist-atheist-Owenite-working-class-radical movement fell quiet, and although the 1850s would witness the foundation of the nation's first secular societies, British atheism as a whole took an altogether more doubtful and melancholic tone.

Science and religion, once again

'The very emblem of all that is solid has moved beneath our feet':
Darwin's ambiguous atheism
Early on in their infidel mission Carlile and Taylor stopped in Cambridge, as much a bastion of Anglican orthodoxy and royalism as Oxford had been during Shelley's brief time there. Setting up an infidel headquarters in the town, they publicly invited the University Vice-Chancellor and Doctors of Divinity to discuss with them 'the merits of the Christian religion', challenging them to refute the charge that the religion was fraudulent, 'nothing more than an emanation from the ancient pagan religion', and that 'such a person as Jesus Christ, alleged to have been of Nazareth, never existed'.[76]

The provocation worked, although not in the intended way. The authorities reacted furiously and evicted the missionaries, who claimed that they had uncovered about 50 students who had avowed infidelity. Charles Darwin, then 20 and unknown, but one day destined to be the pin-up for thinking atheists everywhere, was at that time studying for the Anglican ministry in Cambridge. He would not have been among the 50.

Like most people of his age and class, Darwin was brought up a Christian, although from sceptical stock.[77] Despite this, his nurture was conventionally religious, although he had ended up at Cambridge less through any passionate love of the gospel than because his father, vexed by his son's lack of medical ambition, had insisted he find useful employment, which, for someone of his class, meant the church.

His ministerial career was cut short when the opportunity arose of travelling the world on the *Beagle*, as the self-financing, gentle-manly companion of Captain Robert FitzRoy, a journey that further cooled his already tepid faith. When sailing up the west coast of South America, Darwin experienced an earthquake and volcanic eruption, which shocked him. 'A bad earthquake at once destroys the oldest associations,' he wrote in *The Voyage of the Beagle*. 'The world, the very emblem of all that is solid, has moved beneath our feet like a crust over a fluid'. Perhaps the earth was not tailored to human needs as Cambridge's natural theologians had taught him?

On his return in 1836, he spent three years thinking dangerous thoughts, which culminated in what would, 20 years later, become *On the Origin of Species*. His autobiography, written 40 years later, concentrated his loss of Christian faith into this period, claiming that three reasons – biblical doubts, moral objections and philo-sophical problems – pursued him to unbelief. While he clearly stumbled over each of these issues, it is highly unlikely they all occurred to him during this period.[78] More probably, Darwin fashioned his autobiography so as to bring together all his doubts into a single chapter and timeframe, which he placed during a period of intense and destabilizing intellectual activity.

Darwin's notebooks from this period chart his intellectual journey, recording claims and counter-claims that had long been part of the atheist polemics, and would remain so in Darwin's wake. There was the problem of special creation. Evolution wrecked the idea that God had made each species separately. But then, Darwin reasoned, was that such a great idea? Was it not 'grander' to see all life emerging through a continuous process of law-governed evolution?

Then there was the idea that humans may not, in fact, be that different from other species. 'Man – wonderful man … with divine face turned towards heaven … he is not a deity, his end under present form will come … he is no exception,' Darwin wrote in Notebook C, sounding like an Old Testament prophet.

This upset human pride but there was more. What if key human attributes like thought, morality and religiosity were not distinctively 'spiritual' qualities but rather material outworkings of the evolutionary process? Coming from a worldview in which the material and the spiritual were necessarily distinct and opposed this was a significant challenge. Where did it leave personal morality? Where did it leave human conscience? Where did it leave the Last Judgement?

Darwin's Christian faith didn't die in the 1830s but it showed few signs of life after that, and was finally snuffed out when he witnessed at first hand, the rapid but painful and humiliating death of his eldest daughter, and most loved child, Annie. Darwin's theory of evolution had alerted him to the reality and apparent ubiquity of suffering but he could – or, at least, could try to – rationalize and cope with that. 'From death, famine, rapine, and the concealed war of nature we can see that the highest good, which we can conceive, the creation of the higher animals has directly come,' he wrote at the end of his 1842 'Species' sketch. The key question was, did that 'highest good' justify 'the concealed war of nature'. Darwin's tentative theoretical answer, at least in 1842, was 'yes', but that seems to have teetered during the 1840s and finally fallen with Annie's death in 1851.[79]

Darwin was thus an atheist with regard to the Christian God, but not an atheist period. His beliefs fluctuated during the last three decades of his life. He was, in effect, pulled in two directions. In one of the last letters he wrote, to the philosopher William Graham, author of a book entitled *Creed of Science*, Darwin remarked, 'you have expressed my inward conviction, though far more vividly and clearly than I could have done, that the Universe is not the result of chance'. Yet, he still cavilled. 'There are some points in your book which I cannot digest. The chief one is that the existence of so-called natural laws implies purpose ... I cannot see that there is then necessarily any purpose [to them].'[80]

This was a serious agnosticism, and it was compounded by a typically Darwinian concern. Darwin was not simply agnostic in the sense of not knowing whether or not there was a God. He came to doubt whether the human mind, being evolved from that of a 'lower' animal, could know such things. When reflecting on the universe, he wrote in his autobiography, 'I feel compelled to look to a First Cause having an intelligent mind in some degree analogous to that of man; and I deserve to be called a Theist.' And yet, then there came a monkey puzzle. 'Can the mind of man, which has, as I fully believe, been developed from a mind as low as that possessed by the lowest animal, be trusted when it draws such grand conclusions?'

Darwin thus died a devout sceptic, not only not knowing about God but not knowing whether one could know. It was a problem that would come to haunt atheism, even more than it did theism. If, as Darwin had mused, human knowledge, thought and morality were merely accidents of random mutation and meaningless selection, could they be trusted? Were they anything more than meaningless accidents themselves? The idea that humans were, in effect, no different from animals, long a mainstay of atheist anti-Christian rhetoric, ended up, if taken seriously, sawing through the branch on which the atheists sat.

'It is science that has led to this infidelity': Forging a creation myth
It is ironic, given this subtle agnosticism, not to mention Darwin's belief that it was 'absurd to doubt that a man may be an ardent

Theist & an evolutionist', not to mention his hatred of controversy –
'why should you be so aggressive?' he once asked the atheist Edward
Aveling – that Darwin, and Darwinism, would one day become
the icon of thinking atheism. In reality, the situation was rather
different in the later nineteenth century.

Not only was educated clerical opinion distinctly hesitant about a
literal Genesis and special creation long before Darwin published (the
majority of leading geologists being clerics) but 'with but few exceptions the leading Christian thinkers in Great Britain and America
came to terms quite readily with Darwinism and evolution'.[81]

Darwin's greatest early critics were scientists making their
arguments on scientific grounds, and some of his earliest and most
eager supporters were sincere Christians, like Charles Kingsley
and Frederick Temple in Britain, and Asa Gray in the US. The
infamous Huxley-Wilberforce debate at the British Association for
the Advancement of Science in 1860 was nothing like the 'Science'
vs. 'Religion' cage fight it became in popular myth, and was, in
any case, as much about the social differentiation of science (from
natural theology) and scientists (from clergymen) as it was about
the theory itself.[82]

This is not to say there was no scientific content to late nineteenth-
century atheism. *The Times* wrote its first leading article on the
possibility of conflict in May 1864, and the possibility plagued the
last quarter of the century. 'It is science that, by demonstrating the
insignificance of this globe in the vast scale of creation, has led to
this infidelity,' fretted Lothair in Disraeli's novel of the same name,
published in 1870.[83]

This was the age in which atheism, publicly admissible for the
first time, became conscious of its own history and tradition, both
of which drew heavily on the idea of 'science', albeit tailored to fit
the story. This atheistic self-consciousness had been evolving for
years. As early as 1817, Richard Carlile had run advertisements for
an anti-religious periodical, *The Deist or Moral Philosopher*, under
which title he would publish 'scarce and valuable Deistical tracts,

from the most celebrated and modern writers'.[84] It was the start of an atheistic canon. Thirty years later, the Chartist leader Thomas Cooper lectured on the Early English Freethinkers. In France, Voltaire, D'Alembert, Diderot, Turgot, D'Holbach and Rousseau were celebrated, having fallen into disfavour after the Revolution.

It was also the age that saw W. E. H. Lecky, still only 26, publish his two-volume *History of the Rise and Influence of the Spirit of Rationalism in Europe*, J. M. Wheller his *Biographical Dictionary of Freethinkers of All Ages and Nations*, and John Robertson his various histories of free thought. It was the age when Galileo became a figure of myth and wonder, and Giordano Bruno science's greatest martyr, a statue of him being unveiled in Campo de' Fiori in Rome (where he had been burned nearly 300 years earlier), with 30,000 people marching through the city to hear a speech from anti-clerical orator Giovanni Bovio. Most influentially, it was the age when John William Draper published his *History of the Conflict between Religion and Science* and Andrew Dickson White his *History of the Warfare of Science with Theology in Christendom*, wildly popular tales of how 'Science' and 'Religion', reified into objective entities, had always been opposed to one another. In time, all these histories would come to be heavily criticized as inaccurate and partisan and all but abandoned in academic circles. But they would remain – indeed, still do remain – important sources for the creation myth of science, fighting its way to birth in the shadow of the giant, obscurantist monster of religion.

It was also, not coincidentally, the age in which Pope Pius IX published his *Syllabus of Errors*, which notoriously concluded that the Pontiff ought not 'come to terms with progress, liberalism and modern civilization': the age in which the first Vatican Council dogmatically defined the longstanding doctrine that when the Pope spoke *ex cathedra* in matters of faith and morals, he did so with Christ's gift of infallibility; and the age in which Draper's history was added to the Vatican's Index of Prohibited Books, without, it appears, any sense of irony. The science vs. religion narrative gained purchase not for any overwhelmingly good evidential reasons but because it was articulated with verve just as the papacy was refusing to come to terms with modern civilization. In such circumstances, the myth of conflict and progress seemed not only credible but necessary.

'The process is unstoppable': Freud

Sigmund Freud, the third great icon of this age of atheist promise after Marx and Darwin, grew up in just such an atmosphere. He never had any religious beliefs, nor any doubts that science would one day utterly vanquish religion. 'The scientific mind generates a specific way of approaching the things of this world,' he would write in *The Future of an Illusion*. 'Faced with the things of religion, it pauses, hesitates, and finally here too steps over the threshold. The process is unstoppable'.[85]

Jewish by birth, Freud was the product of a thoroughly non-observant family – 'my father ... let me grow up in complete ignorance of everything that concerned Judaism'[86] – and a culture of medical materialism at the University of Vienna, where he went to study aged 17. He was tempted by theism while in Vienna, in the form of his teacher, the philosopher and former priest Franz Brentano, whom Freud thought 'a damned clever fellow'.[87] It was a brief flirtation, however, which Freud managed to resist until he, like so many before him, discovered Feuerbach. 'Among all philosophers I worship and admire this man the most,' he wrote to Edward Silberstein in 1875.[88]

Feuerbach deepened and gave form to the young man's atheism, supplying him with the idea that religion was an illusion, a projection of human needs and desires. Religious ideas, he said in *The Future of an Illusion*, were illusions, 'fulfilling the oldest, most powerful, most pressing desires of the human race'.[89] This was pure Feuerbach, although Freud would add some psychological depth, and not a little colour, to these already well-established arguments.

Religious belief, Freud argued, was rooted in the unconscious just as other human problems were. 'A personal God is, psychologically, nothing other than an exalted father ... the roots of the need for religion are in the parental complex,' he wrote in his 1910 essay, 'Leonardo da Vinci and a Memory of His Childhood'.[90] Religious ideas – the idea of a benevolent and 'only apparently strict' Providence watching over us – made 'human helplessness bearable'.[91] It allayed fears, secured order, offered protection and provided hope. In short, it did what a parent should for a disturbed child, which was precisely where, according to Freud, it originated.

Humans, he argued, had once lived in hordes that were ruled by a despotic, primal father who enslaved the men and possessed the women. Tyrannized beyond endurance, the men eventually banded together to kill their oppressor, a crime for which they felt such intense guilt that they subsequently deified the murdered father figure, thereafter honouring him through ritual and obedience. Religiosity was thus a kind of collective human neurosis, from which science in general, and psychoanalysis in particular, offered liberation.

Towards the end of his life, Freud took these allegedly scientific ideas further and applied them to Judaism. This primordial parricide Freud found at the root of all religiosity, lay at the root of historical Judaism. Moses, who was not in fact Jewish but an Egyptian, whence he had adopted monotheism, had been murdered by his followers on account of the heavy legal burden he tried to place on them. They, however, felt guilt for their crime and so developed the idea of a messiah who would return to deliver them promised sovereignty in response.

Odd as it may sound, there was more than just demolition in this thesis. Freud saw, in the Jewish insistence on the non-materiality of God, a moment of progress for civilization, as it effected a turn inwards, away from mere appearance towards introspection and intellectual reflection. Religious ideas could sometimes effect progress. This acknowledged, however, Freud's argument did nothing to increase his religious faith, or, for that matter, his historical or scientific authority.

Freud had a high opinion of that authority but acknowledged that he stood on others' shoulders. 'I have said nothing that other, better men have not said before far more completely, forcibly, and impressively,' he wrote in *The Future of an Illusion*. 'I have merely ... added to the critique of my great predecessors some psychological grounds.'[92]

Like them, he was certain that science was driving out the primitive and illusory comforts of mankind's childhood. Like them, he considered his own religious scepticism as indispensable for this scientific progress. 'Why did none of the devout create psychoanalysis?' he asked his friend, the Swiss pastor Oskar Pfister, rhetorically, in 1918. 'Why did one have to wait for a completely godless Jew?'[93] And like them he worried about the consequences of this godless scientific progress on the masses. 'As long as they do not learn that one no longer believes in God, all is well.'[94] In many ways, Freud was or, at least, considered himself to be, the last in the line of continental *philosophes*, enlightening human darkness and defending civilization from all the perils and dangers of religious retardation.

The high point of British atheism

'An unspeakable comfort': Religious atheism

Mrs Humphrey Ward's novel *Robert Elsmere* gripped late Victorian readers. Published in 1888, it had sold over a million copies by the end of the century. It told the story of a young Oxford clergyman, bearing more than a passing resemblance to several real life cases, cast into religious doubt by encountering German thought, which he dealt with by adopting a quasi-Christian social idealism to reassure him of life's purpose and dignity. 'The problem of the world at this moment is – how to find a religion,' the eponymous hero muses at one point, 'some great conception which shall be once more capable, as the old was capable, of welding societies, and keeping man's brutish elements in check.'[95] This was a momentous

struggle, not to be undertaken lightly or satisfied cheaply. 'I …
am not one of those who would seek to minimize the results of
this decline for human life, nor can I bring myself to believe that
positivism or "evolutional morality" will ever satisfy the race.'

Robert Elsmere was sincere, solemn and didactic; Oscar Wilde
once quipped that it was basically Matthew Arnold's *Literature and
Dogma* with the literature left out. Its success was partly due to the
author's earnest handling of a sensitive subject and partly due to its
resonance with so many readers. Biblical criticism and, to a much
lesser extent, evolution had precipitated a crisis of faith, in which
countless sensitive souls wrestled with godlessness, looking for
alternatives with which they could wrest meaning and dignity from
a universe that seemed devoid of both.

Elsmere was right in that 'evolutional morality' did not satisfy,
at least not in Britain, despite the voluminous and comprehensive
writings of Herbert Spencer, the nation's most eminent social
Darwinian, who was seen as an intellectual titan in the last quarter
of the century. Positivism had similarly limited traction. Its British
incarnation originated with Richard Congreve, a history fellow
at Wadham College, Oxford, who had joined the movement in
1854, and been nominated by Comte as the 'spontaneous leader' of
British positivists. Congreve had converted several of his students
and they went on to found the London Positivist Society in 1867.
The Society duly opened a headquarters, which it decorated with
portraits and busts of eminent men, and a table which bore a sacred
positivist formula and was the focus for elaborate rituals and rites
of passage. Their ambition was to replace the Church of England
with the religion of humanity, as Comte had envisaged he would do
with the Roman Catholic Church in France. The British movement
soon endured splits, however, not least because British atheists were
unfamiliar, and not entirely comfortable, with the idea of a planned
society ruled over by a scientific priesthood.

Those who remained faithful morphed into the Ethical
Movement, which sought to offer a credible alternative to religion

without the elaborate intellectual and ritual superstructure of the Religion of Humanity. This movement was longer lived and more popular, but was still riven by different ideas of what it was for.

For some, ethical societies and unions served a narrow practical, social or political purpose. They were, in the words of one-time President of the Union of Ethical Societies Leslie Stephen, a meeting place 'between the expert and specialist on the one side, and on the other, the men who have to apply ideas to the complex concretes of political and social activity'.[96] For others, they were a bulwark against the individualism and industrialization of late Victorian society, a way of nurturing collective public endeavour. For still others – one suspects the majority of those who mourned the loss of their Christian faith – they supplied a more obviously pastoral need.

> For the last four years I have been a member of one of the Ethical Societies and I can speak of the help and strength which it gives me in my duties to attend our Sunday meetings. Not only the addresses, but the instrumental music and singing, inspire me for the world of the coming week and rest me after that of the past. It is an unspeakable comfort to meet there others who are trying to surmount the difficulties of life in the ethical spirit.[97]

As this letter to *Ethical World* suggests, there was not much to distinguish the ethical unions from the churches from which their members were drawn, something that was reinforced when the American-born Stanton Coit took over the running of the movement in the 1890s. Coit was explicit in his desire for ethical churches to replace Christian ones and he shaped the movement's practice accordingly, turning it into a kind of ethical High Church Anglicanism. In 1909, he bought a former Methodist Church in Queensway, London, and fitted it out as befitted an ethical church. He erected statues of Christ, Buddha, Socrates, Pallas Athena and Marcus Aurelius throughout the building, and fitted stained-glass windows commemorating Florence Nightingale, Elizabeth Fry and St Joan. There was also a prominent scripture table, a pulpit and an altar, where Coit would officiate over marriages and funerals in his doctoral gown. This was not Comte's Religion of Humanity although strangers might have been hard-pressed to tell the difference. It seemed that for atheism to flourish, at least within habitually religious cultures, it was inexorably drawn to imitation, inadvertently flattering that which it sought to replace.

'Has not science made the world happy?': Rational atheism
Ethical Unions represented one kind of atheistic response to the Victorian crisis of faith, the kind of 'ethical earnestness', to use Maurice Cowling's phrase, that typified *Robert Elsmere*.[98] They also reflected the sense, keenly felt since atheism's earliest days, that for disbelief to be successful it needed to offer more than disbelief. It needed to offer an alternative: community, ritual, rites of passage, belief or, ideally, all of the above.

Not all atheists agreed. Indeed, some disagreed loudly, denouncing anything that smacked of religious practice as 'castrated church-mongering'. Reason was enough. 'Has not science made the world happy? Is not its very task and joy to make the wheels of life move more smoothly?' asked the prominent Darwinian and atheist Edward Aveling. 'What happiness has any creed yet wrought that can be for one moment compared with the easement given to the hearts of men by the discovery of the electric telegraph'.[99]

This was the creed of the Rationalist Press, which grew out of Charles Watts' earlier publishing venture, the Propagandist Press fund. Both were intended as an alternative to the Society for the Promotion of Christian Knowledge, or SPCK, which had been founded in the 1690s and was still going strong 200 years later. The Rationalist Press boasted a number of eminent honorary members including Emile Zola, Leslie Stephen and the biologist Ernst Haeckel, and became an excellent source for cheap books on science and ethics, in the process helping to form the atheist canon that was emerging at the time.

Its problem was that it never had more than 6,000 members and most of those were middle-class intellectuals rather than the working classes who were apparently in such desperate need of intellectual liberation. The Press was able to rationalize this imbalance by arguing that 'when Rationalists have converted the intellect of the world and made heresy "fashionable", the great multitude will, as sheep, follow their leaders'.[100] However, there is little doubt that its failure to preach to anyone but the rationalist choir was a source of much frustration.

The Rationalists' attitude to religion tended to be one of pity rather than contempt. Given that Christ was uneducated and moved in ignorant circles, they reasoned, he had done an acceptable job. But, if truth be told, he 'revealed nothing of practical value ... [and] taught false notions of existence'. The problem was, 'he had no knowledge of science ... he lacked experimental force'.[101] If only he'd known about the electric telegraph or the microbe, things might have been better. As they were, he and his creed were better put away, like children's toys.

'Ridicule is quite a legitimate weapon': Secular atheism
Others were more militant than pitying. In a footnote in her memoir, *My Apprenticeship*, published in 1926, Beatrice Webb records her first introduction to 'the socialism based on 'scientific materialism', in an interview with Karl Marx's daughter Eleanor, in the refreshment room of the British Museum over 40 years earlier. Eleanor was 'very wrath' about the recent imprisonment of George Foote, editor of *Freethinker*, for blasphemy, and spent the time explaining to Webb why 'ridicule is quite a legitimate weapon' in the battle against religion. 'We think the Christian religion an immoral illusion, and we wish to use any argument to persuade the people that it is false. Ridicule appeals to the people we have to deal with [the working class], with much greater force than any amount of serious logical argument. We want to make them disregard the mythical next world and live for this world'.[102] The idea that the best way to change people's belief was to ridicule them out of it was a

curious one, and would have deleterious consequences in the next century when it failed to work. But it highlights, in this instance, how there were militant atheists for whom positivism, ethical unions and even rationalism were a cop-out.

That angry atheism had subsided a little in the third quarter of the century after the final demise of Owenism and during a generation of comparative economic growth and security. It was never entirely extinguished, however, most of its fury seemingly concentrated into the large and robust frame of Charles Bradlaugh.

We have observed several times in this tale that earnest atheists – and indeed, many of the gentle, melancholic Victorian ones – were often the children of clergy. Bradlaugh was not, but he was nonetheless a religious youth. Born in Hoxton, east London, in 1833, he was an eager Sunday school teacher at St Peter's in Hackney until the point when, while preparing himself for confirmation, he asked the incumbent about some discrepancies within the 39 Articles. The vicar duly complained to Bradlaugh's father about his son's atheistical tendencies and had him suspended. Bradlaugh left St Peter's, and then church altogether, preferring to spend his Sundays listening to freethought lectures. Poverty forced him to enlist, but when a family legacy permitted him to purchase his release, he trained as a legal clerk, picking up skills and knowledge of the law that were to prove useful.

Bradlaugh had started out on the secular lecturing circuit in his late teens, earning the respect of other radicals for his brilliant oratorical skills, his imposing presence and genuine courage. Nicknamed 'Iconoclast' for his forensic and often hyperbolic attacks on Christianity and the Bible, in which he drew on his Sunday school knowledge, he became leader of what was still then a numerically tiny movement after George Holyoake had a nervous collapse in the early 1860s.

The atheist movement had long been marked by petty, and sometimes more significant disputes. George Holyoake had disagreed with Robert Cooper and Charles Southwell over whether it was better to be respectable or radical, and Bradlaugh now disagreed with Holyoake over whether secularism necessitated atheism. The two debated under the title 'Is Secularism Atheism?' in 1870. Holyoake argued that the two were not synonymous and although Bradlaugh recognized that some secularists were not atheist, he contended, with typical force, that 'the logical consequence of the acceptance of secularism must be that the man gets to Atheism if he had brains enough to comprehend'.[103]

Holyoake was the elder statesman of the debate but it was clear that Bradlaugh held the whip hand. It was he who had founded the National Secular Society in 1866, and he who would dominate it for the next 25 years, his annual re-election a mere formality. It was his public atheism and desire for open warfare that would shape the secular movement in the last quarter of the century.

Bradlaugh's arguments were not new and were marked by the exaggerations of a good orator. At the heart of his objection to Christianity, was that it required submission to authority. There were, he argued, two possible intellectual positions in life: 'One, the completest submission of the intellect to authority: to some book, or church, or man. The other, the most thorough assertion of the right and duty of individual thought and judgement.'[104] There was no compromise between the two. Those who felt 'the promotion of Human improvement and Happiness' was mankind's 'highest duty' had only one option they could choose.

As this reasoning suggests, it was less his arguments than the force of his personality that marked out Bradlaugh. As late as 1867, the courts could hold that a contract to let a room to the Secular Society for the purposes of a lecture impugning the character and teachings of Jesus Christ was invalid.[105] George Foote, who set up a separate British Secular Union in 1877, in reaction to Bradlaugh's authoritarian style, was imprisoned for blasphemy in 1881 for his short-lived journal *Freethinker*, the sentence about which Eleanor Marx had been so cross. Until the 1870s secular speakers could expect to be stoned in public. Atheists may not have suffered the way Holyoake had once done, but they remained legally and politically unequal.

It was this that fired Bradlaugh's rage and it was this that came to a head in 1880 when he stood and was elected as MP for Northampton. At first he refused to take the oath of allegiance, asking instead to make a solemn affirmation, as he might in court, as he objected to the Oath's religious content. When, however, he changed his mind, the Commons changed its and he wasn't permitted to take the Oath or his seat.

Public opinion ran high on both sides of the debate, anti-atheist anger stoked by much hysterical Christian indignation. Six years, eight lawsuits, and four re-elections later, Bradlaugh finally assumed his seat. Not surprisingly, interest in the secular movement peaked in the 1880s and membership reached around 4,000, roughly where it stands today. Almost all were men. Debates would attract crowds but many came simply for the show. Membership was often temporary. People joined in a state of fury at some injustice – often the realization that the atheist was not a full citizen. However, once the situation changed, they tended to calm down a bit and found the political or legal situation less egregious than they had imagined. One secular leader once remarked that secular societies were like Turkish baths: good to pass through but not to live in.

The historian Owen Chadwick once remarked that the 1880s was the closest Britain ever came to seeing the working classes go secularist and anti-Christian.[106] Unlike France and Russia, however, they never did, largely because the nation was willing to accommodate heartfelt atheism, like Bradlaugh's, within its structures. Once Bradlaugh had taken his seat, everyone rapidly forgot what the fuss was about, and Parliament passed a new Oaths Act, allowing MPs to affirm rather than swear. In Chadwick's words, 'the old Christian state was dismantled by Christians for the sake of keeping the people Christian'.[107] It worked, at least for a time.

Problems

Nietzsche's dead god

'Casting its first shadow': Nietzsche's early atheism

'If I wage war against Christianity,' Friedrich Nietzsche wrote in his autobiographical text *Ecce Homo*, 'I am the right person to do so, since it never caused me any great misfortune or constricted my life'.[1] *Ecce Homo* was written on the verge of insanity and is marked by moments of delusion. In this instance, however, Nietzsche seems to have been broadly right. 'Throughout our childhood,' his sister Elizabeth once remarked, 'Christianity and religion never seemed to contain any element of restraint'.[2]

Nietzsche's father was a respected Lutheran pastor who died when his son was five. Devout as a child, the philosopher had once planned to enter the priesthood, but he lost his religion in his teenage years in what was a textbook manner for the time. A spirit of adolescent rebellion passed into a more considered analysis of the origins of religion, aided by his skill as a philologist. Strauss' *Life of Jesus* eroded what was left of his beliefs, and by the time he was 20 Nietzsche had abandoned God altogether.

It was not, at the time, a gleeful rejection. 'How could we, armed with the result of mere adolescent broodings, annihilate the authority of two thousand years and the testimony of the greatest minds?' he once asked some school friends rhetorically.[3] Nor was it, in retrospect, a light decision. Perhaps because his childhood faith had been sincere, Nietzsche was never under any illusion about the enormity of what he – and Europe, he believed – was doing. 'The greatest recent event – that "God is dead"; that belief in the Christian God has become unbelievable – is already casting its first shadow over Europe'.[4] With these words Nietzsche became the author of one of the few atheistic aphorisms to compete with Marx's 'opium of the people', although the tone, and expectation, of the two sentiments could not be more different. Whereas Marx saw a new Jerusalem, ascending from the proletarian ground rather than descending from heaven, Nietzsche saw the ruins of a civilization. '[Very few have grasped] how much must collapse because it was built on this faith ... our entire European morality ... [few have grasped] the long dense succession of demolition, destruction, downfall, upheaval that now stands ahead'.[5]

Having abandoned his childhood faith, Nietzsche spent much of the rest of his life wandering, both intellectually and, after resigning his academic post in Basel, physically. He discovered Arthur Schopenhauer in 1865, which was a near religious experience itself. 'I saw a mirror in which I espied the whole world, life, and my own mind depicted in frightful grandeur'.[6] Schopenhauer, who had died five years earlier, was another atheist of independent means and independent mind. His 'gloomy genius', as Nietzsche termed it, saw life as suffering, privation and boredom for which only aesthetic or ascetic practice offered an anaesthetic. Nietzsche was taken with Schopenhauer's atheism, his view of the world and his attempted response.

Nietzsche later embraced positivist ideas and although he would describe Auguste Comte as a great Frenchman beside whom the Germans and English had placed no rival, he was less captivated by the prospect of a humanist religion than by its underlying naturalism, which rejected 'all metaphysical mystification of truth and simplicity'.[7]

In this regard he was typical of his time. Full-blown, baroque positivism never caught on in Germany, but materialist ideas were commonplace within German scientific thought at the time (not that Nietzsche ever really had anything approaching a scientific education himself). Figures like Ernst Haeckel, Darwin's foremost German disciple; Karl Vogt, a professor of zoology and geology;

Friedrich Büchner, whose 1855 publication *Force and Matter* turned him into the pope of scientific materialism; and Jakob Moleschott, lecturer in physiology at Heidelberg – who summed up his thinking in the phrase 'no thought without phosphorous' – planted late nineteenth-century German thought in uncompromisingly materialist territory. In the process, they upset the national stereotype of the German intellectual who was able to read idealism into anything. 'Accustomed to deride Germans for imagining matter not to exist, [contemporary Europeans] were astonished to find Germans who maintained that mind did not exist.'[8]

According to Vogt and his ilk, science had proved the world was nothing more than matter. 'With the most absolute truth and with the greatest scientific accuracy we can say at this day: there is nothing miraculous in the world', Büchner confidently wrote in *Force and Matter*.[9] Matter was eternal, creation impossible. The universe was blind, governed by unalterable law and necessity. Humans were no exception. 'Thoughts come out of the brain as gall from the liver, or urine from the kidneys,' Vogt wrote.[10] 'It used to be said *In the beginning God*,' Feuerbach said reviewing Moleschott. 'Now it is said *In the beginning the belly* ... man is what he eats.'[11] Such beliefs allowed the atheist materialists to dispose of antiquated Christian frivolities such as spirit and soul, God and religion – a disposal that was aided by their robust anti-clericalism – but it also invited the rejection of some of Christianity's other, more troubling, claims, such as free will or the equality of all humans.

The rejection was found liberating. Büchner, writing in *Force and Matter*, captured the way that atheism was experienced as the ultimate rejection of authority. 'Not as the humble and submissive slave of a supernatural master, nor as the helpless toy in the hands of heavenly powers, but as a proud and free son of Nature, understanding her laws and knowing how to tutor them to his own use, does the creature of modern civilisation, the Freethinker, appear'.[12] Owen Chadwick once observed of this German scientific materialism that 'nothing represents better that temporary phase of popular philosophy which combined the contradiction of lowering man to the dust by showing him to be nothing but another animal, while lifting him to the skies and singing his praises as the ruler of the world'.[13] It was a sage observation, except for the word 'temporary'.

'We believe in Olympus – and not in the crucified': An honest revaluation

This flat rejection of supernaturalism underpinned Nietzsche's atheism but it did not dominate it. For a time, when he passed out of his positivistic phase, he discovered Spinoza. He was ecstatic, writing to his friend Franz Overbeck, 'I have a forerunner! ... he denies freedom of the will, purpose, a moral order to the world, the unegoistic evil'.[14]

More important than Schopenhauer or Comte or Spinoza, though, was Richard Wagner under whose spell Nietzsche fell in his 20s. At the time, Wagner's views on Christianity were similar to Nietzsche's own, seeing in it something that had turned earthly life into a 'loathsome dungeon' and left Europeans the legacy of self-contempt.[15] For all of Christianity's failings however, it had at least provided Europe with a myth and sense of cultural unity, the absence of which was resulting in the decay of modern society. Nietzsche was, for some years, a keen advocate of Wagner's attempts to re-articulate a new, quasi-religious myth for Europe. In time he would drift, bitterly, away from the great composer's circle but he never lost the sense that Europe needed a new religion, albeit one shorn of God and the supernatural.

In this too, Nietzsche was a man of his age. The need to shore up or replace the corroded Christian foundations of society pressed upon many later nineteenth-century thinkers. Yet, the way Nietzsche proposed to do this marked him as different, his atheistic vision being at least as much problem as it was promise.

Appointed professor of classical philology at Basel in 1869, Nietzsche became colleagues with another intellectual hero, the historian Jacob Burckhardt, one of the few major historians of the time to reject the Hegelian idea that history was an ever upwards triumph of reason, truth and justice. History, Burckhardt argued, was not the same as progress.

Nietzsche sympathized. He was already convinced that the transition from the classical world to Christianity (note, not to *Christendom* but to Christianity itself) had been a terrible loss and a step backwards. But that did not mean he thought the (essentially Christian) promise of a peaceful, redeemed future was any more credible once secularized. 'These days,' he wrote in *Beyond Good and Evil*, 'people everywhere are lost in rapturous enthusiasms, even in scientific disguise about a future state of society where 'the exploitative character' will fall away ... to my ears that sounds as if someone is promising to invent a life that dispenses with all organic functions.'[16]

It was not so much *that* Europe had lost something in the transition from classical to Christian worlds that marked Nietzsche out as the most original and honest atheist of his time, however. European intellectuals had mourned the passing of classical culture since the fourteenth century. It was *what* it had lost, and what should be done about it.

Nietzsche's anti-Christian rhetoric began early and grew in intensity until, by the time he went mad, it had become an overpowering obsession. By making eternity and the supernatural world the focus of life, Christianity had de-divinized earthly existence, leeching from it the vigour and grandeur that were properly its. The Christian God had destroyed natural virtues of antiquity and in their place burdened the heart with fear and guilt.

In themselves, these were not entirely novel attacks. The idea that Christianity denied this life by celebrating another had been one of the most consistent lines of atheistic attack since the seventeenth century. Nietzsche differed, however, in locating the problem with the Christian *ethics* that had replaced those of antiquity.

Pity, compassion, charity, sympathy: these Christian virtues comprised what Nietzsche called 'slave morality'. The term was contemptuous but also descriptive. According to Nietzsche, the historical origins of this slave morality could be traced beyond Christianity to slavery itself, specifically to the enslavement of the Jews in Babylon 500 years earlier. Having once been sovereign and belligerent, the Jews had found themselves conquered, captured and powerless to challenge their captors in any of the obvious ways. In response, through priestly cunning, they abandoned their more violent god of earlier ages, and worked out a deliberate act of revenge by which they might take power once again. By revaluing basic human values – so powerlessness became humility, impotence goodness, cowardice friendliness – they turned the tables, enervating their oppressors and elevating themselves.

This morality, designed by slaves to emasculate their masters, was adopted and adapted by early Christians, especially in their attribution of equality and free will to all. The former treated the weak as if they were of equal worth as the strong, thereby denigrating life's successes and honouring its failures. The latter burdened the powerful with responsibility and guilt for their acts of oppression, while enabling the weak to represent their weakness as accomplishment, a freely chosen virtue meriting respect, rather than an inadequacy over which they had no choice. The crucifixion was the masterstroke in all this, locating triumph in failure, and placing all men for ever in God's debt. Christianity then spread not due to any genuine moral worth, still less on account of its inherent truth, but through a mixture of fear and guilt, an 'epidemic of panic' about the end of the world, terrifying threats of judgement and eternal damnation, combined with a healthy dose of voluntary martyrdom to make the point.

If the consequent Christian ethics were still honoured by European civilization, it was simply because that civilization had been so corrupted by the Christian God it was now incapable of seeing the world aright. If it could, it would realize that Christianity 'skew[ed] everything self-glorifying, manly, conquering, autocratic, every instinct that belongs to the highest and best-formed type of "human.""[17] It would recognize that pity and compassion were not virtues but causes of suffering, injuring pride and generating resentment among demeaned recipients, contaminating the moral health of those who pitied them, infecting them with a sympathy that led to weakness and death. It would understand that charity was ultimately self-defeating, merely preserving 'too much of what should have perished'.[18]

It fell to Nietzsche to reveal this to contemporaries, to be the one to re-value the world, sweeping away the decaying detritus of Christianity and replacing other-focused slave morality with self-focused master morality. This was where his concept of the will to power came into play. The idea, with its roots sunk somewhere in Darwinism, was that every organism, including human, was driven by an ineradicable lust for strength and supremacy. This was more than mere survival. 'Life itself is essentially a process of appropriating, injuring, overpowering the alien and the weaker, oppressing, being harsh, imposing your own form, incorporating, and, at least, at the very least, exploiting'.[19]

Nietzsche wrote to shock, scandalizing his mother and sister, whose small-minded piety he despised, and upsetting 'the darling "idealists"' who 'wax lyrical about the good, the true and the beautiful'[20] without ever facing up to the fact that the world simply wasn't built that way. In the eternal battle between 'is' and 'ought', Nietzsche sought to show that it was the latter that must conform to the former, rather than the other way around. The future belonged to strength, to self-discipline, to courage, to the will to power, to the Superman, the goal to which humanity was pressing forward.

This was not necessarily selfish in the individualistic sense of the word. However far he drifted from him personally, Nietzsche never abandoned Wagner's sense that civilization needed a new religion to bind society together. Having announced the death of God, the madman in *The Gay Science* asks frantically what festivals and games are necessary to atone for the murder. 'Must we ourselves not become gods simply to appear worthy of it?'[21] The future was religious, just resolutely natural and material, free from any taint of Christianity, its God, or its ethics.

Nietzsche never lost the sense, dominant since his youth, that it was ancient Greece that offered the most fertile model of myth, social unity, natural passion, honest joy and liberation from shame that was needed. The classical world had not sought, unlike naïve Christianity, to eradicate the cruel and violent from human nature, but instead had sublimated it into art, festivals and realistic ethics. The future lay with new rulers, not unlike Plato's philosopher kings, who could lead the people forward to a future that was true to human nature as it was, not as pious idealists imagined it should be. 'We believe in Olympus – and *not* in the crucified.'[22]

Nietzsche was sure that there was no God and if anyone could lay claim to being atheism's prophet it was this eccentric, peripatetic German philologist. Towards the end of the 1880s, he became more egocentric and unhinged, seeing himself as the man who marked a watershed for the West, splitting history in two, ridding Europe of its enervating Christian commitments and effecting the revaluation of values that civilization so badly needed. He came to style himself as the Antichrist, boasting, in a letter to his sister in 1885, 'I find the founder of Christendom superficial in comparison with myself'.[23] The violence of his anti-Christian atheism became concentrated in ever more outrageous and gratuitous sentiments of this kind.

Yet, his sense of a new atheistic dawn remained a constant. Nearly a decade before he went mad he had written that 'there are today among the various nations of Europe perhaps ten to 20 million people who no longer 'believe in God ... [they should] *give a sign* to one another ... they will at once constitute a power in Europe'.[24]

Many other, less original atheists, looked forward to such a dawn. Nietzsche's difference, and his importance, lay in his realization that metaphysics and morals were inseparable, and that to cling to Christian ethics when the Christian religion was defunct was mere cant. The kind of ethical movement popular in Britain at the time revolted him. It was for this reason that he called George

Eliot a 'little moralistic female'. Thus, in answer to the question that gets dragged out in innumerable debates today on the subject, can you have ethics without Christianity, Nietzsche gave the resounding answer 'Yes!', at the same time making the point that you can't have Christian ethics without Christianity (to which he would have added 'and a good thing too'.)

Towards the end of his book *The Antichrist*, Nietzsche outlined various prospective laws against Christianity, such as all priests were to be either expelled or imprisoned and churches razed. In this he would foreshadow much twentieth century atheism, although the twentieth century's atheistic violence would owe more to *scientific* atheism than to Nietzsche's unique and unflinching mixture of classical virtue and Darwinism. Nevertheless, his unflinching gaze into a future that no longer dwelt in the shadow of Christianity was to prove prophetic.

The first death of British atheism

'Social monks': The failure of popular atheism

Although Britain had no comparably original philosophers at the time, its main atheist players and movements were also suffering a crisis of identity. After the climax of George Foote's imprisonment and Charles Bradlaugh's parliamentary seat in the 1880s, public atheism began to lose momentum in Britain. This was partly due to Bradlaugh himself. The problem was not that he began to have doubts about his rightness – Bradlaugh was not a man given to doubting – but that, since he had obtained his parliamentary seat with considerable support from working-class nonconformists in Northampton, he felt slightly awkward about his continued vilification of the Bible. Instead of outright atheist polemic, he turned his prejudices towards Roman Catholicism, which was more to his non-conformist constituents' taste.

Bradlaugh refused to let British secularism accrete any ritual elements. Some secularists confessed to wanting a secular hymn book, music, rational poetry, ceremonies and even to sneaking back to church or chapel for the occasional fillip. Bradlaugh was unmoved, keeping his energies focused on the legal handicaps that were rapidly disappearing. 'Without such wars with other creeds constantly and persistently maintained,' he reasoned, 'secularism has neither force, nor character, nor purpose as a party. To call it 'a new religion' is misleading. It is not a religion.'[25] Secularism was a military endeavour and it needed an enemy. In reality, Bradlaugh bent the rules a little for himself and did officiate at namings, marriages and funerals but he kept the legalistic, combative focus sharp, and even had the Halifax secularist branch expelled for registering itself as a religious institution.

The wells of indignation were running dry, however. It was now clear that you could sit in parliament or attack the fundamentals of Christianity without fear of prosecution. Outdoor militants could still be arrested for offences, but they were more against public order than Christianity *per se*. Secular societies still met, and new ones sprang up, such as in South Wales in 1903–4 in immediate wake of a religious revival there (a good example of their essential parasitism). Atheists endured the abuse of Anti-Infidel Leagues publishing anti-atheist tracts but gave back as good as they got, turning the debate into something of a bar-room brawl.

What had once been outright persecution was now simply part of a culture of difference of opinion, when different people believed different things with the same passion. When the case of *Bowman v Secular Society* came before the House of Lords in 1917 and it was held that opposition to Christianity was not contrary to, or within the reach of, English law, the battle for legal equality was pretty much over and British secular atheism could no longer whip up much indignation in its cause.

In any case, the battle was changing, theological liberalism redrawing the lines in the last decades of the nineteenth century. One J. Whiteley wrote poignantly in the *Secular Review* in June 1878 that 'it is somewhat painful … when, after a vigorous pounding [by an atheist orator] of the doctrines of literal interpretation, eternal punishment, election and reprobation, forensic views of the atonement, etc., etc., the thought arises that, perhaps for 40 miles around, there is not a single man – not even a single clergyman – who would think of controverting a single word'.[27] The secular atheists found themselves tilting at theological windmills.

More than either the legal or theological changes, however, it was the advent and particular nature of British socialism that did for atheism in early twentieth-century Britain. Within a remarkably brief space of time, socialism went from political invisibility to within a whisper of power. Christians, particularly immigrant Catholics and those from certain non-conformist groups, were in the vanguard of the advance. The Labour Church movement was short-lived but popular, its very presence in catalysing the Labour Party itself indicative of the peculiarly close association between socialism and Christianity in Britain.

Some atheists were supportive, but by no means all. The atheistic bodies of the early Edwardian period largely ignored or refused the socialist movement. Bradlaugh, for example, opposed socialism, and refused to support the Employers' Liability Bill, which cost him and the secular movement much working-class support. Secularists were, according to an article in *Truthseeker*, 'too busy discussing the first chapter of Genesis to hear the cry of the outcast, too absorbed in the edifying pastime of proving the impossibility of the Flood story, to heed the bitter wail of the starving workers'.[28]

The Rationalist movement faced the same criticisms. Convinced that reason held the key to the world's problems, it either adopted no particular political positions or, worse, advocated unrealistic or Panglossian solutions to the woes of the time.

The Ethical movement was worse still. This had at least broken through the all-male membership barrier that marked atheist societies at the time, attracting female and, therefore, family support. However, it refused to engage with the emerging Labour movement, either deaf to working-class needs or convinced that they were to be answered by earnest ethical ritual. The working classes looked down their noses at ethicists for their high-minded theorizing and quasi-religious posturing. They wanted concrete activity, not atheists who posed as 'social monks'.[29] The contrast with, say, the slum priest movement or the tough, explicitly Christian commitments of Keir Hardie (himself brought up as an atheist) was instructive.

In a sense, the atheists had become the victim of their own success. Society had become more secularized over the previous century, not so much culturally as structurally and politically. In 1900, unlike 1800, social problems were less likely to be expressed or discussed in religious or even ethical terms. The problem was not so much sin as unjust structures of power or money. If these were the problems, the solutions were no less social and political and economic. The unwillingness or inability of secular, rationalist or ethical groups to seize socialist solutions cost them, not least when there were so many Christians who had done so. Without an obvious enemy in the field, or a charismatic Holyoake or Bradlaugh to inspire loyalty, atheism lost its social presence. In much the same way as Britain's (moderate) toleration of theological latitude in the eighteenth century had drawn pioneering atheist teeth, the political breadth and generosity of late Victorian and Edwardian British Christianity had the same effect for much of the twentieth century.

'Turbulent, restless, inwardly raging': Russell's doomed search for godless certainty

It was curious that these varieties of public atheism – secular, rationalistic, ethical – lost their social presence in Britain just as atheism was finding a more academic voice. Doubt, sometimes verging on despair, had been the principal characteristic of late Victorian intellectual infidelity, rather than outright, let alone buoyant, atheism. That changed, slightly, in the early decades of the new century as a handful of eminent academics, many clustering around Trinity College, Cambridge, pronounced their outright atheism. Being clever academics, however, this atheism was not necessarily straightforward.

John McTaggart Ellis McTaggart was a fellow at Trinity and a member of the Cambridge Apostles, an exclusive university discussion group. A metaphysician, he was a member of the Rationalist Press Association and open about his disbelief in God. He also, however, firmly believed in the existence of a soul and in immortality, and was a keen defender of the Church of England.

His contemporary, G. E. Moore, was one of the founders of analytic philosophy, and also a fellow at Trinity. Moore too was an atheist and open about it. 'I am an infidel, and do not believe that God exists; and I think the evidence will justify my disbelief,' he wrote in the *International Journal of Ethics*.[30] Openness was not the same as clarity, however. 'Just as I think there is no evidence for his existence,' he continued, 'I think there is also no evidence that he does not exist. I am not an atheist in one sense: I do not deny that God exists … I do not believe that he does exist, but also I do not believe that he does not exist'. It was hard to really get behind such a position.

More influential than either was Bertrand Russell, yet another Trinity academic who was to become an icon of British atheism for much of the twentieth century. Russell's atheism was more straightforward than either Moore's or McTaggart's, but that did not mean it was straightforward. Having lost his mother, father and sister before the age of three, Russell was brought up by his grandparents in an atmosphere that was stifling even by late Victorian standards. He abandoned his grandparents' Christianity early and much of the rest of life, intellectual and personal, was spent in search of certainty. 'Christianity has had its day,' he wrote aged 16. 'We want a new form in accordance with science and yet helpful to a good life.'[31] Human reason would deliver us from evil.

The younger Russell was optimistic about the prospect of this. He imagined 'that the human species would become progressively

more humane, more tolerant, and more enlightened' by means
of 'rational knowledge'.[32] He discovered Euclid early on and, like
Hobbes and Darwin before him, was inspired. Euclid's *Elements*
set him on an arduous search for certainty, for 'a mathematics of
human behaviour as precise as the mathematics of machines'.[33]
Ethics would be based on science, which would be based on
mathematics, which would be based on logic. Certainty was
possible.

This search was as much a personal quest as an academic one.
In 1901, Russell had a quasi-mystical experience when staying with
Alfred and Evelyn Whitehead. He recollected in his *Autobiography*
feeling the 'unendurable … loneliness of the human soul', impen-
etrable to all except 'the highest intensity of the sort of love that
religious teachers have preached'. 'Having for years cared only for
exactness and analysis, I found myself filled with semi-mystical
feelings about beauty … and a desire almost as profound as that of
the Buddha to find some philosophy which should make human
life endurable.'[34]

That philosophy was to be found in the Platonic beauty of
mathematics. In contrast to Nietzsche's distaste for the ideal, Russell
believed that 'all knowledge that is concerned with things that
actually exist [is] of very slight value compared to that knowledge
which, like philosophy and mathematics, is concerned with ideal
and external objects, and is freed from this miserable world which
God has made'.[35] It was in this abstract realm that beauty, truth and
goodness were to be located. Mathematics offered some temporary
relief from the confusing pain of being human.[36]

In the long run the search was not successful, either intellectually
or emotionally. In the first case, 20 years after he and Whitehead
published their monumental *Principia Mathematica*, purportedly
grounding mathematics securely in logic, the Austrian logician
Kurt Gödel conclusively proved not only that they had not done
what they set out to do but, worse, that it could not be done.
Certainty, of the type Russell sought, was impossible.

Emotionally, the project fared little better. 'What Spinoza calls "the intellectual love of God" has seemed to me the best thing to live by,' Russell wrote in his *Autobiography*, 'but I have not had even the somewhat abstract God that Spinoza allowed himself to whom to attach my intellectual love … I am conscious that human affection is to me at bottom an attempt to escape from the vain search for God … I have loved a ghost'.[37]

If this melancholic and frustrated mathematical Platonism was the dominant theme of Russell's atheism, there were many subthemes. Russell's tone, and perhaps his opinions, varied not least when there were women involved. He told Ottoline Morrell, during his affair with her, that he wanted 'to preserve much that belongs with religion'.[38] 'Turbulent, restless, inwardly raging – I shall always be – hungry for your God and blaspheming him … . The longing for religion is at times almost unbearably strong'.[39] He even contemplated writing a spiritual autobiography to show how his raging hostility was aimed not at religion per se but at groundless religion. Similarly, in a letter to Constance Malleson, another lover, he confessed how 'the centre of me is always and eternally a terrible pain … a searching for something beyond what the world contains, something transfigured and infinite – the beatific vision – God'.[40]

If this sounds like a soul in search of God, it is balanced by his eloquent essay, 'A free man's worship', written in 1903, in which he stared into a bleakness of eternal solitude and pointlessness and refused to blink.

That man is the product of causes which had no prevision of the end they were achieving; that his origin, his growth, his hopes and fears, his loves and his beliefs, are but the outcome of accidental collocations of atoms; that no fire, no heroism, no intensity of thought and feeling, can preserve an individual life beyond the grave; that all the labours of the ages, all the devotion, all the inspiration, all the noonday brightness of human genius, are destined to extinction in the vast death of the solar system, and that the whole temple of Man's achievement must inevitably be buried beneath the debris of a universe in ruins – all these things, if not quite beyond dispute, are yet so nearly certain, that no philosophy which rejects them can hope to stand.[41]

If this invited a nihilistic or Nietzschean response, Russell avoided both, saying that the 'worship of force' is really 'the result of failure to maintain our own ideals against a hostile universe'. According to Russell, it was only on 'the firm foundation of unyielding despair' that a truly humane and sympathetic life could be built. He did not, however, elaborate on precisely how unyielding despair provided such a firm foundation. Indeed, in its own way, the essay was simply a cry for help. Russell later admitted that it was a kind of 'message to self', exhorting him to treat better his first wife, Alys, whom he was systematically emotionally abusing at the time.

'Nearly all of it was false': The remarkably rapid fall of an ancient atheistic argument

David Berman concludes his book on the history of atheism in Britain by saying that 1927 was probably the high water mark of British atheism, or at least academic atheism, with Russell, McTaggart and Moore among the most respected philosophers in Britain. This may be so but it fails to give sufficient weight to the still more defiantly atheistic tone that academic philosophy took the following decade.

In 1911, Russell was approached by a brilliant and eccentric Austrian student who wanted to know whether he had any talent for philosophy. He did. The student was Ludwig Wittgenstein, at the time studying engineering at Manchester. Russell was intrigued and exasperated in equal measure. 'My German friend threatens to be an infliction … [he is] obstinate & perverse … very argumentative & tiresome. He wouldn't admit that it was certain that there was not a rhinoceros in the room.'[42] At first, he was dubious about his philosophical merits. 'He is armour-plated against all assaults of reasoning. It really is rather a waste of time talking with him.'[43] In a short time, however, Russell changed his mind, and his protégé came not only to impress but surpass him, redirecting the course of philosophy in the process.

Wittgenstein's own religious beliefs were subtle. Nominally Jewish by family background, he had lost whatever Catholic faith he had at school on reading Schopenhauer but retained a stubborn and sincere fascination with and respect for religious belief throughout his life. He read and nearly memorized Tolstoy's *The Gospel in Brief* during the First World War, recommending it to everyone he met and claiming that it 'kept him alive' by leaving 'undisturbed my inner being'.[44]

He spoke of the bleakness of life if Christ had not been resurrected ('We are ... roofed in, as if were, and cut off from heaven'[45]) and talked of faith in gnomic and intriguing terms: 'Faith is faith in what is needed by my *heart*, my *soul*, not my speculative intelligence. For it is my soul with its passions, as it were with its flesh and blood, that has to be saved not my abstract mind ... . Only *love* can believe the Resurrection.'[46] In the last months of his life, he arranged to meet several times with a non-philosophical Catholic priest, not to return to his childhood Catholicism but to hear about the kind of religious life and practice that made religious ideas and language make sense.

This was many years in the future. When he first met Russell, the great logician considered his student 'more terrible' with the Christians than even he had ever been.[47] Accordingly, when Wittgenstein published his *Tractatus Logico-Philosophicus* (the title deliberately echoed Spinoza's *Tractatus*), after which he retired from philosophy believing its central problems solved, it was taken as the foundation stone for a brusquely atheistic philosophical movement.

Soon after the *Tractatus'* publication, a number of philosophers in Vienna took up ideas from his book and developed them into a self-conscious philosophical movement, for which they even issued a manifesto. This 'Vienna Circle' of logical positivists, as it became known, was resolutely anti-metaphysical. They adopted from Wittgenstein the idea that philosophy did not contribute knowledge about the world so much as clarify statements of what was already, supposedly, known.

Those statements fell into two groups: mathematical claims, which could be tested logically, and scientific ones, those claims about the world that were made through the process of the natural sciences and which could therefore be verified or falsified. All other statements were literally meaningless. In one fell swoop, all religious claims (not to mention most philosophical, aesthetic and ethical ones) were dismissed as nonsense.

The Vienna Circle remained largely closed until its thought was introduced to the Anglo-Saxon philosophical world by the young English philosopher A. J. Ayer. Ayer was interested, indeed almost obsessed, by religion from a young age. His first doubts were made on pragmatic rather than philosophical grounds, but as he came to read Russell, Moore and others they morphed, and by the time he was at Oxford he was not only severe in his atheism – 'I came to the conclusion that if one did believe the world had been created, it was much more plausible that it had been created by the devil than by God'[48] – but also relentless, haranguing tutors with his systematic and relentless demands for irrefutable proof. Ayer was, in the words of his tutor Gilbert Ryle, 'an extremely penetrating, and unsentimental thinker'.[49] 'He liked pros and cons, premises, "fors and againsts", proofs and disproofs; and where none were available, possibly suspension of such conversations'.[50]

Ryle directed his protégé to Wittgenstein, whom he finally met in 1932. Wittgenstein liked disciples and Ayer, discipleship not being in his character, resisted the master's spell. He did, however, travel to Vienna (a trip that doubled up as his honeymoon) and met Moritz Schlick, Professor of Philosophy of Science and the Circle's *de facto* leader who invited him to join them. Ayer embraced and popularized the group's logical positivism in his book *Language, Truth and Logic*, which came out in 1936. In it he argued (or, perhaps, asserted) that, as all religious language was unverifiable, it was all basically nonsense. Because it couldn't be verified one way or the other, the statement 'there is a God' was literally meaningless. In the fashion of Moore's sophisticated self-definition, Ayer rejected the label atheist just as he did theist, as to do otherwise would, in his mind, have been to grant God-talk a legitimacy it didn't have.

This was arguably the apex of British philosophical atheism, the logical (as it were) conclusion of atheist ideas critiquing all forms of God-talk that went back to the seventeenth century. It wasn't so much the final nail in God's coffin as the denial there had been a body to bury in the first place. It was not, however, to last.

In the first place, Wittgenstein, who returned to active philosophy in 1929 having decided he hadn't actually solved it, turned sharply against his former self and made it quite clear the ideas on which the Vienna Circle, Ayer and logical positivism were built were simply wrong. Independent of Wittgenstein's change of direction, logical positivism, triumphant for a while, died a sudden death. Post-war philosophers attacked its basic tenets and although these attacks did nothing to rehabilitate God, they did cut the ground from beneath his over-confident detractors.

The abrupt death of logical positivism marked the end of one of the most significant atheist philosophical traditions, one that was as old as modern European atheism itself. Hobbes, Spinoza, D'Holbach, Naigeon, Bentham and many others not so philosophically inclined had all, in their own way, argued that theology was nonsense, treating the mystical as if it were real, the mythical as if it were material. The decline and fall of this philosophical argument was a blow for atheism. Indeed, given the way the argument had long provided the basis for the more substantive attack on spiritual power – religion was wicked because corrupt priests based their power on mythical claims about God and the soul – it was a deeper wound than the merely philosophical.

Ayer himself was naturally reluctant to recognize the demise but even he finally acknowledged what was, by the end of his philosophical career, obvious. When asked by philosopher Bryan Magee in mid-1970s what he now thought were the defects of logical positivism, he admitted, 'Well, I suppose the most important defect was that nearly all of it was false.'[51]

The kingdom of godlessness is at hand

'We ought to deliver a lesson': Preparing for a godless society
On Sunday 9 January 1905 Father Georgy Gapon marched at the head of 150,000 hymn-singing workers to submit a Humble and Loyal Petition to the Tsar at the Winter Palace in St Petersburg. Imperial soldiers blocked their way and fired two warning volleys into the air. The workers continued to advance. The soldiers fired on the crowd and charged. Two hundred workers were killed, many more wounded. Father Gapon survived. 'There is no God any longer,' he later said. 'There is no Tsar.'[52]

The series of rebellions that seized the Russian Empire in 1905 shook both throne and altar but changed little. The Orthodox Church had, in fact, been undergoing reforms for several decades. Father Gapon had received serious, if tacit, support from church authorities, and the 'God-seekers', a loose movement of Russian intellectuals who sought spiritual and religious renewal, had made some headway against the atheism and materialism that was, by the late nineteenth century, the received wisdom among the Russian intelligentsia. The bonds linking political and religious authority remained painfully tight, however. On the eve of the revolution, the Orthodox Church in Russia claimed the allegiance of 100 million believers and boasted 100,000 clergy, 40,000 parish churches, 130 bishops and 67 dioceses. 'If Russia is not your mother, God cannot be your father,' claimed Metropolitan Ioann of St Petersburg.[53]

Orthodoxy's dominance was not complete. Baptists had been present in Russia from the mid-nineteenth century, Pentecostals from around 1910, and there had long been many Muslims and some Buddhists living further east. And across the nation, especially in rural and remote areas, Orthodoxy blended with agricultural pagan cults. Yet it was Orthodoxy that soaked Russian society, from Tsar to peasant, and it was the Orthodox Church that was the threat, to politics, to progress and to the people.

That, at least, was the view of the Revolution's leaders. Vladimir Lenin's atheism was both complex and straightforward. He admired Russia's indigenous radical tradition and in particular Nikolai Chernyshevsky, whose novel *What is to be Done?* helped him define the direction in his life. He spoke highly of the eighteenth-century philosophical materialists and wrote of the need to republish and translate their work. Feuerbach and Marx both strengthened and steered his opinions, not least his belief that God and socialism were totally incompatible: he was disgusted by his experience of English Christian Socialists when in London in 1902. He inherited from all of the above a healthy contempt for religiosity, viewing divine worship as a kind of 'necrophilia' and faith as a kind of virus. 'Any religious idea, any idea of any God at all, any flirtation even with a God is the most inexpressible foulness ... the most dangerous foulness, the most shameful "infection."'[54]

And yet, for all these intellectual forebears, Lenin simply knew God didn't exist and that religion was the root of all evil. He confessed to being an atheist by the age of 16, long before he had read Feuerbach or Marx. His passion sprang from a visceral loathing of the Tsarist state's Orthodox foundations. Religion was simply not a theoretical issue for him. The only relevant question was what could be done to aid its inevitable demise.

His answers to this were cut to fit his audience. To working men he could say that the 'deepest root' of religion was 'the socially downtrodden condition of the working masses and their apparently complete helplessness in face of the blind forces of capitalism'; the solution therefore being the overpowering of capitalism. To the first All-Russian Congress of Working Women in November 1918 he would reason that the 'deepest source of religious prejudice is poverty and ignorance', which made 'propaganda and education' the requisite tactic albeit one deployed 'extremely careful[ly]' so as not to arouse 'popular resentment'.[55] When dealing with the irremediably religious, such as during the show trials of various Orthodox bishops and priests in the early 1920s, he could be more direct. 'The greater the number of representatives of reactionary clergy ... we succeed in shooting, the better. It is precisely now that we ought to deliver a lesson to this public so that they won't dare even think about resistance for several decades.'[56]

Josef Stalin's atheism was more interesting, if only because he had known Orthodoxy from the inside. A devout youth, he was the best reader of psalms in his church and was presented by his school with a Psalter 'for excellent progress, behaviour and excellent recitation and singing'. 'He not only performed the rites but always reminded us of their significance,' said a fellow pupil.[57]

Naturally, Stalin saw the priesthood as his vocation, not least as a means of helping the poor, but under the influence of friends – most of whom were priests' sons – he began to question his vocation and then his faith. The more he read, the more his piety wavered, Darwin having a particular effect on him. His doubts pursued him until, at the age of 14, when lying around with friends talking about the injustice of rich and poor he shocked them by declaring 'God's not unjust, he doesn't actually exist. We've been deceived. If God existed, he'd have made the world more just.'[58]

Unfortunately, the realization came too late to stop him from entering the seminary in Tiflis, a cosmopolitan city rich in unorthodox ideas. While there, he soon moved from atheism to outright rebellion, reading banned books, including Marx, Ernest Renan's *Life of Christ*, and, of course, Chernyshevsky's *What is to be Done?* Eventually and inevitably, he was expelled but he retained a fascination with priests and the power of faith, and appropriated much religious language and imagery for his Bolshevism.

At first, good Marxists that they were, the Bolshevik leaders believed that belief in God would disappear naturally. As Marx had taught, once the revolution had come, man would no longer be alienated and his apparent need for God would vanish. If this weren't enough, science would do the trick. Nikolai Bukharin spoke for many when he said that scientific knowledge 'slowly but surely undermines the authority of all religions'.[59] That recognized, the Orthodox Church was still vast, rich and powerful. The inexorable progress of history would do for God, but that didn't mean his enormous, rotten, tottering structure of ecclesiastical control and reaction couldn't do with a few good kicks.

Shortly after the Revolution, the Bolsheviks moved to separate the Church from the State, passing the innocuous sounding 'Decree on the Freedom of Conscience and on Church and Religious Associations' which appeared to guarantee freedom of both religion and irreligion. Church property was expropriated, including over 2.3 million acres of monastery and convent lands. Clergy were effectively classified as second-class citizens, 'servants of the bourgeosie' in the 1918 Constitution, and had all financial support withdrawn. Church-run schools were transferred to the Commissariat of Enlightenment. Religious instruction of the young was forbidden outside the home and then, three years later, inside it too. Atheistic violence was *ad hoc* and relatively limited at this stage – limited to graffiti on churches, defacing statues and gouging the gems out of sacred objects – although, five years in, over 2,500 priests, 1,900 monks, and 3,000 nuns had been executed.

By this time, official attitudes were beginning to change. On the one hand, re-establishment of diplomatic relationships with Western powers brought pressure to ease attacks on the church. On the other, it was becoming increasingly clear that tactics were not working. The church was massively weakened but belief still persisted. Even some party members were found still to be observing Orthodox rites in secret. 'We have separated the church from the state, but we have not yet separated the people from religion.'[60]

'Religion is poison: protect your children': The militant godless
The result was a move away from violence, for the time being, and
towards a massive outpouring of atheistic propaganda. A resolution
at the 12th Party Congress in April 1923 stated that although
religion would collapse when the economic restructuring of society
had finally been completed, in the meantime the Party required
'intensified, systematic propaganda, graphically and convincingly
revealing to every worker and peasant the lie and contradiction to
his interests of any religion'.[61]

The Godless, an atheist newspaper, had been published from
1922, and over the next five years atheist publishing houses printed
over 1.5 million books and pamphlets. By 1926, there were 68
anti-religious seminaries operating. The Communist Party, the
Komsomol or Young Communist League, trade unions, Red Army,
and schools all indulged in anti-religious propaganda, but it was the
Soviet League of the Militant Godless, established in 1925, ostensibly independent from the Party but in reality closely connected to
it, under which the greatest atheist effort was co-ordinated.

Soviet historians later in the century liked to claim the League's
popularity – and it was popular: by 1932 it had 5.5 million members
– was spontaneous and organic, and evidence of the people's thirst
for godlessness. In reality, it was none of the above. More than half
the members came from the party, which managed and subsidized
its activity. In the words of Daniel Peris, who has charted its history,
the League 'was largely a house of cards – a nationwide Potemkin
village of atheism'.[62]

Orchestrated as it was, the League was still powerful and, in some
ways, successful. It arranged demonstrations, delivered lectures,
established discussion circles, put on evenings and plays, set up
'godless corners', and pinned up (atheist) newspapers in public
places. It choreographed public meetings to press for the closure of
churches and the seizure of their bells for industrialization. It set
anti-religious museums in local history buildings, especially former
churches.

The League deployed a range of messages – political, scientific, anti-theological, anti-clerical, anti-ecclesiastical – which it tailored depending on whether it was targeting educated or illiterate, young or old, rural or urban. The 1924 Congress, for example, decreed that anti-religious propaganda in the countryside should consist primarily of materialist explanations of phenomena of nature and social life. Elsewhere, the argument that belief in God was an exploitative force or that religious leaders were counter-revolutionaries was more powerful.

Tapping into an existing seam of anti-clericalism, it portrayed priests as parasites. There were pictures of clerics as vermin tunnelling under newly electrified Soviet villages. There were reported dialogues, a tactic once popular among Christian apologists, in which priests finally confessed, 'Yes, brothers, the Party secretary has spoken truth. I admit I have deceived you.'[63] There were similar stories of peasants who, having once doubted, fell on their knees and exclaimed 'electricity totally destroyed my faith in God'.[64]

Propaganda made heavy use of ridicule. Aware that religiosity was a disproportionately female phenomenon, propagandists capitalized. In one reasonably typical story, a husband wished to remove the icon from the family apartment only to be refused by his pious wife. One night when the household was asleep he binned it. The following morning, when his wife awoke and asked where it was, he told her, 'It's very likely a miracle. It disappeared on its own, as if it never existed.' His wife, duly convinced, converted, took their daughter to a public lecture on atheism that night and never spoke of icons again.

Campaigns targeted Christmas and Easter in particular, pointing out the pagan origins of such festivals. There were stories of villages that held bonfires of icons and then miraculously prospered in their agricultural production, of saints whose supposedly incorruptible bodies were exhumed only to be revealed as rotting cadavers. Visual imagery was popular for illiterate circles but printed work was also used among them, as peasants often were thought to believe that if something were printed it was by nature true, even sacred. Slogans were short and punchy: 'Science instead of religion'; 'Destroying religion, we say: study science'; 'Religion is poison: protect your children'; 'Terrorists in Cassocks'; 'We want to sweep away everything that claims to be super-natural … '; 'Without God, our affairs are much better'.

The League's activities were not wholly negative. It sought to replace belief in God as well as undermine it. Churchgoing was made as practically difficult as possible, such as by 'encouraging' work on Sundays. People were encouraged to replace religious with secular holidays. Church rituals were replaced with atheist ones, like the 'Octobering' naming ceremony, 'red weddings', and 'civilian funerals'. None of these was ever very popular. Icon corners in houses were replaced by godless or Lenin corners. The image of the new man and woman, *Homo sovieticus* – strong, educated, knowl-edgeable, hard-working, loyal, atheist – was relentlessly broadcast.

Taking their cue from the God-Seekers, a number of leading figures, headed by Anatoly Lunacharsky and Maxim Gorky, sought to invest Marxism with a religious aura. This so-called 'God-building' was to have the full trappings of a socialist religion. After Feuerbach, it was man, in all his glorious, humane, rational, creative potential who was to be the object of worship. After Comte, that worship was to satisfy the emotional, ritual, communal and aesthetic demands that traditional religion so slaked. After Nietzsche, the ultimate goal was to be realized in the superman.

The God-builders would create secular saints, 'examples worthy of being followed by the generations of the future'.[65] Lunacharsky wished to change the commandment to love God above all else into, 'You must love and deify matter above everything else, [love and deify] the corporal nature or the life of your body as the primary cause of things, as existence without a beginning or end, which has been and forever will be'.[66]

Lenin was not impressed. God-building, he believed, was simply an unnecessary and narcissistic flirtation with superstition and obscurantism, an exercise in sugar-coating the poison. God, however rationalized, was a delusion: religion, however dressed up, a sickness. 'The Catholic priest who seduces young girls,' he wrote, 'is far less dangerous ... than a priest without a frock, a priest without a coarse religion, a democratic priest with ideas, who preaches the building and creating of god'.[67] The idea was dropped.

By 1929, when it became clear that even the heroic propaganda of the Soviet League of the Militant Godless had not managed to eradicate belief in God, tactics changed once again. School curricula became officially anti- rather than non-religious. Churches were closed by the thousand, and clergy selected for particular persecution, first forbidden to reside in cities, then singled out as counter-revolutionary threats during the collectivization and dekulakization.[68] The League died a slow death as these more severe measures to build an atheist society did their work.

Having boasted around 54,000 churches, chapels and monasteries on the eve of the Revolution, Orthodox churches and communities could be numbered in their hundreds by 1940. By then, 25 regions had been designated completely churchless. Popular belief is harder to assess, but there is good evidence that, after a quarter of a century of atheistic legislation, propaganda and persecution, belief in God was a waning, fragile and, above all, private thing.

Germany, Britain, France, America: Mid-century

'The most horrible institution imaginable': Reductio ad hitlerum
It was a mark of the sharp downturn in rhetoric between atheists and believers during the New Atheist phenomenon in the early twenty-first century that the Nazis got involved.

In the red corner, there was Richard Dawkins, according to whom Hitler's anti-Semitism 'owed a lot to his having renounced Roman Catholicism'.[69] In the blue, there was Pope Benedict XVI who, in a speech before Queen Elizabeth II, nearly a decade later,

on his state visit to Britain, praised Britain for having coura-
geously withstood 'a Nazi tyranny that wished to eradicate God
from society', which he later termed 'the atheist extremism of the
twentieth century'.[70] The red corner was a little bit upset about
this and Dawkins quickly gave a speech in which he repeated the
idea that 'Hitler was a Roman Catholic', qualifying it by saying 'he
was as much a Roman Catholic as the 5 million so-called Roman
Catholics in this country today'. Some people thought they had
heard Dawkins compare ordinary Catholics with the Nazi leader,
quite erroneously.[71]

Unfortunately for the leading protagonists in this angry debate,
neither has much evidence to support him. Nazism has sadly
little part to play in the history of atheism. Dawkins' (and others')
argument rests almost entirely on the idea that Hitler's various
speeches and public remarks about religion were wholly truthful
and earnest, neither virtues for which he is renowned.

In reality, Hitler was a shallow and opportunistic thinker, willing
to play on hopes and fears of anyone as it was useful, including
Christian ones.[72] During the 1920s, when he needed to smooth his
path to power, Hitler would draw on passages from the Lutheran
Bible, and made great play of the fact he was restoring Protestant
morality to a people who had drifted from it during the corruption
of the Weimar years, and who were now threatened by godless
atheism to the east. 'I am personally convinced of the great power
and deep significance of Christianity,' he said in 1933, the year in
which his party made much of the 450th anniversary of Martin
Luther's birth.[73] German Christians, or at least the majority of them,
welcomed him as an earthly saviour.

In reality, his view of Christianity was as contemptuous as it
was of any view that differed in any way from his own. In true
Nietzschean style he thought that the coming of Christianity was
the 'heaviest blow that ever struck humanity',[74] that the early church
was 'whole-hearted Bolshevism, under a tinsel of metaphysics',[75]
and that Catholic dogma was a ridiculous superstition: 'a negro

with his tabus is crushingly superior to the human being who seriously believes in Transubstantiation'.[76] In early 1937 he declared that 'Christianity was ripe for destruction' and railed against any compromise with 'the most horrible institution imaginable'.[77]

His real beliefs were a mess of nationalism, paganism, social Darwinism and providentialism, locating in the German people and himself a sacred destiny of cleansing and redemption. In Michael Burleigh's words, Hitler 'subscribed to the view that science has largely supplanted Christianity, without rationalism eradicating the need for belief, or undermining the existence of a creator God in whom he continued to believe'.[78] He was, in short, neither an atheist, nor the Catholic of atheist polemic. As usual, the *reductio ad hitlerum* is absurd.

'The Christian contribution to our civilisation': British patriotism
That recognized, neither Hitler nor the Nazi co-option of Christianity is entirely irrelevant to the story of atheism, their impact being largely indirect. In the Soviet Union, as we shall see below, the German invasion precipitated a thaw in state atheism. Stalin loosened the noose around Orthodoxy and drew on its support in the war effort, thereby allowing a short break in the story of atheist repression in Russia.

The impact in Britain was subtler. Winston Churchill was no practising Christian but he knew his Bible and drew on it for his rhetoric of defending Christian civilization. He was not alone. Stanley Baldwin, three times Prime Minister in the interwar years, said in 1934 that 'if freedom has to be abolished and room has to be made for the slave state, Christianity must go because slavery and Christianity cannot live together'.[79] Lord Halifax published a selection of his speeches and broadcasts in August 1940, which sounded a similar note. Arnold Toynbee lectured in the Sheldonian Theatre at Oxford on *Christianity and Civilisation* in May 1940. *The Times* visited the subject in several editorials during the year. The Ministry of Information told its Religious Division to impart 'a real conviction of the Christian contribution to our civilisation and of the essential anti-Christian character of Nazism'.[80]

In this way, the Nazis helped forge a British identity which was (albeit temporarily) self-consciously Christian, or at least providential in the way that American identity had long been. This was not to say that atheism was necessarily un-British. On the contrary, the liberty for which the British knew themselves to be fighting was precisely the liberty to choose one's own personal, as well as political, destiny. Nevertheless, the rhetoric and sentiments did tilt the cultural ground beneath people's feet, as did the experience of war itself, with all its fears and experience of death, and atheism, never a mainstream view, remained a minority pursuit. War Office statistics from 1943, showed that of the 2,476,956 men and women in the army a total of 1,486, or 0.06 per cent, professed to be atheists.[81]

'Atheist humanism was bound to end in bankruptcy': Man dies with God in France

The Nazis had a still different impact in France, where the experience of war precluded any sense of providentialism and instead steered atheist thinkers in an altogether more sober direction, one in which many French intellectuals had been heading before the war.[82] The carnage of the First World War, enabled by technology and associated with modernity, the ensuing uncertainty and depression of the interwar years, and the failures of the secularized Third Republic to prevent them combined with scientific advances relating to indeterminacy and quantum physics[83] to raise serious questions about human progress and the possibility of constructing utopia from the raw material of human reason. Philosophers and writers professed to doubt the idea that there was a fixed identifiable human 'nature' or 'essence' in the first place. The interwar decades were studded with lectures and books on the 'death', or the 'end', or the 'crisis', or the 'suspension', or the 'deconstruction', or the 'devirilization' of man (or 'the last man' or 'the unknown man', etc.). Rarely has a fatality been announced so frequently.

These publications reconceived 'man' as a construct of science and technology, or of religion and history, or of culture and politics – indeed of any range of human activities that tried but failed to determine and define humanity's essence. This could (and often did) sound like ostentatious sophistry but it was nonetheless a serious blow to a tradition of humanistic atheism that traced its origins back to Feuerbach's idea that 'the task of the modern era was the realisation and humanisation of God – the transformation and dissolution of theology into anthropology'.[84] If there was no fixed idea of *anthropos* or the human, there was no fixed idea of the human good, either individual or communal, to journey towards, and no sense that humans had the ethical or rational capacity to reach it, even had they been able to identify where they were headed. This was a different atheist critique to Nietzsche's but hardly less damaging.

None of this reformulation of 'man' resulted in the rebirth of God, although it did give a new lease of life to Catholic humanism. Counter-enlightenment critiques of atheism had long argued that the human, imagined by atheism as an animal without transcendence, was not enough to ground qualities like moral certainty, dependable rationality or unique dignity, qualities that were central to the humanist project. Such criticisms gained strength as this 'atheism that was not humanist' emerged in French thought (to quote the title of a recent book on the subject). In atheism 'man has *literally* been dissolved,' wrote Henri de Lubac in his 1944 book *The Drama of Atheist Humanism*. 'Atheist humanism was bound to end in bankruptcy. Man is himself only because his face is illumined by a divine ray.'[85]

Such arguments were absorbed by many post-war continental atheists, who tended to deflate and redefine their humanistic ambitions rather than abandon them altogether. Thus, in the words of André Malraux, speaking in a UNESCO lecture in November 1946, 'a certain humanism is [now] possible, but ... it is a tragic humanism'.[86] Once upon a time, Maurice Merleau-Ponty wrote, 'human nature had truth and justice for attributes, as other species have fins or wings ... those of us today who are taking up the word 'humanism' again no longer maintain the same shameless humanism of our elders'.[87] The kind of humanism 'which upholds man as the end-in-itself and as the supreme value', Sartre declared in a famous lecture defending existentialism in post-war Paris, was 'absurd'.[88]

The famous existentialist slogan – 'existence precedes essence' – accepted the idea that in a godless universe there was no human nature, no moral order, no meaning to be discovered, and took instead human subjectivity as a starting point for life. The result was a complete freedom to create meaning and identity and purpose, but a freedom marked by a sense of burden, even anguish, rather than triumphant joy, a freedom to which mankind was condemned rather than liberated.

The result was an atheism that hovered between the confident humanistic atheism of the later nineteenth century and the despair that its critics claimed was the only alternative to Catholic humanism. 'Existentialism is nothing else but an attempt to draw the full conclusions from a consistently atheistic position', Sartre claimed. Those conclusions were simultaneously desperate and optimistic.

More interestingly perhaps for our story, was that, according to Sartre at least, this 'consistently atheistic position' had little to do with God. 'Existentialism is not atheist in the sense that it would exhaust itself in demonstrations of the non-existence of God', Sartre commented. Of course, he reasoned, we don't believe he exists, 'but we think that the real problem is not that of His existence: what man needs is to find himself again and to understand that nothing can save him from himself, not even a valid proof of the existence of God'. As it had been way back in the post-Reformation period, atheism was as much – perhaps more – about the nature and future of man, and the society he chose to form, than about whether God existed.

'Worms grovelling for meagre existence': American atheists
Just as foreign affairs shaped atheism in post-war France, so they did in America, although here the impact was not so much to refine atheism as to cripple it.

Nineteenth-century America had not been immune to the intellectual trends of Europe and it was not devoid of atheistic thought. Robert Green Ingersoll, the son of a Presbyterian minister, was an autodidact who schooled himself in Epicurus, Voltaire and Paine. He earned a formidable reputation as a freethinking orator, specializing in anti-clerical and scientific themes, although happier calling himself agnostic than atheist. Elizur Wright was a mathematician and fervent abolitionist. Brought up in a pious Christian family (he once determined to enter ministry himself) he became disgusted by Christian support for slavery and then outraged by the 1873 Comstock Act, which made it illegal to send obscene (meaning rationalist as well as erotic) material through the post. The combination of piety gone sour and moral outrage proved the perfect mixture, and Wright became one of the few late nineteenth-century Americans who campaigned for liberty on openly atheistic as opposed to Christian grounds.

More influential than either of these was Clarence Darrow. Unlike Ingersoll or Wright, Darrow's upbringing was rationalistic and freethinking, and he never had the experience of being a jilted believer. He did, however, develop close connections and a deep affinity for the nascent American labour movement, which he defended in a number of high profile court cases, in the process becoming aware of many churches' intense hostility to the movement. Already antipathetic to religion, he became indignant. Darrow went on to defend John Scopes, the biology teacher charged with teaching evolution in a Tennessee school, in 1925 in a trial that was engineered by the American Civil Liberties Union in order to challenge a Tennessee state law banning the teaching of human evolution.[89] Darrow lost, of course, and Scopes was found guilty, which indeed he was, but Darrow's skill in putting Christian witnesses to the scientific sword in public would be the trial's, and his, main legacy.

There were other atheists, or at least atheistic Americans, in the early twentieth century but America developed no atheistic movement comparable to those in Europe. Felix Adler, a German immigrant, founded the Ethical Culture Movement, and Charles Lee Smith set up The American Association for the Advancement of Atheism but neither grew sizeable and both were fated to die or merge with other groups.

What might (and one day would) be a serious target for American atheism, Christian fundamentalism, was hard to find, at least in mainstream culture, after the Scopes Trial. In any case, the existence and, after 1945, threat of godless communism proved a far more frightening spectre in the public's mind. In 1954, Congress passed a bill that added the words 'under God' to the nation's Pledge of Allegiance, and then again two years later President Eisenhower made 'In God We Trust' the national motto. The Constitution remained unchanged but the moves were indicative of a culture in which it was assumed that to be American was to be anti-communist, which meant, if only by association, anti-atheist.

It was in this atmosphere that the most prominent and pugnacious American atheist of the twentieth century came to fame. Madalyn Murray O'Hair was born in 1919 and joined a number of radical groups in the '40s and '50s before failing to move to the USSR. In 1960, she learned that her son William was saying prayers and reading the Bible as part of his schooling, and although he had no objection to this she most certainly did. At first she wrote to the school asking for her son to be exempt. The school refused but then backed down when O'Hair went public with her story.

O'Hair now had a cause. She soon took over the *Free Humanist* magazine, and founded American Atheists which became the largest American atheist organization (the competition was not great). 'We find the Bible to be nauseating, historically inaccurate, replete with the ravings of madmen,' she told *Life* magazine in April

1963. 'We find God to be sadistic, brutal, and a representation of hatred [and] vengeance. We find the Lord's Prayer to be that uttered by worms grovelling for meagre existence in a traumatic, paranoid world.' It was her objection to that 'grovelling' that would result in her most famous victory.

Using her various organizations to raise money for a legal fund, she took her son's case ultimately to the Supreme Court, which duly found in her favour and effectively banned mandatory Bible reading and prayers in public schools. The case gave her national fame, if not popularity. Her atheist radio programme was widely syndicated and American Atheists claimed nearly 50,000 members. Not satisfied with having liberated America's schoolchildren from the evil of mandatory Bible reading, she sought to liberate all people from God in such a way as would enable them to love one another more fully.

Her story was not to have a happy ending. First, her son William, on whose behalf she had supposedly fought, became a Christian and then campaigned in the 1990s for the reintroduction of prayer in schools. His memoir of growing up with his mother made for agonizing reading. Then people started asking questions about the actual size of O'Hair's organization, she herself was sued for improperly conspiring to gain control of the estates of an atheist publication called *Truth Seeker* and, finally, she disappeared. It later emerged that she was kidnapped, murdered and mutilated, along with her son Jon and granddaughter Robin, by former American Atheists office manager David Roland Waters who had been sacked for financial misappropriation. It was a grim ending to a story that had put atheism on the map in America, if not in the way that most American atheists wanted.

Building godless societies

*'Those who believe in God are becoming fewer': Russia under
Khrushchev*
In September 1943, Stalin invited Metropolitans Sergei, Alexei and
Nikolai to the Kremlin for an evening meeting. In return for the
Church's full and unsparing exertion in the war with Germany, he
was prepared to offer (limited) religious freedom. It was an offer
they couldn't refuse.

The Orthodox leaders fulfilled their promise, portraying the
struggle against Nazis in nationalist religious terms and dutifully
telling the world that there had been no persecution in Russia.
Congregations collected millions of roubles for the Red Army. For
the first time in decades, believers worshipped unmolested, church
bells rang and churches reopened, the number rising from under
1,000 in 1940 to ten times that many a decade later. Such liberty
and patriotism, combined with the natural religiosity inherent in
the insecurity and hardships of war, resulted in a thaw in state
atheism.

It was temporary. Stalin's successor, Nikita Khrushchev, may
not have trained in a seminary but he was no less an atheist than
his predecessor, telling a French journalist in 1958 that, 'there is
no God. I have long ago freed myself from such an idea. I am an
advocate of the scientific worldview. Science and belief in supernatural forces are incompatible and mutually exclusive views.'[90]

Personal commitment translated into the predictable conviction
of religion's impending demise. 'Those who believe in God are
becoming fewer. The vast majority of young people growing up
today do not believe in God. Education, scientific knowledge and
study of the laws of nature leave no room for belief in God.'[91] The
task of building a new, gloriously godless society made of new,
gloriously godless men may have been slower and more problematic
than the early revolutionaries had imagined, but it was coming: by
1980, Khrushchev predicted.

Early on in Khrushchev's reign, in 1954, the Communist Party Central Committee lamented the revitalized church activity since the war, criticized 'shortcomings in scientific atheist propaganda' and called for a renewed attempt to overcome 'religious prejudice'.[92] It was the spur to an intense but brief atheist spasm. Over the next four months the press published numerous crude attacks on religion and popularized scientific research that had supposedly proved the falsity of religious claims. The Education Minister made moves to increase the atheistic content of courses – 'schools must pay very strict attention to rearing our youth in the spirit of militant materialism, in the spirit of atheism'[93] – and there were plans to establish a monthly atheist journal. And then, with equal abruptness, and for no obvious reason, the campaign suddenly broke off and the state returned to the *status quo ante* of diffuse, low level hostility.

It was another five years before Khrushchev launched another atheistic crusade, this time far more vicious and sustained than anything since the 1930s. A *Pravda* editorial of 1959 reminded readers that religion was 'inimical to the interests of the working masses', and that, although we should not insult believers' feelings, the final goal was the 'complete eradication of religious prejudices'.[94] It called on the atheistic faithful to hasten the process.

The press and cinema duly reported lurid stories. A Baptist man murdered his wife for her refusal to convert, while another forbade his children to read any secular literature. There were tales of crazed Pentecostals, drunken, embezzling, lascivious Orthodox priests, ignorant old women prepared to sacrifice grandchildren as a 'gift to the Almighty', and of course, plenty of conversions and defections of those who had come to their scientific senses.

Churches and monasteries were once again closed, and the right to appeal against closures circumscribed. The number of Orthodox churches fell by around 5,000, or nearly half, between 1960 and 1964. It became an offence to teach children religion, to organize pilgrimages, or to carry out any charitable activities in the name of the church. Although precise figures are hard to establish, at least

1,500 believers were sentenced between 1958 and 1964 with some, like Nikolai Khmara, being tortured and killed.

The Orthodox Church once again suffered most acutely, but it did not suffer alone. Other denominations and religions lost over 1,000 places of worship. Baptists, particularly those who showed any signs of resistance, were punished severely, with senior presbyters forbidden to visit their congregations, or to preach or participate in services without express permission. The minimum age for baptism was also increased from 18 to 30.

During the later Khrushchev years, atheist councils began to appear. These were attached to local party organizations and mandated to organize anti-religious activities. The Znanie Society, originally formed in 1947 as a kind of informal successor to the Soviet League of the Militant Godless, which described itself as 'a fighting organ of militant atheism', upped its activities. From a low point of 84,000 in 1956, the number of atheistic lectures given by Znanie members reached over half a million a year by the early 1960s. The Society also launched a journal titled *Science and Religion* in 1960, which published, among other things, discussions of the material origins of life and the universe, attacks on a worryingly modern Pope John XXIII and reprints of Bertrand Russell's 'Why I am not a Christian'. Three years later, the Communist Party's Ideological Commission established an Institute of Scientific Atheism, attached to the Central Committee's Academy of Social Sciences, which was tasked with co-ordinating all the 'scientific work in the field of atheism', and published a biannual collection of essays with atheistic themes.

There was a particular effort to alienate young people from religion. The September 1960 issue of the journal replaced its editorial with a letter to the Education Minister from seven workers calling for a more militant approach to atheism. After giving various examples of children whose lives had been poisoned by religion, they argued that it was time to stand up and move on from 'a position of neutral, religionless education to an active struggle for the education of convinced atheists, militant materialists and worthy members of a future communist society'.[95] On occasion children were removed from their parents when it was deemed their religion made them unfit to raise them, although this seems to have been a rarity. At the level of higher education, a course on the 'basics of scientific atheism' was introduced for all students in 1959, initially on a voluntary basis, although it was made compulsory in 1964 once it became clear that too few students were signing up for it.

There were even attempts, quite contrary to Lenin's express views, to establish new, atheistic rites. The Estonian Central Committee proposed an atheistic alternative to Lutheran confirmation in 1957, with some success, if the subsequent decline in Lutheran confirmations is anything to go by. Similar tactics were less successful in Catholic Lithuania, where the people's attachment to the church's rites was more tenacious. Other rites of passages enjoyed the atheist makeover. Leningrad became the first Soviet city to open a wedding palace in which couples could get married with a more rational and material ritual. Six years later, the city opened a baby palace for a comparable purpose.

The tactics may have lacked the ferocity of the 1920s and '30s but, between them, church closures, media caricatures, materialist lectures, scientific education and atheistic rituals took their toll. The Soviet Union looked like it was on course to become the world's first atheistic society.

'Draw the bow without shooting': China under Mao

It did, however, now have some competition. In 1921, Bertrand Russell and his then lover, soon to be second wife, Dora visited China. Having been to Russia and met with Lenin, among others, the previous year, the great British atheist had become disillusioned with Bolshevism and delivered four lectures, in one day, in Changsha, in which he spoke about his disappointments.

The last of these lectures was on 'Necessary Elements for a Successful Communism' to an audience that included a 26-year-old

Mao Tse-tung. The philosopher spoke 'in favour of communism but against the dictatorship of the workers and peasants', according to Mao's account in a contemporaneous letter. 'He said that one should employ the method of education to change the consciousness of the propertied classes, and that in this way it would not be necessary to limit freedom or to have recourse to war and bloody revolution.' Mao was not persuaded. 'My objections to Russell's viewpoint can be stated in a few words: "This is all very well in theory, but it is unfeasible in practice."'[96]

With a devout Buddhist mother but sceptical father, Mao was moderately pious when younger but lost his Buddhist faith at school. His attitude to religion was initially straightforwardly Marxist, believing that it was simply false consciousness and would die on its own when the economic conditions were right. In a report into the *Peasant Movement in Hunan* in 1927, effectively a treatise on communist organizing among peasantry, Mao explained that, as it was the peasants who made the idols, 'when the time comes they will cast the idols aside with their own hands; there is no need for anyone else to do it for them prematurely'. The Communist Party's propaganda policy in such matters should be, 'draw the bow without shooting, just indicate the motions'.[97] In theory, that was: as his response to Russell's lecture six years earlier shows, Mao was already alert to the need for the enlightened to herd the peasants into the broad, sunlit uplands of godlessness by force.

This was the path already travelled by many Marxists, but Mao's, and indeed Chinese, atheism was animated by another consideration, namely their association of Christianity, especially missionary activity, with Western imperial exploitation. Nowhere was Marx's opium metaphor more resonant than in China, whose experience of Christianity was stained by the Opium Wars of the mid-nineteenth century and the subsequent rise in missionary activity. History provided a rich source of indignation, and propaganda, for the Chinese Communist Party (CCP) when it achieved power in 1949.

Initially, the CCP looked to Russia for guidance in formulating its policy on religion. This was during the temporary and limited thaw in Soviet atheist policy, after the church had helped with the war effort and while there was a growing realization that 30 years of atheist policy had not cured the people of their delusional beliefs. This – plus the fact that there was no equivalent of the Orthodox Church in China, where the majority of people adhered to some form of Taoism, Confucianism or Buddhism, which the communists considered to be more superstitions than religions – meant there was very little Chinese atheist propaganda at first. Instead, the CCP initial line was similar to Lenin's 1918 decree on church and state separation, Article Five of The Common Program passed by the Chinese People's Political Consultative Conference in September 1949 guaranteeing 'freedom of thought, speech, publication, assembly, association ... religious belief, and the freedom of holding processions and demonstrations'.[98]

Such freedom guaranteed, the Party moved quickly against religious bodies, particularly those with any foreign connections. Article Three of the Common Program nationalized all rural land belonging to 'ancestral shrines, temples, monasteries, churches, schools and organizations'. The Christian presence was comparatively small – perhaps 5 million out of 550 million people in 1949 – but it had a social influence out of all proportion, with a large number of churches, hospitals, schools, colleges and publishing houses. It was both a reactionary threat and a rich coffer. Moreover, given that four out of five Catholic bishops, and two out of every five priests, in China were foreign-born, and that the vast bulk of Protestant activity had active connections with overseas mission boards, it was easy to move against the church on anti-imperial or patriotic grounds. The result was not simply the expropriation of land and possessions but a pervasive campaign against nuns and priests in particular, which accused them of everything from murder and cannibalism to conducting medical experiments on babies. Several hundred public executions drove the message home.

Patriotic and revolutionary zeal in the 1950s sought to reorganize religious groups in such a way as to eliminate any foreign influence. Borrowing from what had originally been a Protestant missionary strategy intended for indigenous new churches, the CCP developed the 'three-self formula', whereby religious groups had to be self-governing, self-propagating and self-supporting. Only then, once they had severed all links with reactionary, alien bodies, might they be afforded a measure of religious freedom, although even then religious leaders were commonly brought before cadres of local party functionaries to confess crimes against the people.

Islam, deemed a similarly foreign influence in the west of China, was also persecuted. Buddhism, although not seen as quite as powerful or alien a force (despite being far more numerical, having considerable resources, and originating outside China) was judged to be a source of laxity and parasitism to be stamped out. Taoism was, if anything, even lower than Buddhism, essentially a peasant superstition but one that was still a threat not least because it had no external form that might be readily crushed or controlled by the state. Wherever it could, and whatever people believed, the CCP sought to catalyse the inevitable demise of religion.

By the late '50s it was clear that, enervated as institutional religion had been, belief was proving harder to eradicate. Mao's 1957 *On the Correct Handling of Contradictions* pronounced that 'we cannot abolish religion by administrative decree or force people not to believe in it',[99] and this precipitated the Hundred Flowers Campaign and a degree of liberalization. Moderate and even tolerant views were heard from on high, with Zhou Enlai, the Chinese Premier, famously saying, 'we are going to go on letting you teach, trying to convert the people ... After all we both believe that truth will prevail; we think your beliefs untrue and false, and therefore if we are right, the people will reject them, and your church will decay. If you are right, then the people will believe you, but as we are sure that you are wrong, we are prepared for that risk.'[100] John Stuart Mill couldn't have put it better.

Whether the Hundred Flowers Campaign was a (mis)calculated gamble on the part of the CCP or a cynical plan to entice the snakes out of their caves, as Mao later put it, it was short lived. Opposition was stronger than anticipated. Too many weeds were growing among the flowers. The change in policy was abrupt and total and religious leaders were among the first to be broken in the ensuing Anti-Rightist campaign. By the mid-1960s, it was clear that the people were not going to embrace scientific atheism naturally and the Party stepped up efforts to stamp out religion and inculcate a scientific worldview among the people, culminating in the Cultural Revolution in which the state's Religious Affairs Bureau was closed down, as was every single church and the vast majority of mosques and Buddhist temples. As atheist efforts go, the Cultural Revolution put Khrushchev's and even Stalin's efforts to shame.

'A long, complicated and difficult struggle': Albania under Hoxha
The only country that may have been more successful than China in securing national godlessness was Albania. In the immediate wake of the Second World War, once the communists had murdered their way to power, Enver Hoxha emerged as leader. He initially sought to model the People's Republic of Albania on Stalin's Russia. However, his allegiance to the Soviets foundered after Khrushchev's de-Stalinization and he turned instead to China as a major ally. So it was that Albania managed to get the most extreme form of atheism from two sources.

Most religious property was nationalized when the communists seized power. Religious leaders, in particular those with any foreign links, were stigmatized, expelled or executed, Roman Catholic priests, monks and nuns being particularly vulnerable. Religious institutions had their educational roles removed, followed by their charitable ones. All those that survived had to be officially sanctioned and all appointments and communications, down to parish letters, were to be approved by the government.

Inspired by the Cultural Revolution, the atheistic campaign in Albania turned more violent in 1967, as Hoxha urged young men to spread out across the countryside and 'encourage' conversion. All remaining churches, monasteries and mosques were closed down or converted for secular purposes, and Hoxha confidently declared Albania to be the world's first genuinely atheist state, entirely free of religious institutions, buildings, leaders and worship.

Although not, sadly, of belief: Hoxha, like the Soviets before him, soon realized there was a difference between crushing a church and crushing a faith. 'It is wrong to maintain that religion means church, mosque, priest, imam, [or] icons ... and that if these disappear then automatically religion and its influence of the people will also disappear,' he told the fourth congress of the Albanian Democratic Front. 'We must be realists. The struggle is against habits, traditions, old norms and against religious viewpoints, which are deeply rooted in the course of centuries in the conscience of the people ... [and it has] not come to an end. This is a long, complicated and difficult struggle.'[101]

Decline and fall

'A not insignificant proportion of the population remains believers':
Religion returns in Russia
'A long, complicated and difficult struggle': this was precisely what the Soviet Union itself was discovering. In spite of everything Khrushchev had achieved in his last six years in power, religious belief and practice persisted. His prediction that the truly godless society would be established by 1980 was looking ambitious.

The regime's official position remained unaltered under his successor, Leonid Brezhnev. Official documents and speeches still spoke of the development of the 'new man' under communism. There were resolutions to strengthen atheistic education among workers. *Pravda* still spoke of the inevitability of the demise of religion as a reactionary force. The violence did grind to a halt, however. The closure of churches slowed, arrests ceased, believers were released from camps, and the cruder forms of atheistic propaganda fell silent.

A formal reassessment of atheistic policy in 1965 precipitated a more sustained and scholarly approach to this stubborn problem, and the Party faced up to some serious questions. Why did people persist in rejecting the scientific, material explanation for life? Why would they rather get married in a church than a Soviet wedding palace? Why had they not all embraced atheism after nearly 50 years of relentless propaganda, re-education and official encouragement? A. F. Okulov, then director of the Central Committee's Institute of Scientific Atheism, spoke for a growing number when he complained that 'a superficial approach' to studying religion 'does nothing but harm to atheist work'. Poor understanding of religion merely led atheists into 'boundless fanaticism'.[102]

The same could be said for propaganda. In March 1965, *Science and Religion* published an open letter attacking an atheistic propagandist for her simplistic approach to anti-religious writing which was aimed 'not at religion but at believers', whom she depicted as 'money grabbing, drunken, libertine and parasitic'. Her writing, the letter complained, lacked 'tact and delicacy'.[103]

It would be wrong to suggest that half a century of atheist propaganda had had no effect. In as far as the evidence can be trusted, it shows a marked decline in both religious practice and belief. The majority of remaining believers had chosen to acquiesce to state restrictions on the exercise of faith rather than risk their lives contravening them. Their leaders, for the most part, elected to work with the Party to make the best of a very bad deal. Some heroic individuals remained faithful and resistant but they were a minority, eroded by persecution and execution.

Yet for all this success, atheism had not finally triumphed and Brezhnev's refusal to adopt the brutality of the Stalin or Khrushchev years made the official policy look increasingly vulnerable. The slow thaw in hostility in the early Brezhnev years revealed ever more examples of religious resistance. The Baptists, who had split over the question of whether to accommodate State demands, became bolder and more public in their defiance. The emergence of nationalistic feelings as a challenge to the Soviet State was often rooted in religious identity. Catholics in Lithuania and Poland and, to a lesser extent, Muslims in central Asia drew on belief to define and fortify nationalistic sentiment. Many Christians, especially Pentecostals, emigrated, particularly to the US, drawing attention to the plight of Russian believers in doing so. The brief détente in the mid-1970s had the same effect, as did the presence of the Russian Orthodox Church at the World Council of Churches, although when there it had to tread a difficult line between honesty and loyalty to the regime.

Most humiliatingly, evidence emerged that some communists were actively seeking religious consolation because they found atheism unsatisfactory. In 1968, the Russian intellectual Anatoly Levitin-Krasnov wrote to Pope Paul VI telling him that 'there is a growing number of instances in which the sons of communists, even of old Chekists, are baptised'.[104] A 'growing number' was still a very small number but it was a painful revelation nonetheless.

The authorities were not sure how to respond to this. Some reacted moderately, electing to study, understand and respond 'rationally' to religious resistance, stressing the need for old rituals to be changed slowly. Some were prepared to go further still, and spoke of a 'new type of believer' who was a loyal Soviet while also believing in God. Others were more antagonistic. *Pravda* published letters about how any loosening of freedom for religion would weaken society, as religious leaders would 'morally and even physically cripple people'.[105]

Such problems were exacerbated by the election of John Paul II in 1978, with the Soviet leadership taking a more conservative turn in religious affairs. Vassily Konavlev, senior researcher at the Institute of Scientific Atheism, even went out of his way to praise the achievement of the Stalin era and especially the League of the Militant Godless.

And still, belief remained. In 1983, Konstantin Chernenko ruefully informed the Central Committee that 'a not insignificant proportion of the population remains believers'.[106] A statistical report from the following year revealed that although, over the last five years, the number of infant baptisms in the Russian Orthodox Church had risen by only 2 per cent, the number of adult Baptists had increased by nearly 40 per cent.

At first, for all his liberalizing tendencies, Mikhail Gorbachev showed little interest in changing the Party's atheist position. However, by 1988 he was bowing to the inevitable, made all the more irresistible by the millennial celebrations of the conversion of the Rus. The initial Soviet plan to replace these with a 70th anniversary of Lenin's 1918 law on the separation of church and state was soon abandoned. It was clear to all that the people cared little for Lenin and less for his secularism, but were genuinely moved and motivated by the arrival of Christianity a thousand years earlier. Churches reopened, new communities were founded, religion was, for the first time, seen on television, and state leaders acquiesced in all of the above. When the atheist regime finally crumbled three years later, the Church was left standing.

In September 1918, the dean of the Cathedral of Our Lady of Kazan in St Petersburg had been martyred by revolutionaries, along with his two sons. A few years later, the church's valuables had been confiscated, the church closed and handed over to the Soviet Academy of Sciences which reopened it as a Museum of the History of Religion and Atheism. In November 1990, the first Divine Liturgy in over 70 years was held there. The scenes were ecstatic.

'The construction of a harmonious society': Religion returns in China
The story elsewhere was less dramatic and less conclusive but still instructive. Atheism fell in most former Soviet states, indigenous religions filling the resulting vacuum, sometimes with an authoritarianism and arrogance comparable to their pre-revolutionary incarnations.

In Beijing, official atheist attitudes thawed ever so slightly after Mao's death and China's Religious Affairs Bureau was reopened in 1979. As had happened 20 years earlier in the Brezhnev era in the USSR, a more serious and informed debate about the nature and role of religion developed, not least about what calling religion an 'opium' actually meant. Article 36 of the 1982 People's Republic of China Constitution declared that 'citizens of the People's Republic of China enjoy freedom of religious belief'. At the sixth plenary session of the 16th Central Committee of CCP, President Hu Jintao emphasized the positive role that believers could have in Chinese society, remarking that the Party should 'intensify the unity between believers and non-believers, as well as the unity among people who believe in different faiths, and let religion play its positive role in the construction of a harmonious society'.[107]

Of course, the actual position of the Party was more mixed and complex and not necessarily as friendly. The same 1982 Constitution that afforded religious freedom also required that religious organizations were free from foreign domination, and insisted that 'no one may make use of religion to engage in activities that disrupt public order'. Another document of that year outlining the government's attitude towards religion stated that religion, though a complex historical phenomenon, would eventually disappear in the modern social period but that it would take a long time to do so – religious freedom and the promotion (rather than coercion) of atheism being the best way of catalysing this. Communist Party members still needed to be atheists. Counter-revolutionaries 'hiding behind the façade of religion' were to be prosecuted, religious 'professionals' to be educated in patriotism. All places of worship remained under the administrative control of the Bureau of Religious Affairs. The country's first academic atheist journal, *Science and Atheism*, began in 2002, with an Atheism Magazine, of more popular tone, which included original articles and translations of famous Western atheists, like Richard Dawkins, soon followed. In spite of all this, the numbers of religious believers increased significantly in the decades each side of the millennium and although reliable figures are hard to come by it is thought that there are well over 100 million Christians in China. No matter how stubborn state atheism remained in China, however, it was still generous and tolerant in comparison with its neighbour, North Korea, where Article 68 of the Constitution guarantees that 'citizens have freedom of religious beliefs' but in which any form of religious belief or expression outside tightly drawn and controlled state permission remains forbidden, and members of underground religious groups are arrested.

Yemelyan Yaroslavsky, at the time a leading anti-religion campaigner in the Soviet Union, once remarked that 'religion is like a nail, the harder you hit, the deeper it goes in'.[108] It was a telling observation. The twentieth century saw state-sponsored atheism hammer repeatedly and brutally at belief in God, in Russia, China, Albania, North Korea and elsewhere. It met with considerable success as churches were crushed, leaders silenced, congregations decimated and belief systematically mocked, undermined, contradicted and silenced. Yet, in spite of up to 70 years of propaganda and persecution the final result – with the current exception of North Korea – was a massive, public and humiliating failure, slowly followed by the opening of archives which revealed how very far the promises of atheism had fallen short of their goal.

New dawns

'Is God dead?': The unexpected rise of political religion

Orthodox Christianity reasserted itself in Russia and Eastern Europe after the fall of communism. As the people emerged from the shadow of official atheism, more and more claimed to believe in God, and identified themselves as Orthodox. A law on the freedom of conscience and religious belief was passed in the 1990s providing for religious equality for the first time in Russian history but it was short lived and the *de facto* primacy of the Orthodox Church was re-established by the millennium.

Allying itself with state power, asserting itself as the heart of national identity, and encouraging restrictions on other, particularly foreign, forms of religious association, it was as if the Orthodox Church had learned nothing from the twentieth century. There was no atheist backlash this time. Memories of what it had been like to live in an atheist state were too fresh. But the political reassertion of religion at the end of the century was not limited to Russia and the results elsewhere would give atheism a new lease of life in the twenty-first century.

Religious reassertion hadn't been expected. In 1968, the sociologist Peter Berger had predicted that by the twenty-first century religious believers were likely to be found 'only in small sects, huddled together to resist a worldwide secular culture'.[109] The prediction was hubristic but not exceptional. God, it was widely believed in the secular West, or at least in *bien pensant* circles, was on his death bed.

Even theologians seemed to think so. In April 1966, *Time* magazine ran an iconic cover asking 'Is God dead?' The relevant article was not so much an analysis of whether God still had a place in the modern world – not exactly a front page question by the mid-1960s – but rather a survey of a tiny number of radical Christian theologians who had embraced the death of God and were advocating a non-theistic form of faith, a 'theology without Theos' as the magazine put it.[110] These 'death of God' theologians, or 'Christian Atheists' as they were also called, were never numerous or, for that matter, influential. But they were important, if only because they showed how the lines between religion and atheism, once deemed to be so clear and self-evident, were now blurred and confusing.

The death of God movement did not persuade many Americans but it was credible – just – because political religion in the US, and elsewhere, was at that time comparatively passive and pliable. The Roman Catholic Church had energetically modernized and shown its relevance to the contemporary world in the Second Vatican Council; mainstream Protestant denominations were comfortable if declining, and evangelicals and fundamentalists appeared happy to keep themselves to themselves, licking the wounds that evolution, biblical criticism and the Scopes Trial had inflicted on them. Political religion in the US was tame, or dead.

Of course, it was neither. Five years before the *Time* article, John Whitcomb and Henry Morris had published what was to become a shockingly successful book, *The Genesis Flood: The Biblical Record and its Scientific Implications*, which advocated a young-earth creationism that flew in the face of all scientific progress of the last century and a half. Given that that some early 'fundamentalists', including contributors to the original twelve-volume project *The Fundamentals* such as Benjamin Warfield, James Orr and George Wright, were themselves evolutionists (Warfield called himself a 'Darwinian of the purest water'), this was not an obvious cause for Protestant Christianity to be fighting. But it was to become one of the two most blood-stained battlegrounds in America's coming culture war.

The other was *Roe v Wade*, the 1973 Supreme Court decision, which used the due process clause of the 14th Amendment to secure the right to an abortion nationally. This decision helped effect a rapprochement between America's Protestants and Catholics, hitherto suspicious of one another, and turn them into a political movement to be reckoned with, initially in support of the born-again Jimmy Carter but then, more passionately, for the born-only once Ronald Reagan.

In reality, *Roe v Wade* was not quite the catalyst some claimed, and other liberal legislation, such as the 1972 Equal Rights Amendment, and other causes, such as the fight to retain tax-exempt status for segregated religious schools and colleges, were also important.[111] Whatever the precise causes, the so-called 'Religious' or 'Christian Right' would transform America's religious landscape.

The actual, measurable political success of the movement was questionable. The Religious Right were constantly disappointed by their experiences 'in power', and better mobilized and more vocal when in opposition. Such failure notwithstanding, however, the Religious Right captured the political imagination and public rhetoric and managed to insinuate an association between being Christian (or, at least, theistic), being ethical, and being American, an association that the Founding Fathers had been careful to avoid. Constitutionally, of course, atheists remained as American as believers, but it often didn't feel that way. According to a Gallup/ USA Today poll in 2007, Americans would have rather voted for a presidential candidate who was Catholic, black, Jewish, female, Hispanic, Mormon, thrice-married, 72 years old or homosexual than they would one who was an atheist.[112] Few prejudices were better calculated to stir up a sense of moral indignation.

The comparison between Britain and America over this period is instructive. A year before Reagan was elected, Margaret Thatcher came to power in Britain. Sincerely Christian, she saw Britain's problems as 'spiritual and philosophical' as much as they were political or economic.[113] 'I never thought that Christianity equipped me with a political philosophy,' she told an audience at St Lawrence Jewry in 1977, but 'it did equip me with standards to which political actions must, in the end, be referred'.

For all her earnest and far-from-shallow theological reasoning, however, Thatcher was not carried to power by a religious vote and never managed to capture that vote as Reagan did in America. Indeed, it was Christians, first through the Church of England's *Faith in the City* report, and then through the Keep Sunday Special coalition, who were among her most public critics. As a result, there was never a theo-political nexus in Britain to induce a sense of martyrdom among British atheists as there was in America.

As it transpired, there didn't need to be. The year that saw Thatcher come to power also witnessed the Islamic revolution in Iran and the installation of a republic ordered on strict and often violent theocratic principles. It was to prove, albeit in retrospect, a turning point, as Middle Eastern nations dissociated themselves from the secular, liberal or nationalist ideas that had been dominant since the end of the colonial period and found in Islam an identity to assert against the West.

At first, this was an alarming but mercifully distant feature on the Western political landscape. When, however, Muslims in Britain took offence and then burned Salman Rushdie's novel *The Satanic Verses* it became clear that the issue was both serious and domestic. The Rushdie affair was merely the entrée and, at the turn of the millennium, a strand of political Islam exploded in a series of indiscriminate and highly publicized acts of mass murder. The rise of the American Right had given Western atheists something to get angry about. The rise of militant political Islam allowed them to get apoplectic, which they duly did.

'A display of naked contempt': New Atheism

The term 'New Atheism' was first coined, at least in the modern context, in 2006, although both proponents and opponents quickly came to agree there was nothing new about the arguments.[114] The phenomenon is usually dated to the publication of Sam Harris' book *The End of Faith* in 2004 but it had been latent for some years. In a 1997 Oxford Amnesty Lecture entitled 'What shall we tell the children?', the psychologist Nicholas Humphrey argued that children had a right 'not to have their minds crippled by exposure to other people's bad ideas – no matter who these other people are'. This meant that parents had 'no god-given licence to enculturate their children in whatever ways they personally choose'. Society had a duty to protect children from the atmosphere of 'dogma and superstition' in which their parents might bring them up. Just as no civilized society could countenance female circumcision or allow parents 'to knock their children's teeth out or lock them in a dungeon', so it should no more allow them to teach their children the literal truth of the Bible or deny them their knowledge of Darwin.[115] This was a remarkable view, not least coming in an Amnesty International lecture, and set the tone – and content – for much subsequent New Atheist polemic: extreme hyperbole, absurd comparisons, lazy use of rights language, uncritical self-righteousness and an obsessive interest in how other people – other *religious* people to be precise – brought up their children.

Astonishing as it seems, Sam Harris' contribution to the arguments was even more bombastic. *The End of Faith* book was inspired by the terrorist murders of 9/11 and begun on the following day, opening with a depiction of a young suicide bomber starting out on his mission. Harris' view was clear. 'We are at war with Islam ... [not] with an otherwise peaceful religion that had been "hijacked" by extremists ... [but] with precisely the vision of life that is prescribed to all Muslims in the Koran'.[116]

Harris argued passionately that Islam was incompatible with the values of civil society and that as such the two could not coexist. His own vision of what comprised a civil society was somewhat eccentric, however. Because there was a clear link between religious belief and behaviour, he contended that 'some propositions are so dangerous that it may be ethical to kill people for believing them'.[117] And not just kill: Harris argued that in some circumstances torture was not only permissible but necessary. 'If there is even one chance in a million that he [the terrorist] will tell us something under torture that will lead to the further dismantling of Al Qaeda, it seems that we should use every means at our disposal to get him talking'.[118] In the same vein, Harris also argued that a pre-emptive nuclear strike on a weaponized Islamic state 'may be the only course of action available to us', although he did acknowledge that it would be an 'unthinkable crime'.[119] Execution for one's beliefs, the judicial use of torture, pre-emptive nuclear strikes: Harris achieved the remarkable feat of making an Islamic theocracy look comparatively humane.

In the process, he raised the New Atheist bar very high. Subsequent polemicists would have to try very hard to shock. They did. P. Z. Myers, an American biology professor and blogger, posted evidence of a consecrated Eucharistic host ('goddamned cracker') which he had pierced with a rusty nail and binned with some coffee grounds and banana peel, commenting that he hoped Jesus' tetanus shots were up to date. Baron D'Holbach would have found the joke hilarious.

Others preferred to commit their anger to paper. The respected journalist Christopher Hitchens wrote an uncharacteristically flat book explaining how religion poisoned everything. In this refrain he was echoing a popular New Atheist message that 'religion' (the term was usually left vague) was ethically wicked, constituting a threat to society and making people worse than they would otherwise be. In doing so, the movement had managed to come full circle from the polemics of the sixteenth and seventeenth centuries. Whereas once shelves groaned with tracts explaining how the atheist was the 'most bad man', 'the danger of society' for whom 'truth [was] a fable, and peace a cowardice', now they were full of books explaining that it was the religious person who was a threat to knowledge, peace and society.

Hitchens' book swarmed with sweeping statements, sophistry, non-sequiturs, hyperbole and windmill-tilting, the literary equivalent of being pinned in the corner by a pub bore near closing time. 'Religion is not unlike racism,' Hitchens explained.[120] Those who thought Saddam Hussein's regime was secular 'were deluding themselves'.[121] The German pastor Dietrich Bonhoeffer was motivated by an 'admirable but nebulous humanism'.[122] 'In no real, as opposed to nominal sense ... was [Reverend Martin Luther King] a Christian'.[123]

By no means all New Atheist publications were as absurd. Daniel Dennett, a philosopher of considerable repute, wrote a book on how 'religion' could be understood as a natural phenomenon, studied by scientific methods and explained in evolutionary terms. This was not a particularly contentious idea – as critics pointed out at the time, the human use of music or mathematics was explicable (in one sense at least) by evolution, but that didn't mean music or mathematics were without truth or meaning. Nor was it a particularly offensive one: the eminent sociologist of religion Robert Bellah would subsequently publish a massive (and better evidenced) book about *Religion in Human Evolution*, provoking not scandal but an informed and reasonable debate in religious circles.[124] Evolutionary analysis of religion need not be atheistic.

Reasonableness, however, did not sell books, and the New Atheism spasm was nothing if not an astonishing publishing phenomenon. Beyond the canonical New Atheist texts themselves there were Portable Atheists, Quotable Atheists, Atheist Manifestos, Atheist Handbooks, Atheist Readers, Atheist Primers, Atheist Bibles, Secular Bibles, Manuals for Creating Atheists, Atheist Histories of Belief, Atheist Guides to Christmas, Atheist Guides to Reality, Little Books of Atheist Spirituality, and then, in response, innumerable ripostes and refutations by believers. The 'religious' book market had never looked so healthy.

The most successful of all these publications was Richard Dawkins' *The God Delusion*. Dawkins had earned himself a large, devoted and well-deserved following long before his atheist *magnum opus* through a series of matchless books explaining and defending evolution. A fierce attachment to rationalism, apparently untroubled by a belief in memes,[125] and a gift for metaphor combined to make him the finest science popularizer of his generation and land him a new professorship for the public understanding of science at Oxford University.

That gift for metaphor could prove as misleading as it was enlightening, however. Having been criticized for his use of the word 'robot' to describe human beings in *The Selfish Gene*, Dawkins replied that 'part of the problem lies with the popular, but erroneous, associations of the word "robot"', before going on to tell people what they should understand from the word.[126] When taken to task by the philosopher Mary Midgley for his careless use of the word 'selfish' to describe genes, Dawkins replied, 'In effect I am saying: "Provided I define selfishness in a particular way an oak tree, or a gene, may legitimately be described as selfish."'[127] This lent his arguments a slipperiness that was to prove useful, such as when he described faith as 'one of the world's great evils, comparable to the smallpox virus but harder to eradicate.[128] The idea that anyone should use such a metaphor after what atheist and Nazi regimes had done to various religious groups in the twentieth century beggared belief. But if robot didn't actually mean robot, and selfish didn't actually mean selfish, presumably eradicating the virus of religion didn't meant what it apparently did.

In spite of Darwin's own opinions on the matter, Dawkins was convinced that evolution was in direct competition with God. Religion, he thought, 'is a scientific theory',[129] 'a competing explanation for facts about the universe and life'.[130] More specifically, it is an alternative to natural selection. 'God and natural selection are … the only two workable theories we have of why we exist.'[131]

Dawkins' belief in this was presumably borne of the fact that, over the previous half-century, millions had followed where Whitcomb and Morris had led and did indeed think precisely that. In an increasing number of 'fundamentalist' churches, predominantly but by no means exclusively in America, Darwinism was denounced as irredeemably godless. Dawkins entirely agreed with them. The result was a painful standoff in which one unshakeable set of convictions squared up against the other. As far as the fundamentalists, of both persuasions, were concerned, subtle or sophisticated religious commitments, especially those that understood religiosity as a pattern of life rather than a set of verifiable propositions, were little more than sophistry. The New Atheists, like their opponents, liked their religion undiluted and uncomplicated, and were unwilling to grant to theological (and often philosophical) reasoning the same charity or presumption of intelligence they naturally granted other disciplines. Turning from *The Selfish Gene* to *The God Delusion* was to turn from a judge who was carefully weighing up the evidence before him to one who was wearing a black cap before he entered the courtroom. Religious beliefs were, by definition, simple, propositional and obviously falsifiable. Anything else was casuistry.

It was a problem repeatedly, if fruitlessly, pointed out by critics. 'What Dawkins does too often is to concentrate his attack on fundamentalists. But there are many believers who are just not fundamentalists,' remarked the Nobel prize-winning physicist Peter Higgs.[132] Dawkins's fault, wrote Antony Flew, himself one of the world's most prominent atheists until he decided late in life that the evidence for deism was stronger, was 'his scandalous and apparently deliberate refusal to present the doctrine that he appears to think he has refuted in its strongest form', a failure which indicated 'his insincerity of academic purpose'.[133] Does Dawkins imagine, asked the literary critic Terry Eagleton rhetorically in his review of *The God Delusion*, 'like a bumptious young barrister that you can defeat the opposition while being complacently ignorant of its toughest case?'[134]

It was not Dawkins' verbal shiftiness or intellectual double standards that were most troubling, however, as the way he spoke of those who thought differently. This ran all the way from contemptuous to gratuitously unpleasant. Some targets were predictable. Pope Benedict was a 'leering old fixer'.[135] The Christian philosopher David Bentley Hart was a 'yammering fumblewit'.[136] Others were less so. The eminent philosopher Sir Anthony Kenny was dubbed '[a] "philosopher" with special training in obscurantism', while then Astronomer Royal Sir Martin Rees was called 'a compliant Quisling'.

Less excusably, ordinary believers came under his withering gaze. In a revealing discussion on his website, when he was 'thinking aloud, among friends,' Dawkins suggested that atheists 'should probably abandon the irremediably religious precisely because that is what they are – irremediable'. He was more interested, he wrote, in the 'fence-sitters ... I think that they are likely to be swayed by a display of naked contempt. Nobody likes to be laughed at. Nobody wants to be the butt of contempt'.[137] These sentiments were strangely redolent of the conversation Beatrice Webb had had with Eleanor Marx a century earlier, in which the latter had talked about the need to 'ridicule' people out of their beliefs. The difference was that Marx was talking about ridiculing people's beliefs, whereas Dawkins wanted to humiliate the people themselves.

'A type of atheism that refused to revere humanity would be a genuine advance': Difficult atheism

New Atheism died with a whimper rather than a bang. Christopher Hitchens died tragically early from cancer, Sam Harris published a book which attempted to show how science could determine morality, and Richard Dawkins discovered Twitter. In August 2013, the editor of *New Humanist*, the magazine of the Rationalist Association in Britain, wrote a piece claiming that Dawkins provided 'a case study in how not to do it'. He went on to point out that blanket condemnations of religious groups were morally dubious (as well as counterproductive); that religious believers were in fact no less intelligent than non-believers; and that secularism did not mean excluding religious believers from public life. The tone and arguments could hardly have been more different from those of the New Atheists.[138]

It is hard to tell whether the movement had been successful. Certainly, the number of people calling themselves atheist increased in the first decade of the century. In many Western nations the proportion of atheists had never been higher, and although they were still a minority, particularly in the US, atheism appeared to have the momentum. That recognized, the trend had been identified many years before the millennium. The number of Western atheists had been growing throughout the twentieth century, although not as fast as the number of people who had relinquished religious affiliation – a category with which atheism was often erroneously confused. Rising living standards seemed to be the main driver, although the evidence of a direct correlation between economic growth and 'secularization' became more dubious in the later years of the century, as non-European nations industrialized yet failed to follow the European path. The population of atheists grew most significantly in the decades before the new century, its growth owing much to aggressively politicized religion – always atheism's best recruiting sergeant. Yet, the movement did appear to have some success. It was, for instance, somewhat easier to be an atheist in America in 2013 than it had been a generation earlier. That recognized, the nation does not appear ready to elect its first 'Bright' as President.[139]

Whatever its actual impact had been, New Atheism was certainly successful in occluding other, more traditional types of atheism. These still lurked in the shadows. During Queen Elizabeth II's Jubilee celebrations in 2012, Polly Toynbee, a liberal newspaper columnist and President of the British Humanist Association, wrote an article in which she claimed that 'the tyranny of the monarchy lies not in its residual temporal power but in its spiritual power … subjugat[ing] the national imagination, infantilising us with false imaginings and a bogus heritage of our island story'.[140] It was a courageous article to publish when more or less the entire nation was celebrating the Jubilee. More to the point, it read like something that could have been published during the Diamond Jubilee of 1897.

Other forms of atheism also persisted. New Atheism had made less of an impact on continental Europe than it did in the North Atlantic world, and alternative atheist traditions, particularly those that had developed mid-century, remained strong there. The French philosopher Michael Onfray was sometimes mentioned in the same breath as the New Atheists, but his thought, though no less uncompromising in its rejection of God, was subtly different in its emphasis and perceived implications.

As a rule, French Atheism retained this different tint and remained closer to what the historian Christopher Watkin has called 'ascetic' atheism. This was the tradition in which the true force of Nietzsche's criticism was taken seriously, 'where the same disease that killed God has withered away ideas like Truth, Reason and Humanity', and where 'far from triumphantly acceding to God's vacated throne, Man finds himself unable to survive the divine demise'.[141] This was a 'difficult atheism' because it refused the dishonest platitudes of humanistic atheism,[142] and it stood in direct contrast to what Watkin called 'parasitic' atheism, which tried to preserve a theological structure by replacing divine content with naïve, celebratory humanism.

Such ideas might have been stereotypically French, but they were not confined to France. One of the most effective critics of the lazy and unthinking humanism that marked Anglophone atheism around the turn of the millennium was the British philosopher John Gray, himself an atheist, whose lucid, vigorous prose was everything that post-secular continental philosophers' wasn't.

Gray demolished self-satisfied humanistic atheism with aplomb, attacking it with precisely the same Darwinian weapons that it had used on God. Human uniqueness, he argued, was an essentially religious, indeed a Judeo-Christian idea, which modern-day atheist humanists had clung onto with scant justification. 'The unique status of humans is hard to defend, and even to understand, when it is cut off from any idea of transcendence.'[143] An honest atheistic view, in Gray's mind, should take Darwinism seriously, rather than merely genuflecting before the altar of natural selection while smuggling religious ideas of human significance, dignity and rationality in at the transepts. 'Atheism and humanism … seem to be conjoined when in fact they are at odds … a type of atheism that refused to revere humanity would be a genuine advance.'[144]

Gray's critique pinpointed the problem that had dogged atheism from its earliest days, or at least its earliest public days, namely the simultaneous degradation and elevation of the human. Dawkins was a prime exhibit here. By his reckoning, humans were no more than 'survival machines – robot vehicles blindly programmed to preserve the selfish molecules known as genes'.[145] And yet, as he concluded *The Selfish Gene*, 'we, alone on earth, can rebel against the tyranny of the selfish replicators', or, as he put it more pithily still, we should 'try to teach generosity and altruism, because we are all born selfish'. Here was the definitive humiliation of the human (justified by a particular interpretation of evolution) accompanied by the supreme commission (justified by what beyond mere sentiment is unclear), a problematic combination that had marked much atheist thought since at least the 1740s. Mankind was nothing more than a sophisticated animal, devoid of divine image, eternal soul and, according to many, free will. Yet, he was also uniquely capable of transforming this base metal into transcendent humanist gold. Gray was merely pointing out, in prose as bracing as any New Atheist, that you couldn't do both. 'Humanism is not an alternative to religious belief, but rather a degenerate and unwitting version of it.'[146]

Gray's observation that 'on an evolutionary view the human has no built-in bias to truth or rationality' was far from idiosyncratic.[147] In a similar vein another philosopher, Thomas Nagel, one of the most important analytic thinkers of his generation, published a short book that made the same point albeit from a different direction. As far as Nagel was concerned, the 'materialist neo-Darwinian conception of nature' failed to explain the origins of life, human consciousness, intentionality, meaning and value, and was therefore 'almost certainly false'.

Drawing on the work of Sharon Street[148] among others, Nagel argued that a genuine adherence to evolution by natural selection would 'almost certainly require us to give up moral realism – the natural conviction that our moral judgements are true or false independent of our beliefs'.[149] Like Gray, Nagel was questioning the slapdash way in which naturalism/materialism was judged capable of sustaining value realism. Unlike him, he insisted that a commitment to value realism trumped materialist Darwinism, rather than the other way around.

Nagel argued that mind was not just an 'afterthought or an accident or an add-on' to matter, but 'a basic aspect of nature'.[150] This was an idealism that fitted well with a certain religious view of life but what made Nagel's argument particularly interesting was that he explicitly rejected theism as a possible solution to these problems he was posing, *and* that he had no coherent alternative answer to offer in instead. This was an atheist slicing into atheism's most sacred cow but with nothing to put in its place.

Nagel was predictably eviscerated by some atheist philosophers – Simon Blackburn commented that 'if there were a philosophical Vatican, [Nagel's] book would be a good candidate for going on to the Index'[151] – but his contribution, alongside Gray's, was a welcome return to a more reflective, self-critical and realistic note in atheist thought.

'The stark divide between people of religion and without religion is too crude': Religious atheism
Atheism took another, more fruitful turn in the shadow of New Atheism when a number of sceptics, no more convinced by the existence of God than the New Atheists, began to argue that atheism might actually have something to learn from religion. The idea, sometimes, if unoriginally, called New New Atheism, sought to appreciate and appropriate aspects of religiosity, particularly of religious practice, and although hardly new, or free from condescension, it was a welcome change from rhetoric that insinuated that believers were the moral and intellectual equivalent of plague rats.

At an academic level, the liberal political theorist Ronald Dworkin, delivering the Einstein lectures shortly before he died, argued that 'the familiar stark divide between people of religion and without religion is too crude' and that it was quite possible for atheists to be religious, in a profound rather than trivial sense of that word.[152]

At a more popular level, the writer Alain de Botton published a book on *Religion for Atheists* which suggested atheists were better stealing from religion than mocking it. 'Religion', shorn of its doctrine, claims to truth and all traces of the supernatural, might equip non-believers to live well and wisely, by means of patterns of thought, discipline, community and aesthetic sense honed over centuries. Religious believers debated whether it was better to be patronized or ridiculed.

Where de Botton pointed, some travelled. A New Atheist church was formed in North London, meeting monthly to sing, build community and listen to comedians. Within a year branches had opened in 20 further locations worldwide. It was a kind of resurrection of the ethical church movement of 100 years earlier, tailored to the tastes of the twenty-first century.

In a similar and more earnest vein, humanist associations in Britain and elsewhere recovered from their nadir in the post-war period and started to offer naming ceremonies, funerals and memorials officiated over by accredited humanist 'celebrants' who charged a small fee for their service. On the principle that imitation was the sincerest form of flattery, such activity augured for a more honest conversation between atheists and the religious. The picture was not as rosy worldwide. On the one hand, atheists, like many other religious believers, remained effectively second-class citizens in the majority of Islamic countries. On the other, believers remained vulnerable, sometimes to the point of being brutalized, in the world's remaining atheist regimes.

Ludwig Wittgenstein once commented that doubt was essentially parasitic on faith. 'Doubting and non-doubting behaviour ... there is only the first if there is the second'.[153] Atheism is not doubt. Indeed, some of the atheists discussed in these pages seem to have been congenitally incapable of doubt (or, at least, self-doubt). Nonetheless, Wittgenstein's observation applies just as much to atheism as it does to its more uncertain cousin. After a troubled century in which its former promises not only failed to materialize but mutated into regimes of oppression that not even the religious had managed to achieve, atheism appears to have a renewed future in the twenty-first century. But it does so largely because religion, in its various guises, is once again a dominant feature on our social, political and intellectual landscapes. It is a pleasing irony with which to end. Atheism is here to stay because God is back.

Notes

Introduction

1   See, for example, Dio Cassius, *Epitome*, LXVII.14 and Justin Martyr, *First Apology*, I.V–VI, both quoted in *A New Eusebius: documents illustrating the history of the Church to AD 337* (ed.) J. Stevenson (London: SPCK, 1987), pp. 6, 60–1. See also Athenogoras, *Plea for the Christians*, III in *The Ante-Nicene Fathers: Translations of the Writings of the Fathers down to A.D. 325*, Alexander Roberts and James Donaldson (eds) (Grand Rapids: Eerdmans, 1979–86) pp. 123–48.

2   For a similar accusation against the Jews see Josephus, *Against Apion*, II.148 (Loeb Classical Library) p. 351.

3   *The Martyrdom of Polycarp*, quoted in *A New Eusebius*, pp. 23–30. Some translations, such as Maxwell Staniforth's for Penguin (Early Christian Writings, 1968; rev. 1987) render the relevant Greek text Αιρε τους αθεους as 'Down with the *infidels*' rather than 'atheists', a fact that neatly points to the complexities of the term and its connotations.

4   The way people should have understood and behaved was not, of course, the way they did. In the words of early modern historian Keith Thomas, 'social theory was a poor guide to the way in which many people of the time actually behaved'. Keith Thomas, *The Ends of Life: Road to Fulfilment in Early Modern England* (Oxford: Oxford University Press, 2009), p. 29.

5   John Redwood, *Reason, Ridicule and Religion: the Age of Enlightenment in England, 1660–1750* (London: Thames and Hudson, 1976), p. 9.

6   Taylor's Case 1 Vent 293, quoted in Russell Sandberg, *Law and Religion* (Cambridge: Cambridge University Press, 2011), p. 133.

7   Victoria Frede, *Doubt, Atheism, and the Nineteenth-century Russian Intelligentsia* (Madison: University of Wisconsin Press, 2011), p. 15.

8   The great recent exception here, focused more on the secular mind rather than atheism *per se*, is Charles Taylor's *A Secular Age* (Cambridge, MA:

Harvard University Press, 2007) which sees the development as one of accretion rather than stripping away.

9　　Stephen LeDrew, 'The evolution of atheism: scientific and humanistic approaches', *History of the Human Sciences* 2012, 25(3), pp. 70–87.

10　　See: http://www.atheismresearch.com/

11　　Fritz Mauthner, *Der Atheismus und seine Geschichte im Abendlande* (Reprografischer Nachdruck der Ausgabe Stuttgart/Berlin 1920–3). (Hildesheim: Georg Olms Verlagsbuchhandlung, 1963).

12　　As this book was being completed, Oxford University Press published a substantial *Handbook of Atheism* edited by Stephen Bullivant and Michael Ruse that should fill the gap for the time being.

13　　Anthony Kenny, *A New History of Western Philosophy: Philosophy in the Modern World, Volume IV* (Oxford: Oxford University Press, 2008), p. 318.

Chapter 1 – Possibilities

1　　Roger Ascham, *The Schoolmaster* in *The English Works of Roger Ascham*, William Aldis Wright (ed.) (Cambridge: Cambridge University Press, 1904), p. 236.

2　　Ascham, *English Works*, pp. 229–33.

3　　*Letters de Gui Patin* (ed.), J. H. Reveillé-Parise (Paris, 1846) III.80, quoted in Michael Hunter and David Wootton (eds), *Atheism from the Reformation to the Enlightenment* (Oxford: Clarendon, 1992), p. 56.

4　　Voltaire, *Oeuvres complètes des Voltaire*, Vol. 8, *Histoire de Jenni* (Paris: Desoer, 1817), p. 366, quoted in Blom, *Wicked Company: Freethinkers and Friendship in pre-Revolutionary Paris* (Phoenix, 2012), p. 89.

5　　Richard Popkin, *The History of Scepticism: From Savonarola to Bayle* (Oxford: Oxford University Press, 2003), p. 101.

6　　Marin Mersene, *Quaestiones celeberrimae in Genesim … In hoc volumine athei, et deistae impugnatur, et expugnatur …* (Paris, 1623), quoted in Alan Charles Kors, *Atheism in France, 1650–1729: Vol. 1. The Orthodox Sources of Disbelief* (Princeton, NJ: Princeton University Press, 1990), p. 30.

7　　Jonathan Israel, *Enlightenment Contested: Philosophy, Modernity, and the Emancipation of Man, 1670–1752* (Oxford: Oxford University Press, 2006), p. 164. Averroism is the school of thought combining Aristotelianism with Islam, named after the twelfth-century philosopher Ibn Rushd or Averroës.

8　　Michael J. Buckley, *At the Origins of Modern Atheism* (New Haven and London: Yale University Press, 1987), p. 10.

9   Quoted in Michael Hunter, 'The Problem of "Atheism" in Early Modern England', in *Transactions of the Royal Historical Society*, Fifth Series, Vol. 35 (1985), p. 138.

10   Buckley, *Origins*, p. 10.

11   *Ibid.*

12   E. A. Strathmann, *Sir Walter Ralegh: A Study in Elizabethan Skepticism* (New York: Columbia University Press, 1951), pp. 46–52.

13   Quoted in Keith Thomas, *Religion and the Decline of Magic* (London: Weidenfeld and Nicolson, 1971), p. 167.

14   G. E. Aylmer, 'Unbelief in Seventeenth-century England', in *Puritans and Revolutionaries: Essays in Seventeenth-century History Presented to Christopher Hill*, Donald Pennington and Keith Thomas (eds) (Oxford: Clarendon Press, 1978), pp. 22–46.

15   Kors, *Atheism*, pp. 17–42.

16   Christopher Haigh, *The Plain Man's Pathways to Heaven: Kinds of Christianity in Post-Reformation England, 1570–1640* (Oxford: Oxford University Press, 2007), p. 169.

17   Thomas, *Religion*, p. 167.

18   Hunter and Wootton, *Atheism*, p. 79.

19   Robert Burton, *The Anatomy of Melancholy*, (Oxford, 1621), III, p. 249.

20   Nicholas Breton, *The Good and the Badde, or Descriptions of the Worthies and Unworthies of this Age* (1616), quoted in *The Broadview Anthology of Seventeenth-Century Verse and Prose*, Alan Rudrum, Joseph Black, and Holly Faith Nelson (eds) (Ontario: Broadview Press Ltd, 2000), p. 15.

21   Charles Blount, *The Two First Books of Philostratus, Concerning the Life of Apollonius Tyaneus* (London, 1680), p. 81.

22   Francis Bacon, 'Of Atheism', in *Francis Bacon: The Major Works* (Oxford: Oxford University Press, 2008), pp. 371–2.

23   Laurent Pollot, *Dialogues contre la pluralité des religions et l'athéisme* (La Rochelle, 1595), 97r, quoted in Kors, *Atheism*, p. 28.

24   David Derodon, *L'athéisme convaincu* (Orange, 1659), pp. 148–51, quoted in Kors, *Atheism*, p. 31.

25   Pierre Bayle, *An Historical and Critical Dictionary, selected and abridged … in Four Volumes* (London: Hunt & Clarke, 1826), I.162.

26   Thomas Nash, *Works*, Vol. 1, R. B. McKerrow (ed.) (Bullen, 1904), pp. 114–29.

27   Pierre Viret, *Deux dialogues: L'alcumie du purgatoire; L'homme naturel, 1544, 1561*, Jacques Courvoisier (ed.) (Lausanne, 1971), p. 32, quoted in Kors, *Atheism*, p. 26.

28   A legendarily decadent king of Assyria.

29 Molière, Don Juan, I.i, in *Don Juan and Other Plays* (Oxford: Oxford University Press, 2008).

30 *Histoire des Ouvrages des Savans*, Henri Basnage de Beauval (ed.) (1689), pp. 81–2, quoted in Kors, *Atheism*, p. 39.

31 David Derodon, *L'athéisme convaincu* (Orange, 1659), quoted in Kors, *Atheism*, p. 23.

32 René Rapin, S. J., *Oeuvres de P[ère] Rapin*, 3 Vols (The Hague, 1725), I. 422, quoted in Kors, *Atheism*, p. 17.

33 John Milton, *The Christian Doctrine*, in *The Works of John Milton* (eds), J. Handord and W. Dunn (New York, 1933), IV.29; quoted in David Berman, *A History of Atheism in Britain: From Hobbes to Russell* (London: Routledge, 1990), p. 158.

34 Israel, *Enlightenment Contested*, p. 164.

35 William Blackstone, *Commentaries on the Law of England* (Oxford, 1769), IV.4, p. 44.

36 Lucien Febvre, *The Problem of Unbelief in the Sixteenth Century: the Religion of Rabelais* (Cambridge, MA and London: Harvard University Press, 1982).

37 'Febvre believed that until Gassendi and Descartes unbelief was necessarily handicapped because the philosophy and science of the day made it impossible to separate successfully the natural from the supernatural, a necessary preliminary to denying persuasively the existence of the supernatural'. See David Wootton, 'Lucien Febvre and the problem of unbelief in the early modern period', *The Journal of Modern History*, Vol. 60, No. 4 (December 1988), pp. 702–3.

38 Hunter and Wootton, *Atheism*, p. 25.

39 Quoted in Anne Hudson, *The Premature Reformation: Wycliffite Texts and Lollard History* (Oxford: Clarendon Press, 1988), p. 384.

40 John Edwards, 'Religious faith and doubt in late medieval Spain: Soria circa 1450–1500', *Past and Present*, No. 120 (August 1988), pp. 3–25.

41 Quoted in Febvre, *Problem of Unbelief*, p. 130.

42 For an illuminating survey see Haigh, *Plain Man's Pathways*.

43 Quoted in Thomas, *Religion*, p. 169.

44 *Ibid.*

45 Quoted in Nicholas Davidson, 'Marlowe and Atheism', in D. Grantley and P. Roberts (eds), *Christopher Marlowe and English Renaissance Culture* (Aldershot: Scolar, 1996), p. 137.

46 See Davidson, 'Marlowe and Atheism', p. 141. Marlowe's beliefs about Christ and St John were unusual and offensive, but not unique. Forty years earlier one Francesco Calcagno had been denounced in Brescia for saying that Christ 'often had carnal knowledge of St John'.

47   Charles Nicholl, '"By my onely meanes sett down": The Texts of Marlowe's Atheism' in Takashi Kozuka and J. R. Mulryne, *Shakespeare, Marlowe, Jonson: New Directions in Biography* (Aldershot: Ashgate, 2006).

48   Geoffroy Vallée, *La béatitude des chestiens ou le fléo de la foy (1573)*, quoted in Kors, *Atheism*, p. 27.

49   Hunter and Wootton, *Atheism*, p. 25.

50   M. Hunter, 'The Problem of "Atheism" in Early Modem England', *Transactions of the Royal Historical Society*, 5th Series, 35 (1985), pp. 135–57; David Wootton, 'Lucien Febvre and the problem of unbelief in the early modern period', *The Journal of Modern History*, Vol. 60, No. 4 (December 1988), pp. 695–730.

51   It is thus to be distinguished from Academic scepticism which positively asserted that *no* knowledge was possible.

52   See C. B. Schmitt, 'The Rediscovery of Ancient Skepticism in Modern Times', in M. Burnyeat (ed.), *The Skeptical Tradition* (Berkeley: University of California Press, 1983), pp. 226–41.

53   See Anthony Grafton, *New World, Ancient Texts: The Power of Tradition and the Shock of Discovery* (Cambridge, MA: Harvard University Press, 1995).

54   Jonathan Israel, *Radical Enlightenment: Philosophy and the Making of Modernity 1650–1750* (Oxford: Oxford University Press, 2001), p. 544.

55   Thomas More, *Utopia* (Penguin Classics, 2003), p. 101.

56   François Garasse, *La Doctrine curieuse des beaux esprits de ce temps* (Paris, 1623), quoted in Tulio Gregory, 'Pierre Charron's 'Scandalous Book', in Hunter and Wotton, *Atheism*, p. 87.

57   Pierre Charron, *De la sagesse*, II.2.306, in Hunter and Wootton, *Atheism*, p. 90.

58   Charron, *De la sagesse*, II.2.308, p. 92.

59   Charron, *De la sagesse*, II.3.325, p. 92.

60   Charron, *De la sagesse*, I.16.132, p. 92.

61   Charron, *De la sagesse*, II.5.346–7, p. 92.

62   Charron, *De la sagesse*, II.5.342–4, p. 98.

63   David Hume, *The Natural History of Religion*, in David Hume, *Dialogues and Natural History of Religion* (Oxford World's Classics, 1998), p. 132.

64   See, for example, Maurizio Viroli, *Machiavelli's God* (Princeton: Princeton University Press, 2010).

65   *Confession of the Faith of the Protestant Churches of France*, 1559; Institutes of the Christian Religion, I.7.4.

66   Martin Luther, *On the Bondage of the Will* (1525).

67   Robert Ferguson, *The Interest of Reason in Religion* (London, 1675) quoted in Popkin, *Scepticism*, p. 74.

68   Popkin, *Scepticism*, p. 53.

69   cf. I Corinthians 1.

70   Michel de Montaigne, *An Apology for Raymond Sebond*, in *Complete Essays* (London: Penguin, 1993), p. 557.

71   Popkin, *Scepticism*, p. 82.

72   René Descartes, *Meditations on First Philosophy* (Cambridge: Cambridge University Press, 1996), p. 12–15.

73   Objections to the Meditations and Descartes's Replies, at www.earlymod-erntexts.com, 1, p. 6

74   *Ibid.*

75   Popkin, *Scepticism*, p. 155.

76   Stephen Gaukroger, *Descartes: An Intellectual Biography* (Oxford: Clarendon Press, 1995).

77   Popkin, *Scepticism*, p. 168.

78   Buckley, *Atheism*, p. 67.

79   On the pelican see the Aberdeen Bestiary, quoted in Peter Harrison, 'The Bible and the Emergence of Modern Science', *Science and Christian Belief* (2006), 18, p. 121.

80   Harrison, 'Emergence', p. 126.

81   Stephen Greenblatt, *The Swerve: How the Renaissance Began* (London: Vintage, 2012), p. 233.

82   Francis Bacon, *The Advancement of Learning*, I.vi.16, in Bacon, *Works*, p. 153.

83   Stephen Gaukroger, *The Emergence of a Scientific Culture Science and the Shaping of Modernity*, 1210–1685 (Oxford: Oxford University Press, 2005), p. 23.

84   Bacon, *Advancement,* in Bacon, *Works*, p. 153.

85   *Ibid.*

86   Origen, *On First Principles*, IV.iii.4.

87   Thomas Burnet, *The Sacred Theory of the Earth*, 2nd ed. (London, 1691), p. 16.

88   2 Esdras 14.21–2.

89   Noel Malcolm, 'Leviathan, the Pentateuch, and the Origins of Modern Biblical Criticism', in *Leviathan After 350 Years*, Tom Sorell and Luc Foisneau (eds) (Oxford: Oxford University Press, 2004), p. 245.

90   e.g. Numbers 21.14.

91   Malcolm, 'Leviathan', p. 249.

92   Nash, *Works*, I, 172.

93   Popkin, *Scepticism*, p. 222.

94   Popkin, *Scepticism*, p. 237.

95   *Ibid.*

96   Christopher Hill, *The English Bible and the Seventeenth Century Revolution* (London: Allen Lane, 1993), p. 232.

97   Thomas Hobbes, *Leviathan* (Oxford World's Classics, 1998), I.5, p. 31.

98   Hobbes, *Leviathan*, IV.46, p. 447.

99   Hobbes, *Leviathan*, I.4, p. 26.

100   Hobbes, *Leviathan*, I.3, p. 19.

101   Thomas Hobbes, *Thomas White's 'De mundo' Examined*, (trans.) Harold Whitmore Jones (London, Bradford University Press, 1976), pp. 326, 341, 391.

102   Hobbes, *Leviathan*, III.34, p. 262.

103   Hobbes, *Leviathan*, Introduction, p. 7.

104   Hobbes, *Leviathan*, II.29, p. 218.

105   Hobbes, *Leviathan*, III.5, p. 272.

106   Hobbes, *Leviathan*, III.32, p. 248.

107   Hobbes, *Leviathan*, III.32, p. 249.

108   Hobbes, *Leviathan*, III.37, p. 291.

109   Hobbes, *Leviathan*, III.37, p. 291.

110   Hobbes, *Leviathan*, III.32, p. 196.

111   Hobbes, *Leviathan*, I.7, p. 44.

112   Noel Malcolm (ed.), *The Correspondence of Thomas Hobbes* (Oxford: Clarendon Press, 1994), p. 120.

113   Writing to Matthew Wren, Bishop of Ely, in October 1651; quoted in Richard Tuck, 'The "Christian Atheism" of Thomas Hobbes', in Hunter and Wootton, *Atheism*, p. 111.

114   Edward, Earl of Clarendon, *A Brief View and Survey of the Dangerous and Pernicious Errors to Church and State, in Mr. Hobbes's Book, Entitled 'Leviathan'* (Oxford, 1676), pp. 72–3.

115   Thomas Hobbes, *Mr. Hobbes Considered in his Loyalty, Religion, Reputation, and Manners. By way of Letter to Dr. Wallis* (London, 1662), p. 37.

116   Quoted in A. P. Martinich, *Hobbes: A Biography* (Cambridge: Cambridge University Press, 1999), p. 326.

117   Thomas Hobbes, 'Six lessons to the Savilian professors of mathematics', in Hobbes, *The Collected English works of Thomas Hobbes*, William Molesworth (ed.) (London: Routledge/Thoemmes, 1997) Vol. 7, p. 350.

118   Martinich, *Hobbes*, p. 330.

119   Charles Wolseley, *The Reasonableness of Scripture-Belief* (London, 1672).

120   Martinich, *Hobbes*, p. 350.

121   See S. A. Lloyd, *Ideals as Interests in Hobbes's 'Leviathan': The Power of Mind over Matter* (Cambridge and New York: Cambridge University Press, 1992); A. P. Martinich, *The Two Gods of 'Leviathan': Thomas Hobbes on Religion and Politics* (Cambridge and New York: Cambridge University Press, 1992).

122   See Peter Geach, 'The Religion of Thomas Hobbes', in *Religious Studies* (1981) 17: 549–58.

123   See Richard Tuck in Hunter and Wootton, *Atheism*; Berman, *History*; Quentin Skinner, *Reason and Rhetoric in the Philosophy of Thomas Hobbes* (Cambridge and New York: Cambridge University Press, 1996). See Douglas M. Jesseph, 'Hobbes's Atheism', in *Midwest Studies in Philosophy*, XXVI (2002), pp. 140–66 which provides a good overview of opinions, before arguing forcibly that Hobbes was indeed an atheist.

124   British Library, MS. Harl. 7257 (Journal of the House of Commons), f.220r.

125   Quoted in Martinich, *The Two Gods*, p. 339.

126   Quoted in Steven Nadler, *A Book Forged in Hell: Spinoza's Scandalous Treatise and the Birth of the Secular Age* (Princeton, NJ: Woodstock: Princeton University Press, 2011), p. 231.

127   Benedict de Spinoza, *Theological-Political Treatise* (Cambridge: Cambridge University Press, 2007), p. 30.

128   Spinoza, *Theological-Political Treatise*, p. 35.

129   Spinoza, *Theological-Political Treatise*, p. 84.

130   Spinoza, *Theological-Political Treatise*, p. 106.

131   Spinoza, *Theological-Political Treatise*, p. 108.

132   Spinoza, *Theological-Political Treatise*, p. 101.

133   Spinoza, *Theological-Political Treatise*, p. 97.

134   Spinoza, *Theological-Political Treatise*, p. 132.

135   The Remonstrants were themselves an offshoot of Dutch Calvinists, taking their name from the Remonstrance, a declaration dating from 1610 and signed by numerous 'moderates', which rejected a number of Calvinist doctrines and called for greater theological toleration.

136   Nadler, *A Book Forged*, p. 231.

137   Spinoza, *Theological-Political Treatise*, p. 161.

138   Spinoza, *Theological-Political Treatise*, p. 184.

139   Spinoza, *Theological-Political Treatise*, p. 195.

140   *Ibid.*

141   Spinoza, *Theological-Political Treatise*, p. 196.

142   Benedict de Spinoza, *Ethics* (Penguin, 1996), p. 20.

143   Spinoza, *Theological-Political Treatise*, p. 197.

144   Spinoza, *Theological-Political Treatise*, pp. 197-8.

145   Spinoza, *Theological-Political Treatise*, p. 199.

146   Spinoza, *Theological-Political Treatise*, p. 200.

147   Spinoza, *Theological-Political Treatise*, p. 201.

148   Spinoza, *Theological-Political Treatise*, p. 208.

149   Spinoza, *Theological-Political Treatise*, p. 238.

150 See *Treatise Political*, in Spinoza, *Complete Works*, Michael L. Morgan (ed.) (Indianapolis, IN: Hackett Publishing, 2002), pp. 676–754.
151 Quoted in Israel, *Radical Enlightenment*, p. 607.
152 George Berkeley, *Alciphron or: The Minute Philosopher, In Seven Dialogues* (London: J. Tonson, 1732) VII.26.
153 Quoted in Nadler, *A Book Forged*, p. 50.
154 Richard Blackmore, *Creation. A philosophical poem. In seven books* (London: S. Buckley; J. Tonson, 1712), p. 101.
155 Quoted in Nadler, *A book forged*, p. 174.
156 Israel, *Radical Enlightenment*, p. 698.
157 Israel, *Radical Enlightenment*, p. 695.
158 Nadler, *A book forged*, p. 55.
159 Israel, *Radical enlightenment*, p. 703.
160 Popkin, *Scepticism*, p. 289.
161 Philip Blom, *Wicked Company*, p. 40.
162 Quoted in Kors, *Atheism*, p. 36.
163 John Locke, *A Letter Concerning Toleration* in *Two Treatises of Government and A Letter Concerning Toleration,* Ian Shapiro (ed.) (New Haven: Yale University Press, 2003), p. 246.
164 Popkin, *Scepticism*, p. 295.

Chapter 2 – Pioneers

1 T. B. Macaulay, *The History of England* (5 Vols; London 1849–65), iv. 781–4.
2 Hunter and Wootton (eds), *Atheism from the Reformation to the Enlightenment* (Oxford: Clarendon, 1992) p. 225.
3 Hunter and Wootton, *Atheism*, p. 240.
4 *Some Considerations about the Danger of going to Plays. In a Letter to a Friend* (London, 1704).
5 John Milton, *Of True Religion, Heresy, Schism, Toleration* (1673), p. 16.
6 Song by Lord Vaughan, quoted in Redwood, *Reason, Ridicule and Religion: the Age of Enlightenment in England, 1660–1750* (London: Thames and Hudson, 1976), p. 213.
7 Quoted in Peter Harrison 'Religion and the Early Royal Society', in *Science and Christian Belief* (2010) 22, p. 3.
8 Robert Boyle, *Some Physico-Theological Considerations about the Possibility of the Resurrection* (London: T. N. for H. Herringman, 1675), preface.
9 See http://www.stmarylebow.co.uk/#/boyle-lecture-2/4535373186

10 *Physico-Theology, or a Demonstration of the Being and Attributes of God from his Works of Creation* (London: W. Innys, 1716), p. 467.

11 William Whiston, *A New Theory of the Earth* (London, 1696), p. 26.

12 Arianism takes its name from the third- to fourth-century presbyter Arius, whose heretical views on the subordinate nature of Christ were denounced at the Council of Nicaea in 325 but whose ideas and followers remained a significant force in late antiquity.

13 Baruch Spinoza, *Theological-Political Treatise* (Cambridge: Cambridge University Press, 2007) pp. 20–1.

14 Quoted in Redwood, *Religion*, p. 141.

15 *A Letter to the Moral Philosopher Being a Vindication of a Pamphlet, entitled, The Immorality of the Moral Philosopher* (London, 1717), p. 37. Emphases added.

16 Anthony Ashley Cooper, 3rd Earl of Shaftesbury, *A Letter Concerning Enthusiasm* (London, 1707).

17 John Trenchard, *Natural History of Superstition* (London, 1709).

18 Thomas Chubb, *Some Short Reflections on the Grounds and Extent of Authority and Liberty, with Respect to Civil Government* (London, 1728), p. 458.

19 Antony Collins, *A Discourse of the Grounds and Reasons of the Christian Religion in 2 parts* (London 1724), p. vi.

20 Matthew Tindal, *Reasons against Restraining the Press* (London, 1704), p. 7.

21 *Memoirs of the Life and Writings of Matthew Tindall, LL.D. with a History of the Controversies Wherein he was Engaged* (London: E. Curll, 1733), pp. 44–5.

22 Antony Collins, *A Discourse of Free-Thinking* (London, 1713), p. 105.

23 Quoted in Roy Porter, *Enlightenment: Britain and the Creation of the Modern World* (London: Allen Lane, 2000), p. 102.

24 See: http://www.newtonproject.sussex.ac.uk/prism.php?id=44

25 Original letter from Isaac Newton to Richard Bentley, dated 10 December 1692; Source: 189.R.4.47, ff. 4A-5, Trinity College Library, Cambridge, UK.

26 Isaac Newton, Principia Mathematica, III, p. 545.

27 John Locke, *Two Treatises of Government* and *A Letter Concerning Toleration*, Ian Shapiro (ed.) (New Haven: Yale University Press, 2003), p. 215.

28 Quoted in Porter, *Enlightenment*, p. 97.

29 Valentin Loescher, *Praenotiones* (Wittenberg, 1708), pp. 20–2, quoted in Jonathan Israel, *Enlightenment Contested: Philosophy, Modernity, and the Emancipation of Man 1670–1752* (Oxford: Oxford University Press, 2006), p. 164.

30 Friedrich Wilhelm Stosch, *Concordia rationis et fidei* (1692), quoted in Israel, *Enlightenment Contested*, p. 182.

31 Israel, *Radical Enlightenment*, p. 502.

32 Socinians were highly unorthodox Christians who, following the ideas of

the sixteenth-century scholar Fausto Sozzini, rejected the Trinity and the divinity of Christ but maintained a belief in God. Ashkenazi Jews take their name from Ashkenaz, son of Gomer (Genesis 10.3) and were to be found in the Central Europe where they settled from the early Middle Ages.

33   The Jesuits, or Society of Jesus, were founded in 1534 by Ignatius Loyola and defined, among other things, by a special vow of obedience to the pope, from whom they received formal approval six years later. Jansenism was a movement, rather than an order, which developed a century later, primarily in France, which placed a particular emphasis on human sin and divine grace, and thereby ran into constant conflict with Jesuits (and others in the church hierarchy) who saw in their teaching distinct affinities with Calvinism.

34   Jean Meslier, *Testament: Memoir of the Thoughts and Sentiments of Jean Meslier* (Amherst, NY: Prometheus Books, 2009) I, 3. I am very grateful to Charles Devellennes for being able to read his unpublished doctoral thesis, 'The Emergence of Self-Avowed Atheism: The Political Philosophies of Meslier and Holbach' (University of Kent, 2011) on which the following pages dealing with Meslier and D'Holbach draw.

35   Meslier, *Testament*, I, 23–4.

36   Quoted in Philip Blom, *Wicked Company: Freethinkers and Friendship in pre-Revolutionary Paris* (London: Phoenix, 2012), p. 87.

37   Quoted in Blom, *Wicked Company*, p. 87.

38   Meslier, *Testament*, I, 80.

39   Meslier, *Testament*, I, 153.

40   Meslier, *Testament*, I, 209.

41   Meslier, *Testament*, I, 298.

42   Meslier, *Testament*, I, 369.

43   Meslier, *Testament*, I, 113.

44   Meslier, *Testament*, I, 140.

45   Voltaire's letter to Helvétius, 1 May 1763 in Paul Henri Thiry, Baron D'Holbach, *Le Bon Sens du curé J. Meslier, suivi de son Testament.* Paris: 1802, p. 12.

46   Voltaire cited in Meslier, *Testament*, III, 486.

47   Aram Vartanian, 'Trembley's Polyp, La Mettrie, and Eighteenth-Century French Materialism', *Journal of the History of Ideas*, Vol. 11, No. 3 (June 1950), p. 259.

48   Vartanian, 'Trembley's Polyp', p. 259.

49   Georges-Louis Leclerc, Comte de Buffon, *Histoire naturelle* (Paris: De l'Imprimerie Royale, 1949–89), Vol. 2, 17, quoted in Denis Alexander and Ronald Numbers (eds), *Biology and Ideology: From Descartes to Darwin* (Chicago, IL.: University of Chicago Press, 2010), p. 45.

50   Vartanian, 'Trembley's Polyp', p. 268.

51   Not to mention the 11 accompanying volumes with 2,900 engravings.

52   Blom, *Wicked Company*, p. 100.

53   Diderot, *Correspondance*, 15 [Letter from Diderot to Voltaire, 11 June 1749].

54   Blom, *Wicked Company*, p. 75.

55   Paul Henri Thiry D'Holbach, *Théologie portative*, in Paul Henri Thiry D'Holbach, *Œuvres Philosophiques, Tome I*, Jean Pierre Jackson (ed.) (Paris: Alive, 1998) p. 609, quoted in Devellennes, *The Emergence of Self-Avowed Atheism*.

56   D'Holbach, *La Contagion Sacrée*, p. 148, quoted in Devellennes, *The Emergence of Self-Avowed Atheism*.

57   Paul Henri Thiry D'Holbach, *Tableau des Saints*, in Paul Henri Thiry D'Holbach, *Œuvres Philosophiques, Tome III*, Jean Pierre Jackson (ed.) (Paris: Alive, 2001), p. 56, quoted in Devellennes, *The Emergence of Self-Avowed Atheism*.

58   Paul Henri Thiry D'Holbach, *Histoire critique de Jésus-Christ*, in Paul Henri Thiry D'Holbach, *Œuvres Philosophiques, Tome II*, Jean Pierre Jackson (ed.) (Paris: Alive, 1999), p. 761, quoted in Devellennes, *The Emergence of Self-Avowed Atheism*.

59   Hunter and Wootton, *Atheism*, pp. 280–1.

60   Claude Adrien Helvétius, *On the Mind* (London, 1807), II, 6, pp. 62–3.

61   Paul Henri Thiry D'Holbach, *Système Social*, in Paul Henri Thiry D'Holbach, *Œuvres Philosophiques 1773–1790*, Jean Pierre Jackson (ed.) (Paris: Coda, 2004), quoted in Hunter and Wootton, *Atheism*, p. 299.

62   Paul Henri Thiry D'Holbach, *Politique Naturelle*, in Paul Henri Thiry D'Holbach, *Œuvres Philosophiques, Tome III*, Jean Pierre Jackson (ed.) (Paris: Alive, 2001), p. 382, quoted in Devellennes, *The Emergence of Self-Avowed Atheism*.

63   D'Holbach, *Politique Naturelle*, p. 370.

64   Claude Adrien Helvétius, *A Treatise on Man: his Intellectual Faculties and his Education* (London: Albion Press, 1810), Vol. 2, p. 206.

65   D'Holbach, *Christianity Unveiled*, Chapter XVI.

66   Helvétius, *On the Mind* p. 363.

67   Isaiah Berlin, *Freedom and Its Betrayal*, Henry Hardy (ed.) (London: Pimlico, 2003).

68   *Ibid.*, p. 24.

69   Blom, *Wicked Company*, p. 251.

70   Paul Henri Thiry, Baron D'Holbach, *System of Nature; or, the Laws of the Moral and Physical World* (London, 1797), Vol. 1, p. 109.

71 Quoted in Israel, *Enlightenment Contested*, p. 718.

72 La Mettrie, *Machine Man and Other Writings* (Cambridge: Cambridge University Press, 1996), p. 23.

73 Mettrie, *Machine Man,* p. 25.

74 Quoted in Israel, *Enlightenment Contested*, p. 718.

75 *L'Art de Jouir,* (anon.), The Art of Pleasure (1751).

76 Blom, *Wicked Company*, p. 61.

77 Mettrie, *Machine Man*, p. xxiv.

78 Blom, *Wicked Company*, p. 138.

79 David Hume, *An Enquiry concerning Human Understanding* (Oxford: Oxford University Press, 2008), Sec. XII, p. 109.

80 *New Letters of David Hume*, Raymond Klibansky and E. C. Mossner (eds) (Oxford: Clarendon Press, 1954), p. 26.

81 *The Letters of David Hume*, J. Y. T. Grieg (ed.) (Oxford: Clarendon, 1932) Vol. 1, p. 498.

82 Hume, *An Enquiry,* Sect. X, p. 90.

83 James Boswell, *Life of Samuel Johnson* (Oxford World's Classics, 1998), p. 426.

84 *New Letters of David Hume*, pp. 82–3.

85 See David O'Connor, *Hume on Religion* (London: Routledge, 2001), p. 4.

86 David Hume, *The Natural History of Religion*, in *Philosophical Essays on Morals, Literature, and Politics* (Philadelphia: Edward Earle, 1817), Vol. II, p. 369.

87 Ernest Campbell Mossner, 'The religion of David Hume', *Journal of the History of Ideas*, Vol. 39, No. 4 (October–December 1978), p. 653.

88 David Hume, 'Of Superstition and Enthusiasm'.

89 Latitudinarianism was originally a pejorative term used to describe certain Anglicans in the later seventeenth century who placed their emphasis on reason, rather than revelation, and accordingly downplayed the importance of doctrine and church strictures.

90 David Hume, 'Of miracles' in *Philosophical Essays concerning Human Understanding*. X.91.

91 Hume, 'Of miracles', X.92.

92 Hume, 'Of miracles', X.101.

93 Nicholas Phillipson, *David Hume: The Philosopher as Historian* (New Haven: Yale University Press, 2012), p. 14.

94 Hume, *Natural History*, p. 429.

95 David Hume, *A Treatise Concerning Human Nature* (London: Penguin Classics, 1985), p. 319.

96 Hume, *Natural History*, p. 429.

97   Hume, *Treatise*, III.i.i, p. 509.

98   Quoted in E. C. Mossner, 'Hume as literary patron: a suppressed review of Robert Henry's history of Great Britain 1773', *Modern Philology*, 1942, 361–82.

99   David Hume, *The History of England in Three Volumes, Henry VII to Mary*, Chapter XXIX, available at http://www.gutenberg.org/

100 Edward Gibbon, *Memoirs of My Life*, G. A. Bonnard (ed.) (London: Nelson, 1966), pp. 135–6.

101 Edward Gibbon, *The History of the Decline and Fall of the Roman Empire* (London: Allen Lane, 1994), Chapter LII.

102 Gibbon, *History*, XXXV.

103 Gibbon, *History*, XXVIII.

104 Gibbon, *History*, XV.

105 Gibbon, *History*, XVI.

106 Gibbon, *History*, XX.

107 Gibbon, *History*, XX.

108 Gibbon, *History*, XXIII.

109 Gibbon, *History*, LI.

110 Gibbon, *History*, XXIII.

111 Gibbon, *History*, XXXVIII.

112 John Ogilvie, *An Inquiry into the Causes of the Infidelity and Scepticism of the Times, with Occasional Observations on the Writings of Herbert, Shaftesbury, Bolingbroke, Hume, Gibbon, Toulmin, etc.* (London, 1783), p. 2.

113 Gibbon, *History*, p. 916, n. 13.

114 Gibbon, *History*, p. 983.

115 J. G. A. Pocock, 'Gibbon and the primitive church' in *History, Religion, and Culture: British intellectual history, 1750–1950*, Stefan Collini, Richard Whatmore and Brian Young (eds) (Cambridge: Cambridge University Press, 2000), p. 59.

116 Quoted in John Fea, *Was America Founded as a Christian Nation?* (Louisville, KY: Westminster John Knox Press, 2011), p. 237.

117 George Washington, Farewell Address, 17 September 1796, quoted in Arlin M. Adams and Charles J. Emmerich, *A Nation Dedicated to Religious Liberty: The Constitutional Heritage of the Religion Clauses* (Philadelphia: University of Pennsylvania Press, 1990), p. 114.

118 Short of the reference to the Year of our Lord in Article VII.

119 Quoted in Fea, *America*, p. 7.

120 Quoted in Fea, *America*, p. 17.

121 Alexis de Tocqueville, *Democracy in America* (London: Penguin Classics, 2003) I.17.

Chapter 3 – Promises

1   Voltaire, *Philosophical Dictionary*, Peter Gay (trans) (New York: Basic Books, 1962), II, 473.

2   Alphonse Aulard (ed.), *La Société des jacobins* (Paris: Librairie Jouaust, 1889–97), XIV, 461–2, quoted in Charles A. Gliozzo, 'The Philosophes and Religion: Intellectual Origins of the Dechristianization Movement in the French Revolution', *Church History*, Vol. 40, No. 3 (September 1971), p. 277.

3   Blom, *Wicked Company*, p. 307.

4   Marquis de Sade, *Justine, or the Misfortunes of Virtue* (Oxford: Oxford University Press, 2012), p. 59.

5   Marquis de Sade, *Letters from Prison* (London: Harvill, 2000), p. 336.

6   De Sade, *Letters*, p. 336.

7   Marquis de Sade, *Juliette* (New York: Grove Press, 1968), p. 269.

8   Immanuel Kant, *Prolegomena to Any Future Metaphysics,* Gary Hatfield (ed.) (Cambridge: Cambridge University Press, 2004), p. 10.

9   Allen W. Wood, *Kant's Rational Theology* (Ithaca: Cornell University Press), pp. 95–146.

10 Immanuel Kant, *Critique of Practical Reason*, Mary Gregor (ed.) (Cambridge: Cambridge University Press, 1997), p. 103.

11 There is a significant literature on this. See, for example, Lara Denis, 'Kant's Criticisms of Atheism', *Kant-Studien* 94 (2):198–219 (2003); Stijn van Impe, 'Kant's Moral Theism and Moral Despair argument against Atheism', *The Heythrop Journal*, (2011), pp. 1–12; John Hare, 'Kant on the Rational Instability of Atheism', in *God and the Ethics of Belief: New Essays in Philosophy of Religion*, Andrew Dole and Andrew Chignell (eds) (Cambridge: Cambridge University Press, 2005), pp. 202–18; Charles F. Kielkopf, *A Kantian Condemnation of Atheistic Despair* (New York: Peter Lang, 1997).

12 Immanuel Kant, *The Critique of Pure Reason* (London: Penguin Classics, 2007), Appendix, Chapter II. The Canon of Pure Reason.

13 Immanuel Kant, *Critique of Judgement* (Indianapolis, IN: Hackett Publishing Co., 1987.), p. 342.

14 Kant, *Critique of Judgement*, p. 342.

15 Immanuel Kant, *Lectures on Ethics* (Cambridge: Cambridge University Press, 2007), p. 292.

16 Anthony Kenny, *A New History of Western Philosophy, Volume 3: The Rise of Modern Philosophy* (Oxford: Oxford University Press, 2008), p. 330.

17 Alister McGrath, *The Twilight Of Atheism: The Rise and Fall of Disbelief in the Modern World* (London: Rider, 2005), p. 53.

18   http://www.marxists.org/archive/marx/works/1843/10/23.htm

19   Ludwig Feuerbach, *The Essence of Christianity*, Marian Evans (trans.) (London: John Chapman, 1854), p. 12.

20   Quoted in Frede, *Doubt, Atheism*, p. 210. Herzen's letters and diary entries from the time tell a rather different story.

21   Karl Marx, Foreword to *The Difference Between the Natural Philosophy of Democritus and the Natural Philosophy of Epicurus*, in Karl Marx and Friedrich Engels, *On Religion* (New York: Dover Publications Inc., 2008), pp. 14–15.

22   Karl Marx, *A Contribution to the Critique of Hegel's Philosophy of Right*, in Marx and Engels, *On Religion*, p. 41.

23   See Owen Chadwick, *The Secularization of the European Mind in the 19th Century* (Cambridge: Cambridge University Press, 1975), p. 49.

24   Karl Marx, *The Communism of the Paper* Rheinischer Beobachter, in Marx and Engels, *On Religion*, pp. 82–3.

25   Karl Marx and Friedrich Engels, *The Communist Manifesto* (London: Penguin, 1967), p. 241.

26   Karl Marx, *Das Kapital*, in Marx and Engels, *On Religion*, p. 135.

27   Marx and Engels, *The Communist Manifesto*. p. 247.

28   Quoted in Frede, *Doubt, Atheism*, p. 94.

29   Frede, *Doubt, Atheism*, p. 29.

30   Frede, *Doubt, Atheism*, p. 102.

31   Frede, *Doubt, Atheism*, p. 93.

32   Frede, *Doubt, Atheism*, p. 103.

33   Frede, *Doubt, Atheism*, p. 111.

34   Dobroliubov's loss of faith was also prompted by personal loss, his parents dying early and leaving eight orphaned children, his seminary teacher's efforts to console, with reassurance about God's wisdom and Providence, not exactly helping.

35   Matthew Turner, *Answer to Dr Priestley's Letters to a Philosophical Unbeliever* (London, 1782), p. xvii.

36   Augustin Barruel's, *Memoirs Illustrating the History of Jacobinism* (London, 1797), p. xxi, quoted in Eileen Groth Lyon, *Politicians in the Pulpit: Christian Radicalism in Britain from the Fall of the Bastille to the Disintegration of Chartism* (Aldershot: Ashgate, 1999), p. 44.

37   Edmund Burke, Reflections on the Revolution in France (Harmondsworth: Penguin, 1968), p. 262.

38   Quoted in Chadwick, *Secularization*, p. 148.

39   Quoted in Thomas Jefferson Hogg, *The Life of Percy Bysshe Shelley* (London: Edward Moxon, 1858), Vol. 2, p. 128.

40 F. L. Jones (ed.), *The Letters of Percy Bysshe Shelley* (Oxford: Oxford University Press, 1964), I, pp. 27–8. see also Richard Holmes, *Shelley: The Pursuit* (Penguin, 1987), Chapter 2 especially.

41 Shelley, *Letters*, I, pp. 27–8.

42 Shelley, *Letters*, I, p. 47.

43 Shelley, *Letters*, I, p. 51.

44 Shelley, *Letters*, I, p. 215.

45 Holmes, *Shelley*, p. 54.

46 Shelley, *Letters*, I, p. 66.

47 Friedrich Engels, *The Condition of the Working Classes* (Oxford: Oxford World's Classics, 2009), p. 136.

48 Quoted in Edward Royle, *Radical Politics 1790–1900 Religion and Unbelief* (London: Longman, 1971), p. 6.

49 Thomas Paine, *The Age of Reason* (Minneola, NY: Dover Publications, 2004), p. 21.

50 John Quincy Adams, *Memoirs of John Quincy Adams: Comprising Portions of His Diary from 1795 to 1848* (J. B. Lippincott & Company, 1874) Vol. 3, p. 564.

51 Philip Schofield, 'Political and Religious Radicalism in the thought of Jeremy Bentham', *History of Political Thought*, 20 (1999), p. 281.

52 See Philip Schofield, *Bentham: A Guide for the Perplexed* (London: Continuum, 2009), Chapter 5.

53 Schofield, *Bentham*, p. 122.

54 Quoted in James E. Crimmins, 'Bentham on Religion: Atheism and the Secular Society' in *Journal of the History of Ideas*, Vol. 47, No. 1 (January–March 1986), p. 95. See also James E. Crimmins, 'Bentham's Political Radicalism Reexamined', in *Journal of the History of Ideas*, Vol. 55, No. 2 (April 1994), pp. 259–81.

55 Written between 1811 and 1821, they were not deposited with his papers in UCL library but eventually found their way to the British Library.

56 Crimmins, 'Bentham on Religion', p. 103.

57 Crimmins, 'Bentham on Religion', p. 105.

58 Berman, *Atheism*, p. 203.

59 *Ibid.*

60 Martin Priestman, *Romantic Atheism: Poetry and Freethought, 1780–1830* (Cambridge: Cambridge University Press, 1999), p. 214.

61 Priestman, *Romantic Atheism*, p. 205.

62 Joshua Muravchik, *Heaven on Earth: The Rise and Fall of Socialism* (London: Politico's, 2004), p. 37.

63 *Ibid.*

64 *Ibid.*

65 *Ibid.*

66   Muravchik, *Heaven on Earth*, p. 38.

67   Owen Chadwick, *The Victorian Church* (London: Adam & Charles Black, 1966–70), Vol. 1, p. 358.

68   Susan Budd, *Varieties of Unbelief: Atheists and Agnostics in English Society, 1850–1960* (London: Heinemann, 1977), p. 27.

69   *Counsellor*, No. 2, September 1861, p. 7, quoted in Budd, *Varieties*, p. 29.

70   *Reasoner*, No. 89, 1848, pp. 151–2, quoted in Budd, *Varieties*, p. 28, fn. 40.

71   *Reasoner*, 15 December 1852, pp. 430–1, quoted in Budd, *Varieties*, p. 34.

72   In a footnote, Holyoake notes 'I do not remember using this phrase, but as the witnesses reported it perhaps it was so; but I still incline to the opinion that it was an expression they fell upon in stating their impressions of the meeting to their employers, and all working in one office, they fell into one story, either through inadvertence or from precaution'. See George Holyoake, *The History of the Last Trial by Jury for Atheism in England: a Fragment of Autobiography* (London: James Watson, 1850).

73   See Nick Spencer, *Freedom and Order: History, Politics and the English Bible* (London: Hodder and Stoughton, 2011), Chapter 9 for more on these.

74   Chadwick, *Victorian Church*, Vol. 1, p. 333.

75   Michael Burleigh, *Earthly Powers: Religion and Politics in Europe from the Enlightenment to the Great War* (London: HarperCollins, 2005), p. 242.

76   Adrian Desmond and James Moore, *Darwin* (Harmondsworth: Penguin, 1992), pp. 70–3.

77   His maternal grandfather, Josiah Wedgewood, was a Unitarian, his paternal one, Erasmus Darwin, a notorious freethinker, and his father was (probably) an atheist.

78   In the words of his biographer Janet Browne, the autobiography 'was just as much an exercise in camouflage – a disguise – as it was a methodical laying out of the bare bones of his existence.' Browne, *Charles Darwin: Voyaging* (London: Jonathan Cape, 1995), p. xi.

79   See my *Darwin and God* (London: SPCK, 2009), and more recently John Van Whye and Mark J. Pallen's '"The Annie Hypothesis": Did the Death of His Daughter Cause Darwin to "Give up Christianity"?', *Centaurus* 54 (2012), pp. 1–19, which argues Darwin had fully abandoned his Christianity some time before Annie's death.

80   Charles Darwin to William Graham, 3 July 1881. See the Darwin Correspondence Project (darwinproject.ac.uk).

81   J. R. Moore, *The Post-Darwinian Controversies* (Cambridge: Cambridge University Press, 1979), p. 92.

82   See John Hedley Brooke, 'The Wilberforce-Huxley Debate: Why Did it Happen?', in *Science & Christian Belief*, Vol. 13, No 2, October 2001, pp. 127–41.

83   Benjamin Disraeli, *Lothair* (London: Longmans, Green, & Company, 1911), p. 409.

84   Priestman, *Romantic Atheism*, p. 212.

85   Sigmund Freud, *The Future of an Illusion* (Harmondsworth: Penguin, 2008), p. 48.

86   Sigmund Freud to J. Dwossis, 15 December 1930, quoted in Peter Gay, *A Godless Jew: Freud, Atheism and the Making of Psychoanalysis* (New Haven and London: Yale University Press, 1987), p. 125.

87   Sigmund Freud to Eduard Silberstein, 5 March 1875, quoted in Gay, *A Godless Jew*, p. 38.

88   Sigmund Freud to Eduard Silberstein, 7 March 1875, quoted in Gay, *A Godless Jew*, p. 53.

89   Freud, *The Future of an Illusion*.

90   Sigmund Freud, *Leonardo da Vinci and a Memory of His Childhood* (London: W. W. Norton, 1964), p. 80.

91   Freud, *The Future*, pp. 20–1.

92   Quoted in Gay, *A Godless Jew*, p. 42.

93   Sigmund Freud to Oskar Pfister, 9 October 1918, quoted in Gay, *A Godless Jew*, p. 37.

94   Freud, *The Future of an Illusion*.

95   Mrs Humphrey Ward, *Robert Elsmere* (Brighton: Victorian Secrets, 2007) p. 412.

96   Quoted in Budd, *Varieties*, p. 203.

97   Letter from F. N. B., *Ethical World*, 9 April 1898, p. 238, quoted in Budd, *Varieties*, p. 213.

98   Maurice Cowling, *Religion and Public Doctrine in Modern England, Volume II: Assaults* (Cambridge: Cambridge University Press, 1985).

99   E. B. Aveling, *A Godless Life the Happiest and Most Useful* (London: Freethought Publishing Company, 1882), pp. 7–8.

100   *Literary Guide*, 15 December 1889, p. 3, quoted in Budd, *Varieties*, p. 131.

101   C. A. Watts, *The Meaning of Rationalism* (London: Watts, 1905), quoted in Budd, *Varieties*, p. 135.

102   Beatrice Webb, *My Apprenticeship* (Cambridge: Cambridge University Press [for] the London School of Economics and Political Science, 1979), pp. 301–2.

103   Quoted in Budd, *Varieties*, p. 47.

104   Budd, *Varieties*, p. 44.

105   *Cowan vs. Milbourne* (1867) L.R. 2 Ex. 230.

106   Chadwick, *Victorian Church*, Vol. 2, p. 293.

107   Chadwick, *Secularization*, p. 93.

Chapter 4 – Problems

1 Friedrich Nietzsche, *Ecce Homo*, Sect. 1.7.

2 Quoted in Julian Young, *Friedrich Nietzsche: a Philosophical Biography* (Cambridge: Cambridge University Press, 2010), p. 5.

3 Young, *Friedrich Nietzsche*, p. 35.

4 Friedrich Nietzsche, *The Gay Science* (Cambridge: Cambridge University Press, 2001), Sect. 343.

5 *Ibid.*

6 Young, *Friedrich Nietzsche*, p. 81.

7 Friedrich Nietzsche, *Daybreak: Thoughts on the Prejudices of Morality* (Cambridge: Cambridge University Press, 1997), p. 215; Young, *Friedrich Nietzsche*, p. 242.

8 Chadwick, *The Secularization of the European Mind in the 19th Century* (Cambridge: Cambridge University Press, 1975), p. 173.

9 Chadwick, *Secularization*, p. 171.

10 Chadwick, *Secularization*, p. 166.

11 Chadwick, *Secularization*, p. 169.

12 Chadwick, *Secularization*, p. 171.

13 *Ibid.*

14 Young, *Friedrich Nietzsche*, p. 319.

15 Young, *Friedrich Nietzsche*, p. 113.

16 Friedrich Nietzsche, *Beyond Good and Evil* (Cambridge: Cambridge University Press, 2001), Section 259.

17 Nietzsche, *Beyond Good and Evil*, Sect. 62.

18 *Ibid.*

19 Nietzsche, *Beyond Good and Evil*, Sect. 259.

20 Nietzsche, *Beyond Good and Evil*, Sect. 39.

21 Nietzsche, *The Gay Science*, Sect. 125.

22 Quoted in Young, *Nietzsche*, p. 518.

23 Young, *Nietzsche*, p. 378. The letter admittedly does also have Nietzsche say that 'some of the best minds in Germany believe that I am mad or even say that I will die in a madhouse'.

24 Nietzsche, Daybreak, Sect. 96.

25 Budd, *Varieties*, p. 51.

26 *Bowman vs. Secular Society* [1917] A.C. 406.

27 J. Whiteley, *Secular Review*, 8 June 1878, p. 354, quoted in Budd, *Varieties*, p. 47.

28 S. Standring, *Truthseeker*, August 1894, p. 11, quoted in Budd, *Varieties*, p. 70.

29 H. Snell, 'Is the Ethical Movement Practical?', Democracy, 21 September 1901, p. 528, quoted in Budd, *Varieties*, p. 253.

30 G. E. Moore, 'The Value of Religion', in *International Journal of Ethics*, 1901, 12 (1), p. 88.

31 Ray Monk, *Bertrand Russell: The Spirit of Solitude* (Vintage, 1997), p. 32.

32 Monk, *Spirit of Solitude*, p. 27.

33 Monk, *Spirit of Solitude*, p. 26.

34 Bertrand Russell, *Autobiography* (London: Routledge Classics, 2010), p. 133.

35 Russell, *Autobiography*, p. 149.

36 Monk, *Spirit of Solitude*, p. 159.

37 Monk, *Spirit of Solitude*, p. 41.

38 Monk, *Spirit of Solitude*, p. 209.

39 Monk, *Spirit of Solitude*, p. 243.

40 Monk, *Spirit of Solitude*, p. 317.

41 Bertrand Russell, *A Free Man's Worship, and Other Essays* (London: Unwin Books, 1976).

42 Ray Monk, *Ludwig Wittgenstein: The Duty of Genius* (Vintage, 1991), p. 39.

43 Monk, *Ludwig Wittgenstein*, p. 40.

44 Monk, *The Duty of Genius*, p. 116.

45 Ludwig Wittgenstein, *Culture and Value* (Chicago: University of Chicago Press, 1980), p. 33.

46 *Ibid.*

47 Monk, *Duty of Genius*, p. 44.

48 Ben Rogers, *A. J. Ayer: a Life* (London: Vintage, 2000), p. 34.

49 Rogers, *Ayer*, p. 65.

50 *Ibid.*

51 Bryan Magee, *Men of Ideas: Some Creators of Contemporary Philosophy* (New York: Viking Press, 1978), p. 131.

52 Simon Sebag Montefiore, *Young Stalin* (Phoenix, 2008), p. 130.

53 Christopher Marsh, *Religion and the State in Russia and China: Suppression, Survival, and Revival* (London: Continuum, 2011), p. 50.

54 James A. Thrower, *Marxism-Leninism as the Civil Religion of Soviet Society: God's Commissar* (Lampeter: Edwin Mellen Press Ltd, 1992), p. 39.

55 Marsh, *Religion and the State*, p. 54.

56 Robert Service, *Lenin* (London: Pan Books, 2010), p. 442.

57 Montefiore, *Young Stalin*, p. 41.

58 Montefiore, *Young Stalin*, p. 47.

59 Quoted in Daniel Peris, *Storming the Heavens: The Soviet League of the Militant Godless* (Ithaca, NY: London: Cornell University Press, 1998), p. 23.

60 David Powell, *Antireligious Propaganda in the Soviet Union: A Study in Mass Persuasion* (Cambridge: MIT Press, 1975), p. 22.

61 Peris, *Storming the Heavens*, p. 31.

62 Peris, *Storming the Heavens*, p. 9.

63 Peris, *Storming the Heavens*, p. 76.

64 Peris, *Storming the Heavens*, p. 94.

65 Quoted in Marsh, *Religion and the State*, p. 40.

66 Quoted in Dimitry V. Pospielovsky. *A History of Soviet Atheism in Theory, and Practice, and the Believer, Vol. 1: A History of Marxist-Leninist Atheism and Soviet Anti-Religious Policies* (New York: St. Martin's Press, 1987) p. 94.

67 Marsh, *Religion and the State*, p. 41.

68 Dekulakization was the murderous Soviet campaign against wealthier peasants, who were stigmatized as class enemies, nearly two million of whom were deported and/or liquidated in the early 1930s.

69 Richard Dawkins, *A Devil's Chaplain* (London: Weidenfeld and Nicolson, 2003), p. 158.

70 Pope Benedict XVI's Speech to The Queen, Palace of Holyrood House, Edinburgh, Thursday, 16 September 2010, http://www.thepapalvisit.org.uk/Replay-the-Visit/Speeches/Speeches-16-September/Pope-Benedict-XVI-s-Speech-to-The-Queen

71 http://www.guardian.co.uk/commentisfree/belief/2010/sep/22/ratzinger-enemy-humanity

72 As Michael Burleigh has written 'there is something faintly ridiculous about the weight of learning brought to bear in the last six decades on this less than fascinating figure, a cavernous blank behind the impassioned postures'. See Michael Burleigh, *Sacred Causes: Religion and Politics from the European Dictators to Al Qaeda* (London: HarperPress, 2006), p. 94.

73 Quoted in John S. Conway, *The Nazi Persecution of the Churches, 1933–1945* (London: Weidenfeld & Nicolson, 1968), p. 25.

74 Quoted in Mordecai Paldiel, *Churches and the Holocaust: Unholy Teaching, Good Samaritans, and Reconciliation* (Jersey City: Ktav, 2006), p. 29.

75 Burleigh, *Sacred Causes*, p. 101.

76 *Ibid.*

77 Ian Kershaw, *Hitler 1936–1945: Nemesis* (Harmondsworth: Penguin, 2001), p. 40.

78 Burleigh, *Sacred Causes*, p. 100.

79 *The Times*, 3 December 1934, quoted in Philip Williamson, 'Christian Conservatives and the Totalitarian Challenge, 1933–40', in *The English Historical Review*, Vol. 115, No. 462 (June 2000), p. 617.

80 Ian McLaine, *Ministry of Morale: Home Front Morale and the Ministry of Information in World War II* (London: Allen and Unwin, 1979), p. 151.

81 Michael Snape, *God and the British soldier: Religion and the British Army in the First and Second World Wars* (Abingdon: Routledge, 2005), p. 146.

82 On this generally see Stefanos Geroulanos, *An Atheism that is not Humanist Emerges in French Thought* (Stanford, CA: Stanford University Press, 2010).

83 Which, one suspects, the French philosophers in question understood about as thoroughly as does the present author.

84 Ludwig Feuerbach, *Principles of the Philosophy of the Future* (Hackett Publishing, 1986), p. 5.

85 Henri de Lubac, *The Drama of Atheism Humanism* (San Francisco: Ignatius, c. 1995), p. 67.

86 Geroulanos, *An Atheism that is not Humanist*, p. 209.

87 Geroulanos, *An Atheism that is not Humanist*, p. 15.

88 See Jean-Paul Sartre, *Existentialism Is a Humanism* (Cambridge MA: Yale University Press, 2007).

89 See Edward Larson, *Summer for the Gods: The Scopes Trial and America's Continuing Debate Over Science and Religion* (New York: Basic Books, 2006).

90 *Pravda*, 27 March 1958 quoted in John Anderson, *Religion, State and Politics in the Soviet Union and Successor States* (Cambridge: Cambridge University Press, 1994), p. 15.

91 *Pravda*, 29 November 1957, in John Anderson, *Religion, State and Politics*, p. 15.

92 John Anderson, *Religion, State and Politics*, p. 7.

93 John Anderson, *Religion, State and Politics*, p. 40.

94 John Anderson, *Religion, State and Politics*, p. 19.

95 John Anderson, *Religion, State and Politics*, p. 40.

96 Monk, *Spirit of Solitude*, p. 592.

97 Marsh, *Religion and the State*, pp. 162–3.

98 *Ibid.*, p. 162.

99 Mao Tse-Tung, *On the Correct Handling of Contradictions among the People* (Peking: Foreign Languages Press, 1957), p. 16.

100 Donald E. MacInnis, *Religious Policy and Practice in Communist China – A Documentary History* (London: Hodder & Stoughton, 1972), p. 24.

101 Quoted in Marsh *Religion and the State*, p. 184.

102 John Anderson, *Religion, State and Politics*, pp. 70–1.

103 John Anderson, *Religion, State and Politics*, p. 70.

104 Quoted in Marsh, *Religion and the State*, p. 83.

105 *Pravda*, 30 June 1977, quoted in John Anderson, *Religion, State and Politics*, p. 79.

106 *Pravda*, 15 June 1983, quoted in John Anderson, *Religion, State and Politics*, p. 77.

107 Marsh, *Religion and the State*, p. 239.

108 Quoted in Marsh, *Religion and the State*, p. 65.

109 He later recanted in his 1999 book entitled *The Desecularisation of the World: Resurgent Religion and World Politics*: 'the assumption that we live in a secularised world is false: The world today, with some exceptions … is as furiously religious as it ever was, and in some places more so than ever' (p. 2).

110 'Toward a Hidden God', *Time Magazine*, April 1966.

111 See, for example, Daniel K. Williams, *God's Own Party: The Making of the Christian Right* (New York: Oxford University Press, 2010); Randall Balmer, *Thy Kingdom Come: An Evangelical's Lament* (New York: Basic Books, 2006); Ruth Murray Brown, *For A Christian America: A History Of The Religious Right* (New York: Prometheus Books, 2002).

112 Jeffrey M. Jones, 'Some Americans Reluctant to Vote for Mormon, 72-Year-Old Presidential Candidates'. Gallup Poll, 20 February 2007: http://www.galluppoll.com/content/?ci=26611&pg=1

113 See, for example, her first Conference address as Conservative Party leader in 1975. See also Margaret Thatcher, *The Path to Power* (London: HarperCollins, 1995), pp. 305–6.

114 See Thomas Zenk, 'New Atheism', in *Oxford Handbook of Atheism*, Stephen Bullivant and Michael Ruse (eds) (Oxford: Oxford University Press, 2013), pp. 249–50. Also, Gary Wolf, 'The Church of the Non-Believers', *Wired*, Issue 14.11, November 2006.

115 Nicholas Humphrey, 'What shall we tell the children?' in *The Values of Science*, Wes Williams (ed.) (Oxford: Westview Press, 1998), pp. 58–79.

116 Sam Harris, *The End of Faith: Religion, Terror and the Future of Reason* (London: Free Press, 2006), p. 109.

117 Harris, *The End of Faith*, pp. 52–3.

118 Harris, *The End of Faith*, pp. 198–9.

119 Harris, *The End of Faith*, p. 129.

120 Christopher Hitchens, *God is Not Great: How Religion Poisons Everything* (London: Atlantic Books, 2007), p. 35.

121 Hitchens, *God is Not Great*, p. 25.

122 Hitchens, *God is Not Great*, p. 7.

123 Hitchens, *God is Not Great*, p. 176.

124 See http://www.firstthings.com/blogs/firstthoughts/2013/07/31/remembering-robert-bellah-a-symposium-on-his-last-book/

125 Memes, for the uninitiated, are very small units of transmission. They cannot be seen, heard, sensed or detected in any way. They have no explanatory or predictive power.

126 Richard Dawkins, *The Selfish Gene* (Oxford: Oxford University Press, 1989), p. 270. As Andrew Brown has observed, 'This lofty condescension – "popular, but erroneous" – is difficult for a popular writer to maintain.

Who is he to tell us what the erroneous associations of the word "robot" are?' Andrew Brown, *The Darwin Wars: How Stupid Genes became Selfish Gods* (London: Simon & Schuster, 1999), p. 40.

127   Richard Dawkins, 'In defence of selfish genes', *Philosophy* (1980) 56, pp. 556–73. There is a curious and presumably unintentional echo of Humpty Dumpty from Lewis Carroll's *Through the Looking Glass* in these sentiments. '"When I use a word", Humpty Dumpty said in rather a scornful tone, "it means just what I choose it to mean – neither more nor less".'

128   Richard Dawkins, *The Humanist* 57, January/February 1997.

129   Richard Dawkins, 'A scientist's case against God', Speech at Edinburgh International Science Festival, 15 April 1992.

130   Richard Dawkins, 'A Reply to Poole', *Science & Christian Belief* (1995) 7, pp. 45–50.

131   Richard Dawkins, *The Extended Phenotype* (Oxford: Oxford University Press, 1982), p. 181.

132   http://www.elmundo.es/elmundo/2012/12/27/ciencia/1356611441.html; http://www.guardian.co.uk/science/2012/dec/26/peter-higgs-richard-dawkins-fundamentalism

133   Antony Flew, 'A Reply to Richard Dawkins', *First Things*, December 2008; http://www.firstthings.com/article/2008/11/001-documentation-a-reply-to-richard-dawkins-38

134   http://www.lrb.co.uk/v28/n20/terry-eagleton/lunging-flailing-mispunching

135   http://www.guardian.co.uk/commentisfree/belief/2010/sep/22/ratzinger-enemy-humanity

136   '"Listen to the stumbling, droning inarticulacy," he continued, "the abysmal lack of anything approaching wit or intelligence. Imagine this yammering fumblewit coming up against Christopher Hitchens, or Dan Dennett, or PZ Myers – doesn't it make your mouth water?"'

137   The original discussion appears to have been taken down but Dawkins' sentiments can be read here: http://www.theguardian.com/commentisfree/andrewbrown/2009/apr/30/religion-atheism-dawkins-contempt

138   Daniel Trilling, Beyond Dawkins, http://rationalist.org.uk/articles/4271/beyond-dawkins

139   A Bright, for the uninitiated, is (yet) another name for an atheist, coined in 2002/3 presumably on the basis that people who are not atheists are dim.

140   http://www.theguardian.com/commentisfree/2012/may/31/queen-diamond-jublilee-why-celebrate

141   Christopher Watkin, *Difficult Atheism: Post-theological Thought in Badiou, Nancy and Meillassoux* (Edinburgh: Edinburgh University Press, 2011), p. 6.

142 And presumably partly because the relevant thinkers write so impenetrably. See Christopher Watkin, *Difficult Atheism*, and Martin Hägglund, *Radical Atheism: Derrida and the Time of Life* (Stanford, CA: London: Stanford University Press, 2008).

143 John Gray, *The Silence of Animals: On Progress and Other Modern Myths* (London: Allen Lane, 2013), p. 77.

144 Gray, *The Silence of Animals*, p. 81.

145 Dawkins, *Selfish Gene*, p. xxi.

146 John Gray, *Heresies: Against Progress and Other Illusions* (Cambridge: Granta Books, 2004), p. 48.

147 Gray, *The Silence of Animals*, p. 78.

148 Sharon Street, 'A Darwinian Dilemma for Realist Theories of Value', *Philosophical Studies* 127, no. 1 (January 2006), pp. 109–66.

149 Thomas Nagel, *Mind and Cosmos: Why the Materialist Neo-Darwinian Conception of Nature is Almost Certainly False* (New York: Oxford University Press, 2012), p. 28.

150 *Ibid.*, p. 16.

151 Simon Blackburn, 'Thomas Nagel: a philosopher who confesses to finding things bewildering', New Statesman, 8 November 2012: http://www.newstatesman.com/culture/culture/2012/11/thomas-nagel-philosopher-who-confesses-finding-things-bewildering

152 Ronald Dworkin, *Religion without God* (Cambridge, MA: Harvard University Press, 2013), p. 2.

153 Ludwig Wittgenstein, *On Certainty* (Oxford: Blackwell, 1974), sect. 354.

Index

Act of Toleration 85
Adams, Samuel 130
Adler, Felix 228
Advancement of Learning (Bacon, Francis) 33
Age of Reason (Paine, Thomas) 166
agnosticism 182
Aikenhead, Thomas 70–2, 86
Albania 237–8
Alexander I 154
Alexander II 159
alienation 150
Allen, Ethan, *Reason the Only Oracle of Man* 129
America 129–32, 227–9, 244–6
American Association for the Advancement of Atheism 228
American Atheists 228–9
American Civil Liberties Union 227
Analysis of the Influence of Natural Religion on the Temporal Happiness of Mankind (Bentham, Jeremy) 170
animals 98
Anglican Church 72–3
Annet, Peter 160
Answer to Dr Priestley's Letters to a Philosophical Unbeliever (Turner, Matthew) 161
Antichrist, The (Nietzsche, Friedrich) 203
Antidote against Atheism (More, Henry) 31, 76
Anti-Persecution Union 178
Apollonius Tyraneus 80–1, 127–8
apology for Raymond Sebond, An (Montaigne, Michel de) 26–7
Apostolic Constitutions 78

Arianism 78
ascetic atheism 254
atheism *see also* New Atheism and New New Atheism
  ascetic 254
  Christian 244
  definitions 4–8
  etymology of 13
  parasitic 254–5
  practical 6–7
  theoretical 6–7
    L'athéisme convaincu (Derodon, David) 3
atheisms xviii
atheist societies 175–7, 188–9
atomism 14–16
Austria 211–12
Autobiography (Russell, Bertrand) 208–9
Averroism 2, 260n. 7
Ayer, A. J. 212
  Language, Truth and Logic 212–14

Bacon, Francis 15, 33, 34
  Advancement of Learning 33
Bacon, Nicholas 3
Baines Note 11
Baldwin, Stanley 223
Barbarians, the 127
Barre, Jean-François de la 93
Bauer, Bruno 147–8
Bayle, Pierre 63–9
  Dictionnaire historique et critique 6, 63–8
  Various Thoughts on the Occasion of A Comet 64
Beccaria, Cesare 104

Bekker, Balthasar 2
Bellah, Robert 249
   Religion in Human Evolution 250
Benedict XVI 221–2, 252
Bentham, Jeremy 167–71
   *Analysis of the Influence of Natural
      Religion on the Temporal Happiness
      of Mankind* 170
   *Church-Of-Englandism and Its
      Catechism Examined* 170
   Constitutional Code 170–1
   *Introduction to the Principles of Morals
      and Legislation, An* 168, 170
   'Jug. Util.' 170
   Not Paul, But Jesus 168
   'Of Ontology' 167
   Swear Not At All 170
Bentley, Richard 84
   Confutation of Atheism 76
Berger, Peter 244
Berlin, Isaiah 110–11
Beyond Good and Evil (Nietzsche,
      Friedrich) 199
Bible, the 32–6 *see also* scripture
   textual criticism and 38–45, 47–9, 53–6
Bayle, Pierre and 61–2, 65
Bill of Rights 85
*Biographical Dictionary of Freethinkers
      of All Ages and Nations* (Wheller,
      J. M.) 184
Blackmore, Richard, *Creation, The* 60
Blackstone, William, *Commentaries on the
      Law of England* 7, 160
Blasphemy Act 1661 71
Blasphemy Act 1697 86
Blount, Charles 5, 80–1
   Great is Diana of the Ephesians 81
   *Miracles, No Violations of the Laws of
      Nature* 81
Bolshevism 216–17
Boulainvilliers, Henri de, *Vie de
      Mahomed* 63
Bowman v Secular Society 204
Boyle, Robert 76
Boyle lectures, the 76–7
Botton, Alain de 257
   Religion for Atheists 257
Bradlaugh, Charles 192–4, 203–4, 205
   'Is Secularism Atheism' 193

Bramhall, John 50
   Catching of Leviathan, The 50
Brentano, Franz 185
Breton, Nicholas
   *Good and the Badde, or Descriptions of
      the Worthies and Unworthies of this
      Age, The* 4–5
Brezhnev, Leonid 238–9
Brianchaninov, Ignatii 157
Britain *see* Great Britain
Bruno, Giordano 184
   *Expulsion of the Triumphant Beast,
      The* 33
Büchner, Friedrich 197
   Force and Matter 197
Buddhism 236
Buffon, Georges-Louis Leclerc, Comte de
      101, 103
   Histoire naturelle 101
Bukunin, Michael 151
Burckhardt, Jacob 199
Burnet, Thomas 78, 79
   Sacred Theory of the Earth 35–6
Byckenell, Ralph 3

Caius, John 3
Calvin, John 10
   *True Meaning of the System of Nature,
      The* 172
Calvinism 102
Cambridge Apostles 207
Candide (Voltaire) 91
Cappel, Louis 39
Carlile, Richard 172–3, 179–80, 183–4
Casmir, Count 89
Castellio, Sebastian 23
Catching of Leviathan, The (Bramhall,
      John) 50
Catholicism 24–6
   Bible, and the 39–41
   France and 133–4, 137–8
   paganism and 81
CCP (Chinese Communist party) 234–7,
      242
Cerne Abbas circle 2–3
Chadwick, Edwin 171
Chambers, Ephraim, *Cyclopaedia* 102
Charles V 127
Charron, Pierre 17, 28

De la sagesse 17–18

Chartism 179

Chaumette, Gaspard 134–5

Chernyshevsky, Nikolai 158–60

What is to be Done?: Tales of the New People 159–60

China 16, 234–7, 242–3

Chinese Communist party (CCP) 234–7, 242

Christian Atheists 244

Christian Philosopher, The (Mather, Cotton) 129

Christian Right, the 245–6

Christianisme dévoilé (Christianity Unveiled) (D'Holbach, Paul-Henri Thiry, Baron d') 104–5

Christianity *see also* Anglican Church *and* Catholicism *and* Protestantism *and* Orthodoxy

America and 129–132

China and 234–5

crisis in 22–6

Diderot, Denis and 102

dominance of 13

early years of xv

European culture and xv–xviii

French Revolution and 134

Gibbon, Edward and 124–8

Hitler, Adolf and 222–3

Holbach, Paul-Henri Thiry, Baron d' and 106–7

Hume, David and 117–21

Meslier, Jean and 95–7

morality and 200

Nietzsche, Friedrich and 199–203

Sade, Donatien Alphonse François, Marquis de and 135

Christianity and Civilisation (Toynbee, Arnold) 223

christicole 96

Christ's Tears over Jerusalem (Nashe, Thomas) 2, 6

Church-Of-Englandism and Its Catechism Examined (Bentham, Jeremy) 170

Churchill, Winston 223

Clarendon, Earl of 50

classical heritage 13–14

classical world, the 199, 202

Coit, Stanton 189–90

Collegiants 55

Collins, Antony, *Discourse of Free-Thinking* 83

Commentaries on the Law of England (Blackstone, William) 7, 160

communism 97, 109, 152–3, 228, 233–4

Communist Manifesto (Mark, Karl) 153

Communist Party, the 218, 231, 232 *see also* Chinese Communist Party

Comte, Auguste 139, 140–1

Condillac, Étienne Bonnot de 104

Condorcet, Marie Jean Antoine Nicolas de Caritat, Marquis de 104

confessional theology 77

Confutation of Atheism (Bentley, Richard) 76

Confutation of Atheism, A (Dove, John) 3

Congreve, Richard 188

Constantine I 126–7

Constitution, American 131–2

Constitution of the Confederate States of America 132

Constitutional Code (Bentham, Jeremy) 170–1

Contemporary 159

Contribution to the Rectification of the Public's Judgment of the French Revolution (Fichte, Johann Gottlieb) 145

Cooper, Thomas 184

Correspondance littéraire 103

Cotes, Roger 36

Coventry Mutual Improvement Society 176

Coward, William 79–80

Grand Essay: or a Vindication of Reason and Religion against the Impostures of Philosophy 80

Second Thoughts concerning the Human Soul 79–80

Creation, The (Blackmore, Richard) 60

creation myths xii–xiv

creationism 245

Creed of Science (Graham, William) 182

creeds xviii

Critical History of the Old Testament (Simon, Richard) 43

Critique of All Revelation (Fichte, Johann Gottlieb) 144

Critique of Hegel's Philosophy of Law (Marx, Karl) 151

Critique of Pure Reason (Kant, Immanuel) 142

Cudworth, Ralph 5
  True Intellectual System of the Universe 5

Cultural Revolution, the 237

Cyclopaedia (Chambers, Ephraim) 102

D'Abillon, André 12
  Divinité défendue contre les athées, La 3

D'Alembert, Jean-Baptiste le Rond 102, 103

D'Alembert's Dream (Diderot, Denis) 15, 115–16

Darrow, Clarence 227–8

Darwin, Charles 180–3
  On the Origin of the Species 180
  Voyage of the Beagle, The 180

Dawkins, Richard 221–2, 250–3, 255
  God Delusion, The 250–1
  Selfish Gene, The 250–1, 255

De la sagesse (Charron, Pierre) 17–18

De l'esprit (On the Mind) (Helvétius, Claude Adrien) 15, 110, 111

De rerum natura (Lucretius, NAME) 14–16

de Sade *see* Sade

De Tribus Impostoribus 61

deism 80–3
  America and 129
  Germany and 88–9

Deist or *Moral Philosopher, The* 183

Deistical Society of New York, the 129

democracy 109

Dennett, Daniel 249

Derodon, David 5
  L'athéisme convaincu 3

Descartes, René 29–30
  Meditations 30

determinism 57

D'Holbach, Paul-Henri Thiry, Baron d' 103–9, 112, 116–17
  Christianisme dévoilé (Christianity Unveiled) 104–5
  Portable Theology 105
  Système de la nature (System of Nature, The) 104–5, 112, 135, 161

Dialogue between a Priest and a Dying Man (Sade, Donatien Alphonse François, Marquis de) 135–6

Dialogues Concerning Natural Religion (Hume, David) 119–20

Dictionnaire historique et critique (Bayle, Pierre) 6, 63–8

Diderot, Denis 98–9, 101–3, 115, 122, 154
  D'Alembert's Dream 15, 115–16
  Encyclopédie 99, 102, 104
  Letter on the Blind For the Use of Those Who See 101, 115
  Pensées philosophiques 99, 101

Diegesis; being a Discovery of the Origin, Evidence, and Early History of Christianity, The (Taylor, Robert) 173

Discourse of Free-Thinking (Collins, Antony) 83

Discourse on the Present State of England, A 2

Discourses on Livy (Machiavelli, Nicolo) 21

divine providence 79

Divinité défendue contre les athées, La (D'Abillon, André) 3

doctrinal wars 24

Don Juan (Molière) 6

Dove, John, *Confutation of Atheism, A* 3

Draper, John William, *History of the Conflict between Religion and Science* 184

Du Marsais, César Chesneau 113
  Examen de la Religion 61
  Le Philosophe 115

Dubroliubov, Nikolai 158–9

Dutch Republic, the 91–2 *see also* Holland

Dworkin, Richard 257

Eagleton, Terry 252

Ecce Homo (Nietzsche, Friedrich) 195

economics 167

Edelman, Johann Christian 89
  Revealed Face of Moses, The 88

Edict of Nantes 85

education 110, 155, 231–3, 238–9

Encyclopaedia Britannica 162–3

Encyclopédie (Diderot, Denis) 99, 102, 104

End of Faith, The (Harris, Sam) 247–8

Engels, Friedrich 146–7
  Progress of Social Reform On the Continent 146–7
  Schelling and Revelation 147

England 2–3, 9–10 *see also* Great Britain
    Anglican Church 72
    Coward, William 79–80
    Glorious Revolution in 85
    Locke, John 85–6
    natural theology and 77–9
    Newton, Isaac 84–5
    Reformation, and the 25
    Restoration, and the 72–5
    Rochester, Earl of 74–5
    Royal Society, the 75–6
Enquiry Concerning Human Understanding
    (Hume, David) 117
*Enquiry into the Origin of Honour; and the
    Usefulness of Christianity in War*
    (Mandeville, Bernard) 83
equality 109–110
Erasmus, Desiderius 38
    Novum instrumentum (New
        Instrument) 38
Essai sur l'étude de la Littérature (Gibbon,
    Edward) 125
Essay Concerning Human Understanding
    (John Locke) 85, 164
Essay on the Formation of Character
    (Owen, Robert) 174
Essays (Montaigne, Michel de) 27
Essence of Christianity, The (Feuerbach,
    Ludwig) 148–9
Essenes 88
Estlin, John, *Nature and Cause of Atheism,
    The* 161
Ethical Culture Movement, the 228
Ethical Movement, the 188–90, 205–6
Ethics (Spinoza, Benedict) 57
Europe 22–6
evolution 100, 181, 250–1, 256
Examen de la Religion (Du Marsais, César
    Chesneau) 61
existentialism 226
Expulsion of the Triumphant Beast, The
    (Bruno, Giordano) 33
Ezra (the scribe) 40–1

*Fable of the Bees, or, Private Vices,
    Public Benefits* (Mandeville,
    Bernard) 82–3
faith 105, 119
Febvre, Lucien, *Problem of Unbelief in the*

*Sixteenth Century: the Religion of
    Rabelais, The* 8
Feuerbach, Friedrich, *Religion of the
    Future, The* 157
Feuerbach, Ludwig 148–9
    *Thoughts on Death and
        Immortality* 148–9
Fichte, Johan Gottlieb 144–5
    *Contribution to the Rectification of the
        Public's Judgment of the French
        Revolution* 145
    Critique of All Revelation 144
    *Reclamation of the Freedom of Thought
        from the Princes of Europe, who
        have hitherto Suppressed it* 145
fideism 27
First Great Awakening, the 129
Fisher, Samuel 44
    Rustick's Alarm to the Rabbies, The 44
Flew, Antony 252
Foote, George 191, 193
Force and Matter (Büchner, Friedrich) 197
foreign cultures 16–19
Fouché, Joseph 134
Founding Fathers 130–1
France 1, 92–9, 101, 137–41, 224–6
    Edict of Nantes 85
    French atheism 254, 160–3
    French Revolution 133–4, 137, 145, 161
    intellectual life in 103–4, 108–10, 128,
        134, 137–9
    Reason in 134–5
    Reformation, and the 25
Franklin, Benjamin 130
Frazer 72
Frede, Victoria xvi
Frederick II (the Great) 89–90, 116
*Free Thoughts on Religion, the Church and
    National Happiness* (Mandeville,
    Bernard) 83
free will 111–12
freedom 82, 110–11
'freeman's worship, A' (Russell,
    Bertrand) 209–10
Freethinker 85, 193
Freud, Sigmund 185–7
    Future of an Illusion, The 185, 187
    'Leonardo da Vinci and a Memory of
        His Childhood' 186

Friedrich Wilhelm IV 147–8
fundamentalism 245, 251–2
Future of an Illusion, The (Freud,
    Sigmund) 185

Galiani, Ferdinando 104
Galileo 184
Gapon, Georgy 214
Garasse, Francois 1
Gascoigne, George 3
Gassendi, Pierre 15–16, 29
Gaukroger, Stephen 30
Gay Science, The (Nietzsche, Friedrich) 202
*Genesis Flood: The Biblical Record and
    its Scientific Implications, The*
    (Whitcomb, John and Morris,
    Henry) 245
Germany 2, 86–91, 142–53
  Bauer, Bruno 147–8
  Engels, Friedrich 146–7
  Feuerbach, Ludwig 148–9
  French Revolution and 145
  Hegel, Georg Wilhelm Friedrich 145–7,
    156
  Marx, Karl 148, 149–53
  materialism in 196–8
  Nazism 221–3
  Pietism and 142
  Reformation, and the 25
  science in 196–8
  theology in 146
Gibbon, Edward 104, 123–9
  *History of the Decline and Fall of the
    Roman Empire, The* 124–8
  Essai sur l'étude de la Littérature 125
Glorious Revolution, the 85
God 138, 142–3, 149
  death of 243–4
God Delusion, The (Dawkins,
    Richard) 250–1
Gödel, Kurt 208
Godless, The 218
God-seekers 214
*Good and the Badde, or Descriptions of the
    Worthies and Unworthies of this
    Age, The* (Breton, Nicholas) 4–5
Gorbachev, Mikhail 241
gospels, the 106
government 108–9, 122

Graham, William, *Creed of Science* 182
Gray, John 255–7
Great Britain 160–85 *see also* England
  atheist press in 176–7, 190–1
  atheist publications in 184
  atheist societies in 175–7, 188–9
  Ayer, A. J. 212–14
  Bentham, Jeremy 167–71
  Bradlaugh, Charles 192–4, 203–4, 205
  Carlile, Richard 172–3, 179–80, 183–4
  colonies and 129
  Darwin, Charles 180–3
  economics 167
  Ethical movement in 188–90, 205–6
  French atheism and 160–3
  Gray, John 255–7
  Holyoake, George Jacob 176–9
  liberty and 85–6
  Nazism and 223–4
  Owen, Robert 173–5
  positivism in 188
  Rationalist movement in 205
  religious moderation and 123
  Russell, Bertrand 207–10
  science and 183
  secular movement, and the 191–4,
    203–5
  Shelley, Percy Bysshe 163–6
  socialism and 205
  Southwell, Charles 176
  Taylor, Robert 173, 179–80
  Thatcher, Margaret and 246
  toleration and 85–6
  working classes in 165–6, 171–2, 174–5,
    194, 205–6
Great is Diana of the Ephesians (Blount,
    Charles) 81
Grecian History (Stanyan, Temple) 99
Greenham, Richard 2
Grimm, Friedrich Melchior, Baron von 103

Haeckel, Ernst 196
Halifax, Edward Frederick Lindley Wood,
    Lord 223
Hardie, Keir 206
Harriot, Thomas 3
Harris, Sam 253
  End of Faith, The 247–8
Hart, David Bentley 252

Hébert, Jacque 134
Hegel, Georg Wilhelm Friedrich 145–7,
    156
Hegelianism 146–8, 150
Helinant 9
Hell-fire clubs 75
Helvétius, Claude Adrien 109–11
    On the Mind (De l'esprit) 15, 110, 111
    *Treatise on Man: His Intellectual
        Faculties and His Education, A* 110
heresy 13
Herzen, Alexander 149, 156
    My Past and Thoughts 149
Hess, Moses 151
Higgs, Peter 251
Hilton, John 10
Histoire naturelle (Buffon, Georges-Louis
    Leclerc, Comte de 101
History of England (Hume, David) 123
*History of the Conflict between Religion
    and Science* (Draper, John
    William) 184
*History of the Decline and Fall of the
    Roman Empire, The* (Gibbon,
    Edward) 124
*History of the Last Trial by Jury for Atheism
    in England* (Holyoake, George
    Jacob) 177–8
*History of the Rise and Influence of the
    Spirit of Rationalism in Europe*
    (Lecky, W. E. H.) 184
*History of the Warfare of Science with
    Theology in Christendom* (White,
    Andrew Dickson) 184
Hitchens, Christopher 249, 253
Hitler, Adolf 221–3
Hobbes, Thomas 45–52, 56, 59
    Germany and 89
    Leviathan 45, 47–50, 81
Hobbism 51
Hogg, Thomas Jefferson 163–4
Holland 2, 25, 92
Holyoake, George Jacob 176–9, 192–3
    *History of the Last Trial by Jury for
        Atheism in England* 177–8
    'Home Colonisation as a means of
        superseding Poor Laws and
        Emigration' 177–8
    'Is Secularism Atheism' 193

'Home Colonisation as a means of
    superseding Poor Laws and
    Emigration' (Holyoake, George
    Jacob) 177–8
Hooke, Robert 77
Hoxha, Enver 237–8
Hu Jintao 242
humanism 19–20, 224–6, 255–6, 258 *see
    also* Erasmus, Desiderius
humans 107–8, 111
    as machines 113, 115–16
Hume, David 104, 116–23
    Dialogues Concerning Natural Religion
        119–120, 122
    *Enquiry Concerning Human
        Understanding* 117
    History of England 123
    Natural History of Religion 118, 121–2
    'Of Miracles' 119
    'Of Parties in General' 122
    'On the immortality of the soul' 120–1
    *Philosophical Essays concerning Human
        Understanding* 119
    Treatise Concerning Human Nature 119
Humphrey, Nicholas 247
Hundred Flowers Campaign, the 237
Huxley–Wilberforce debate 183

Ingersoll, Robert Green 227
Inquiry Concerning Virtue and Merit, An
    (Shaftesbury, Anthony Ashley-
    Cooper, 3rd Earl of) 99
*inquiry into the causes of the infidelity and
    scepticism of the times, An* (Ogilvie,
    John) 128
*Introduction to the Principles of Morals and
    Legislation, An* (Bentham, Jeremy)
    168, 170
Investigator 178
Iran 246
Islam 62–3, 105, 127, 236, 246–8
Italy 1, 3

Jansenism 99
Jay, John 130
Jefferson, Thomas 130, 131–2
Jesuits 269n. 33
Jew of Malta, The (Marlowe,
    Christopher) 22

Jews 9–10, 186
  Holbach, Paul-Henri Thiry, Baron d'
    and 106
  Meslier, Jean and 95
  scripture and 39–40
  slavery and 200
John Street Literary Institution 175
Journet, Noël 41–2
'Jug. Util.' (Bentham, Jeremy) 170
Julian the Apostate 127
justice 7

Kant, Immanuel 142–4
  Critique of Pure Reason 142
  'On the Basis of Our Belief in a Divine
    Governance of the World' 144–5
  Religion within the Bounds of
    Reason 144
Katenev, Vasilii 157
Kenny, Anthony 252
  New History of Western
    Philosophy xx–xxi
Khrushchev, Nikita 230–1, 238
Knutzen, Matthias 2, 87–8
Konavlev, Vassily 240
Kyd, Thomas 11

La Mettrie, Julien Offray de 112–16, 135
  L'Homme Machine (Man a
    Machine) 113
  Natural History of the Soul 113
  System of Epicurus 15
La Mothe Le Vayer, François de 28
La Peyrère, Isaac 28, 42–3
  Prae-Adamitae (Men before Adam) 42
language 107, 111
Language, Truth and Logic (Ayer, A. J.)
    212–13
latitudinarianism 271
Lau, Theodore Ludwig 88–9
Le Philosophe (Du Marsais, César
    Chesneau) 115
Lecky, W. E. H., History of the Rise and
    Influence of the Spirit of Rationalism
    in Europe 184
Leibniz, Gottfrien von 56, 91
Lenin, Vladimir 160, 215–16, 220–1
'Leonardo da Vinci and a Memory of His
    Childhood' (Freud, Sigmund) 186

Letter Concerning Enthusiasm, A
    (Shaftesbury, Anthony Ashley-
    Cooper, 3rd Earl of) 81
Letter Concerning Toleration (Locke,
    John) 67, 85–6
Letter on the Blind For the Use of Those
    Who See (Diderot, Denis) 101
Letters from Rome (Middleton,
    Conyers) 81
Letters to Serena (Tolland, John) 81, 103
Leuckfeld, Johann Georg 87
Leviathan (Hobbes, Thomas) 45, 47–50, 81
Leviathan drawn out with a hook (Ross,
    Alexander) 50
Levitin-Krasnov, Anatoly 240
L'Homme Machine (Man a Machine) (La
    Mettrie, Julien Offray de) 113
libertines érudits 28
libertinism 7, 58, 75, 115 see also vice
  Meslier, Jean and 97
liberty 85–6
Licensing Act 1662 72, 85
Life of Apollonius Tyraneus
    (Philostratus) 80
Life of Jesus, Critically Examined, The
    (Strauss, David) 147
Linn, William 131
Locke, John 85–6
  Essay Concerning Human Understanding
    85, 164
  Letter Concerning Toleration 67, 85–6
  Two Treatises of Government 85
Loescher, Valentin 87
  Praenotiones 89
logical positivism 211–14
Lollardy 9
London Positivist Society 188
Louis XIV 92
Lovett, William 179
Low Countries, the 91–2 see also Holland
Lucretius, De rerum natura (On the Nature
    of Things) 14–16
Lunacharsky, Anatoly 220
Luther, Martin 22–3

Machiavelli, Nicolo 19, 21–2
  Discourses on Livy 21
  Prince, The 19–21
Maillet, Benoît de 100

Telliamed, or Conversations between an Indian Philosopher and a French Missionary on the Diminution of the Sea 100
Man a Machine (L'Homme Machine) (La Mettrie, Julien Offray de) 113
Mandeville, Bernard 82–3
  Enquiry into the Origin of Honour; and the Usefulness of Christianity in War 83
  Fable of the Bees, or, Private Vices, Public Benefits 82–3
  Free Thoughts on Religion, the Church and National Happiness 83
  Modest Defense of Public Stews 83
manuscripts, clandestine 60–1
Mao Tse-tung 234–7
  On the Correct Handling of Contradictions 236
  Peasant Movement in Hunan 234
Marlowe, Christopher 10–11
  Jew of Malta, The 22
Marmontel, Jean-François 103
Marx, Eleanor 191
Marx, Karl 148, 149–53
  Communist Manifesto 153
  Critique of Hegel's Philosophy of Law 151
Marxism 97, 220
Masius, Andreas 40
materialism 46–7, 99, 107–8, 112–16, 152
  Germany and 196–8
mathematics 208
Mather, Cotton, *Christian Philosopher, The* 129
Mauthner, Fritz xix
McTaggart, John McTaggert Ellis 207
Meditations (Descartes, René) 30
Mémoire (Meslier, Jean) 61, 94–8, 104
Men before Adam (La Peyrère, Isaac) 42
Menocchio 12
Mersenne, Marin 1, 29
Meslier, Jean 94–8, 109
  Mémoire 61, 94–8, 104
Middleton, Conyers 81
  Letters from Rome 81
Milton, John 73
miracles 48, 54, 81
  Hume, David and 119
  Meslier, Jean and 95

Miracles, No Violations of the Laws of Nature (Blount, Charles) 81
Moderator between an Infidel and an Apostate, The (Woolston, Thomas) 81
Modest Defense of Public Stews (Mandeville, Bernard) 83
Moleschott, Jacob 197
Molière, *Don Juan* 6
Montaigne, Michel de 17, 26
  apology for Raymond Sebond, An 26–7
  Essays 27
Moore, G. E. 207
morality 82–3
More, Henry 30–1
  Antidote against Atheism 31, 76
More, Thomas, *Utopia* 17
Morellet, André 103
Mornay, Philip of, *Woorke concerning the trewness of the Christian Religion, written in French: Against Atheists, Epicures, Paynims, Jews, Mahumetists, and other Infidels, A* 3
Morris, Henry (and Whitcomb, John), *Genesis Flood: The Biblical Record and its Scientific Implications, The* 245
My Apprenticeship (Webb, Beatrice) 191
My Past and Thoughts (Herzen, Alexander) 149
Myers, P. Z. 248–9

Nagel, Thomas 256–7
Naigeon, Jacques-André 15, 108
Nashe, Thomas
  Christ's Tears over Jerusalem 2, 6
  Pierce Penilesse 42
National Association of Evangelicals 132
National Reform Association 132
National Secular Society 193
Natural History of Religion (Hume, David) 118, 121–2
Natural History of Superstition (Trenchard, John) 81
Natural History of the Soul (La Mettrie, Julien Offray de) 113
natural philosophy 79, 87, 99–101
natural theology 77–9, 120–1
nature 32–6, 136

Nature and Cause of Atheism, The (Estlin, John) 161

Naudé, Gabriel 28

Nazism 221–4

'Necessary Elements for a Successful Communism' (Russell, Bertrand) 234–5

Necessity of Atheism, The (Shelley, Percy Bysshe) 164–5

Netherlands, the *see* Holland

New Atheism 247–54 *see also* New New Atheism

New Harmony, Indiana, USA 175

New History of Western Philosophy (Kenny, Anthony) xx–xxi

New Lanark, Scotland 174

New Moral World 175

New New Atheism 257–8

New Poor Law, the 167, 171

Newton, Isaac 36, 84–5
    Principia Mathematica 36, 84–5

Nicholas I 154, 155–6, 157–8

Nietzsche, Friedrich 195–6, 198–203
    Antichrist, The 203
    Beyond Good and Evil 199
    Ecce Homo 195
    Gay Science, The 201

North Korea 243

Not Paul, But Jesus (Bentham, Jeremy) 168

Nouveau Christianisme (Saint-Simon, Hendri de) 139

Novum instrumentum (New Instrument) (Erasmus, Desiderus) 38

oaths 7

'Of Miracles' (Hume, David) 119

'Of Ontology' (Bentham, Jeremy) 167

'Of Parties in General' (Hume, David) 122

Ogarev, Nikolai 156

Ogilvie, John, *An inquiry into the causes of the infidelity and scepticism of the times* 128

O'Hair, Madalyn Murray 228–9

O'Hair, William 228–9

Okulov, A. F. 239

'On the Basis of Our Belief in a Divine Governance of the World' (Fichte, Johann Gottlieb) 144–5

On the Correct Handling of Contradictions (Mao Tse-tung) 236

'On the immortality of the soul' (Hume, David) 120–1

On the Mind (*De l'esprit*)(Helvétius, Claude Adrien) 15, 110

On the Nature of Things (Lucretius) 14–16

On the Origin of the Species (Darwin, Charles) 180

'on the sufficiency of natural religion' (Diderot, Denis) 99

Onfray, Michael 254

Oracle 176

Origen 35

Orleans, Philippe II, Duke of 92–3

Orthodoxy 154–6, 214–17, 241, 243–4
    Khrushchev, Nikita and 230–2
    numbers 221, 231–2, 241
    Stalin, Josef and 223, 230

Owen, Robert 173–4
    Essay on the Formation of Character 174
    Second Lecture on the New Religion 173

paganism 43, 81, 127, 219–20

Paine, Thomas 130, 166–7
    Age of Reason 166

Pallavicino, Ferrante 3

Palmer, Elihu 129

parasitic atheism 254–5

Pascal, Blaise 37
    Pensées 37

Peasant Movement in Hunan (Mao Tse-tung) 234

Pensées (Pascal, Blaise) 37

Pensées philosophiques (Diderot, Denis) 99, 101

Pfister, Oskar 187

Philippe II, Duke of Orleans 93

Philosophical Essays concerning Human Understanding (Hume, David) 119

philosophy 64

Philostratus, *Life of Apollonius Tyraneus* 80

'Physico-Mathematical Experimental Learning' 75

physico–theology 78–9

Pierce Penilesse (Nashe, Thomas) 42

Pietism 142

Pius IX, *Syllabus of Errors* 184

Platonism 105

Pocock, John 129–30
political authority 47–50
Political Treatise (Spinoza, Benedict) 59
Polycarp xv
polygenism 42
polyps 99–100, 116
Popkin, Richard 24
Portable Theology (D'Holbach, Paul-Henri Thiry, Baron d') 105
positivism 138–41, 188, 196
practical atheism 6–7
Prae-Adamitae (La Peyrère, Isaac) 42
Praenotiones (Loescher, Valentin) 89
Priestley, Joseph 161
priests 102
Prince, The (Machiavelli, Nicolo) 19–21
Principia Mathematica (Newton, Isaac) 36, 84–5
Principia Mathematica (Russell, Bertrand and Whitehead, Alfred) 208
Problem of Unbelief in the Sixteenth Century: the Religion of Rabelais, The (Febvre, Lucien) 8
Progress of Social Reform On the Continent (Engles, Friedrich) 146–7
Propagandist Press fund 190
prophecy 54
Protestantism 24–6, 85
  Bible, the and 39, 41
providentialism 131
Prussia 148, 153 *see also* Germany
Prussian Academy of Sciences 87
publications 85, 176–7, 184, 190–1, 250
Pyrrhonian scepticism 14 *see also* scepticism

Rabelais, Françoise 8
Raleigh, Walter 2
Rational Society, the 175
Rationalist movement, the 205
Rationalist Press, the 190–1
Raynal, Thomas 103–4
reason xiii, 24, 26–7, 58, 64 *see also* Rationalist movement, the *and* revelation *and* science
  deism and 82, 83
  France and 134–5
  Sade, Donatien Alphonse François, Marquis de and 136

Reason the Only Oracle of Man (Allen, Ethan) 129
Reclamation of the Freedom of Thought from the Princes of Europe, who have hitherto Suppressed it (Fichte, Johann Gottlieb) 145
Rees, Martin 252
Reflections on French Atheism and on English Christianity (Richards, William) 161
Reformation, the 10, 22–5
  England and 25
  scripture and 22–3, 32–3
Reimann, Friedrich 2
Reimann, Jakob 87
relativism 102
religion 18, 213 *see also* Catholicism *and* Christianity *and* Protestanism
  Dawkins, Richard and 251
  death of 108, 114
  France and 138
  Freud, Sigmund and 186
  Hume, David and 121–2
  Marx, Karl and 150–2
  New Atheism and 249
  Spinoza, Benedict and 57, 59
Religion for Atheists (de Botton, Alain) 257
Religion in Human Evolution (Bellah, Robert) 250
Religion of the Future, The (Feuerbach, Friedrich) 157
Religion within the Bounds of Reason (Kant, Immanuel) 144
religiosity 186
Religious Right, the 245–6
Remonstrants, the 55
Republican 172
Restoration, the 72–5
resurrection 169
Revealed Face of Moses, The (Edelman, Johann Christian) 88
revelation 48, 54, 80, Meslier, Jean and 95
Rheinische Zeitung 153
Richards, William, *Reflections on French Atheism and on English Christianity* 161
Robert Elsmere (Ward, Mrs Humphrey) 187–8
Robertson, John 184
Robespierre, Maximilien 134

Rochester, John Wilmot, 2nd Earl of 74–5
    Satyr Against Reason and Mankind, A
        74–5
Roe v Wade 245
Roman Empire, the 125–7
Ross, Alexander, *Leviathan drawn out with
        a hook* 50
Rousseau, Jean-Jacques 103–4, 134
Royal Society, the 75–6
Rushdie, Salman 247
Russell, Bertrand 207–10, 233
    Autobiography 208–9
    'freeman's worship, A' 209–10
    'Necessary Elements for a Successful
        Communism' 234–5
    Principa Mathematica 208
Russia 153–60, 214–21, 223, 230–3, 243 *see
        also* Soviet Union, the
Rustick's Alarm to the Rabbies, The (Fisher,
        Samuel) 44

Sacred Theory of the Earth (Burnet,
        Thomas) 35–6
Sade, Donatien Alphonse François,
        Marquis de 135–7
    *Dialogue between a Priest and a Dying
        Man* 135–6
Sage and the Atheist, The (Voltaire) 1
Saint-Roch church 133
Saint-Simon, Henri de 139–40
    Nouveau Christianisme 139
Satyr Against Reason and Mankind, A
        (Rochester, John Wilmot, 2nd Earl
        of) 74–5
Saunderson, Nicholas 102
Scargill, Daniel 51
scepticism 23–31, 144
    libertines érudits and 28
    Montaigne, Michel de and 26–7
    Pyrrhonian 14
Schelling and Revelation (Engels,
        Friedrich) 147
Schlick, Moritz 212
Schmidt, Johann Lorenz 88, 89
Schopenhauer, Arthur 196
science xiii–xiv, 29, 32–8, 183–7, 196–8 *see
        also* Boyle lectures, the *and* natural
        theology *and* Royal Society, the

Science and Atheism 242
Science and Religion 232–3, 239
Scopes, John 227
Scotland 70–2
    Blasphemy Act 1661 71
scripture 22–3, 32–3 *see also* Bible, the
Sebond, Raimond 26
    Theologia Naturalis 26–7
Seckendorff, Veit Ludwig von 87
Second Lecture on the New Religion (Owen,
        Robert) 173
*Second Thoughts concerning the Human
        Soul* (Coward, William) 79–80
secular movement, the 53–4, 191–4,
        203–5
    evolution 100
    France and 138–41
    Germany and 87, 196–8
    Great Britain and 183–4
    Maillet, Benoît de and 100
    polyps and 99–100
    transformism and 100
    Trembley, Abraham and 99–100
Selfish Gene, The (Dawkins, Richard)
        250–1, 255
Semer, Thomas 9
Servetus, Michael 23
Sextus Empiricus 23–4
Shaftesbury, Anthony Ashley-Cooper, 3rd
        Earl of
    *Inquiry Concerning Virtue and Merit,
        An* 99
    Letter Concerning Enthusiasm, A 81
Shaposhnikov, Petr 157
Sharples, Eliza 172
Shelley, Percy Bysshe 163–6
    Necessity of Atheism, The 164–5
Simon, Richard 43–4
    Critical History of the Old Testament 43
slave morality 200
Smith, Adam 104
Smith, Charles Lee 228
social order 82
socialism 105
Society for Reformation of Manners,
        the 72
Society for the Love of Wisdom, the 154,
        155–6

Society for the Promotion of Christian Knowledge, the 72, 190
Socinians 268n. 32
soul, the 79–80, 120–1
South Place Society 175
Southwell, Charles 176
Soviet League of the Militant Godless, the 218–21
Soviet Union 238–41 *see also* Russia
Spain 1, 9
Spencer, Herbert 188
Speshev, Nikolai 158
Spinoza, Benedict 52–60
    Ethics 57
    Germany and 88
    Political Treatise 59
    Tractatus Theologico-Politicus 52–6, 60, 62, 81
Stalin, Josef 216, 223, 230
Stanyan, Temple, *Grecian History* 99
Stephen, Leslie 189
Stosch, Friedrich Willhelm 88
Strauss, David 147
    Life of Jesus, Critically Examined, The 147
superstition 61–2, 64, 81, 118, 127
Swear Not At All (Bentham, Jeremy) 170
Switzerland 25
Syllabus of Errors (Pius IX) 184
Symbolum sapiente 88
System of Epicurus (La Mettrie, Julien Offray de) 15
Système de la nature (*System of Nature, The*) (D'Holbach, Paul-Henri Thiry, Baron d') 104–5, 112, 135, 161

Taoism 236
Taylor, Robert 173, 179–80
    Diegesis; being a Discovery of the Origin, Evidence, and Early History of Christianity, The 173
Taylor, Thomas 9
Telliamed, or Conversations between an Indian Philosopher and a French Missionary on the Diminution of the Sea (de Maillet, Benoît) 100
Temple of Reason, The 129
Thatcher, Margaret 246

Theologia Naturalis (Sebond, Raimond) 26–7
Theophilanthropy 166
Theophrastus redivivus 61
theoretical atheism 6–7
Thirty Years War, the 25, 89
Thomasius, Christian 90–1
Thoughts on Death and Immortality (Feuerbach, Ludwig) 148
Tillotson, John 83
Tindal, Matthew 83, 89
Toland, John, *Letters to Serena* 81, 103
toleration 85–6, 92
Tolstov, Aleksei 157
torture 248
Tostado Ribera de Madrigal, Alfonso 39
Tostatus 39
Toynbee, Arnold, *Christianity and Civilisation* 223
Toynbee, Polly 254
Tractatus Logico-Philosophicus (Wittgenstein, Ludwig) 211
Tractatus Theologico–Politicus (Spinoza, Benedict) 52–6, 60, 62, 81
Traité des Trois Imposteurs (*Treaty of the Three Imposters*) 61–2, 88
transformism 100
Treatise Concerning Human Nature (Hume, David) 119
Treatise of Government (Locke, John) 85
Treatise on Man: His Intellectual Faculties and His Education, A (Helvétius, Claude Adrien) 110
Treaty of Westphalia 89
Trembley, Abraham 99–100, 116
Trenchard, John, *Natural History of Superstition* 81
Trinity, the 38, 78
Trinitarianism 127
True Intellectual System of the Universe (Cudworth, Ralph) 5
True Meaning of the System of Nature, The (Carlile, Richard) 172
Turgot, Anne-Robert-Jacques 104
Turner, Matthew, *Answer to Dr Priestley's Letters to a Philosophical Unbeliever* 161

Universal Community Society of Rational Religionists 174, 175
utilitarianism 97–8, 169–71, 173
Utopia (More, Thomas) 17

Vallée, Geoffrey 11
Vanini, Giulo Cesare 11–12
Various Thoughts on the Occasion of A Comet (Bayle, Pierre) 64
Vaux, Clothilde de 140–1
Via et L'Esprit de Mr, Benoit de Spinosa 61–2
vice 82–3, 112
Vie de Mahomed (Boulainvilliers, Henri de) 63
Vienna Circle, the 211–12
Viret, Pierre 6
Voëtius, Gisbert 30
Vogt, Karl 196–7
Voltaire (François–Marie Arouet) 86, 94, 98–9, 134
  Candide 91
  Sage and the Atheist, The 1
Voyage of the Beagle, The (Darwin, Charles) 180

Wachter, Johann 88
Wagner, Gabriel 88
Wagner, Richard 198
Ward, Mrs Humphrey, *Robert Elsmere* 187–8
Washington, George 130
Watkin, Christopher 254
Watts, Charles 190
Webb, Beatrice, *My Apprenticeship* 191
Weber, Immanuel 87
Werthem Bible 88

What is to be Done?: Tales of the New People (Chernyshevsky, Nikolai) 160–1
Wheller, J. M., *Biographical Dictionary of Freethinkers of All Ages and Nations* 184
Whiston, William 77–8
Whitcomb, John (and Morris, Henry), *Genesis Flood: The Biblical Record and its Scientific Implications, The* 245
White, Andrew Dickson, *History of the Warfare of Science with Theology in Christendom* 184
Whitehead, Alfred, *Principia Mathematica* 208
Wilkes, John 104
Wilmot, John 74–5
  Satyr Against Reason and Manind, A 74–5
Witherspoon, John 130
Wittgenstein, Ludwig 210–12, 213, 258
  Tractatus Logico-Philosophicus 211
Wolff, Christian 90
Wolffe, Christian 16
Woodward, John 77
Woolston, Thomas, *Moderator between an Infidel and an Apostate, The* 81
Woorke concerning the trewness of the Christian Religion, written in French: Against Atheists, Epicures, Paynims, Jews, Mahumetists, and other Infidels, A (Mornay, Philip of) 3
Wright, Elizur 227

Yaroslavsky, Yemelyan 243

Znanie Society 232